The United Nations and Human Rights

Julie Mertus' highly acclaimed text continues to be the only completely up-to-date comprehensive yet succinct guide to the United Nations human rights system.

Today, virtually all UN bodies and specialized agencies are undertaking efforts to incorporate the promotion or protection of human rights into their programs and activities. *The United Nations and Human Rights* examines these recent initiatives within the broader context of human rights practice, including the promotion of individual rights, management of international conflict, and the advancement of agendas of social movements.

The fully revised and updated second edition not only provides a complete guide to the development, structure and procedures within the UN human rights system, but also reflects the vital changes that have occurred within the UN system, devoting considerable attention to expanding the range of issues discussed, including:

- new developments in the Office of the High Commissioner for Human Rights
- the current controversy surrounding the new Human Rights Council
- an expanded treatment of economic and social rights.

A superb addition to any human rights syllabus, this book maintains its position as essential reading for students and practitioners of human rights, international relations, and international law.

Julie A. Mertus is Professor and Co-Director of the M.A. program in Ethics, Peace, and Global Affairs at American University, Washington D.C. She is author or editor of over two dozen academic articles and six books, including *Bait and Switch: Human Rights and U.S. Foreign Policy* (Routledge, 2004) which was named "Human Rights Book of the Year" by the American Political Science Association.

Routledge Global Institutions

Edited by Thomas G. Weiss
The CUNY Graduate Center, New York, USA
and Rorden Wilkinson
University of Manchester, UK

About the Series

The "Global Institutions Series" is designed to provide readers with comprehensive, accessible, and informative guides to the history, structure, and activities of key international organizations. Every volume stands on its own as a thorough and insightful treatment of a particular topic, but the series as a whole contributes to a coherent and complementary portrait of the phenomenon of global institutions at the dawn of the millennium.

Books are written by recognized experts, conform to a similar structure, and cover a range of themes and debates common to the series. These areas of shared concern include the general purpose and rationale for organizations, developments over time, membership, structure, decision-making procedures, and key functions. Moreover, current debates are placed in historical perspective alongside informed analysis and critique. Each book also contains an annotated bibliography and guide to electronic information as well as any annexes appropriate to the subject matter at hand.

The volumes currently published include:

33 The United Nations and Human Rights (2009)
A guide for a new era, 2nd edition
by Julie A. Mertus (American University)

32 The International Organization for Standardization and the Global Economy (2009)
Setting standards
by Craig N. Murphy (Wellesley College) and JoAnne Yates (Massachusetts Institute of Technology)

31 Shaping the Humanitarian World (2009)
by Peter Walker (Tufts University) and Daniel G. Maxwell (Tufts University)

30 Global Food and Agricultural Institutions (2009)
by John Shaw

29 Institutions of the Global South (2009)
by Jacqueline Anne Braveboy-Wagner (City College of New York, CUNY)

28 International Judicial Institutions (2009)
The architecture of international justice at home and abroad
by Richard J. Goldstone (Retired Justice of the Constitutional Court of South Africa) and Adam M. Smith (Harvard University)

27 The International Olympic Committee (2009)
The governance of the olympic system
by Jean-Loup Chappelet (IDHEAP Swiss Graduate School of Public Administration) and Brenda Kübler-Mabbott

26 The World Health Organization (2009)
by Kelley Lee (London School of Hygiene and Tropical Medicine)

25 Internet Governance (2009)
The new frontier of global institutions
by John Mathiason (Syracuse University)

24 Institutions of the Asia-Pacific (2009)
ASEAN, APEC, and beyond
by Mark Beeson (University of Birmingham)

23 UNHCR (2008)
The politics and practice of refugee protection into the twenty-first century
by Gil Loescher (University of Oxford), Alexander Betts (University of Oxford), and James Milner (University of Toronto)

22 Contemporary Human Rights Ideas (2008)
by Bertrand G. Ramcharan (Geneva Graduate Institute of International Studies)

21 The World Bank (2008)
From reconstruction to development to equity
by Katherine Marshall (Georgetown University)

20 The European Union (2008)
by Clive Archer (Manchester Metropolitan University)

19 The African Union (2008)
Challenges of globalization, security, and governance
by Samuel M. Makinda (Murdoch University) and Wafula Okumu (McMaster University)

18 **Commonwealth (2008)**
Inter- and non-state contributions to global governance
by Timothy M. Shaw (Royal Roads University)

17 **The World Trade Organization (2007)**
Law, economics, and politics
*by Bernard M. Hoekman (World Bank) and Petros C. Mavroidis
(Columbia University)*

16 **A Crisis of Global Institutions? (2007)**
Multilateralism and international security
by Edward Newman (University of Birmingham)

15 **UN Conference on Trade and Development (2007)**
*by Ian Taylor (University of St. Andrews) and Karen Smith (University
of Stellenbosch)*

14 **The Organization for Security and Co-operation in Europe (2007)**
by David J. Galbreath (University of Aberdeen)

13 **The International Committee of the Red Cross (2007)**
A neutral humanitarian actor
*by David P. Forsythe (University of Nebraska) and
Barbara Ann Rieffer-Flanagan (Central Washington University)*

12 **The World Economic Forum (2007)**
A multi-stakeholder approach to global governance
by Geoffrey Allen Pigman (Bennington College)

11 **The Group of 7/8 (2007)**
by Hugo Dobson (University of Sheffield)

10 **The International Monetary Fund (2007)**
Politics of conditional lending
by James Raymond Vreeland (Georgetown University)

9 **The North Atlantic Treaty Organization (2007)**
The enduring alliance
*by Julian Lindley-French (Center for Applied Policy, University of
Munich)*

8 **The World Intellectual Property Organization (2006)**
Resurgence and the development agenda
by Chris May (University of the West of England)

7 **The UN Security Council (2006)**
Practice and promise
by Edward C. Luck (Columbia University)

6 **Global Environmental Institutions (2006)**
by Elizabeth R. DeSombre (Wellesley College)

5 **Internal Displacement (2006)**
Conceptualization and its consequences
by Thomas G. Weiss (The CUNY Graduate Center) and David A. Korn

4 **The UN General Assembly (2005)**
by M.J. Peterson (University of Massachusetts, Amherst)

3 **United Nations Global Conferences (2005)**
by Michael G. Schechter (Michigan State University)

2 **The UN Secretary-General and Secretariat (2005)**
by Leon Gordenker (Princeton University)

1 **The United Nations and Human Rights (2005)**
A guide for a new era
by Julie A. Mertus (American University)

Books currently under contract include:

Transnational Organized Crime
by Frank Madsen (University of Cambridge)

The Organisation for Economic Co-operation and Development
by Richard Woodward (University of Hull)

Regional Security
The capacity of international organizations
by Rodrigo Tavares (United Nations University)

Global Institutions and the HIV/AIDS Epidemic
Responding to an international crisis
by Franklyn Lisk (University of Warwick)

African Economic Institutions
by Kwame Akonor (Seton Hall University)

Non-Governmental Organizations in Global Politics
by Peter Willetts (City University, London)

The International Labour Organization
by Steve Hughes (University of Newcastle) and Nigel Haworth (University of Auckland Business School)

The Regional Development Banks
Lending with a regional flavor
by Jonathan R. Strand (University of Nevada)

Multilateral Cooperation Against Terrorism
by Peter Romaniuk (John Jay College of Criminal Justice, CUNY)

Peacebuilding
From concept to commission
by Robert Jenkins (The CUNY Graduate Center)

Governing Climate Change
by Peter Newell (University of East Anglia) and Harriet A. Bulkeley (Durham University)

Millennium Development Goals (MDGs)
For a people-centered development agenda?
by Sakiko Fukada-Parr (The New School)

Human Development
by Maggie Black

Human Security
by Don Hubert (University of Ottawa)

Global Poverty
by David Hulme (University of Manchester)

UNESCO
by J. P. Singh (Georgetown University)

UNICEF
by Richard Jolly (University of Sussex)

Organization of American States (OAS)
by Mônica Herz (Instituto de Relações Internacionais)

The UN Secretary-General and Secretariat, 2nd edition
by Leon Gordenker (Princeton University)

FIFA
by Alan Tomlinson (University of Brighton)

International Law, International Relations, and Global Governance
by Charlotte Ku (University of Illinois, College of Law)

Preventive Human Rights Strategies in a World of New Threats and Challenges
by Bertrand G. Ramcharan (Geneva Graduate Institute of International and Development Studies)

Humanitarianism Contested
by Michael Barnett (University of Minnesota) and Thomas G. Weiss (The CUNY Graduate Center)

Forum on China-Africa Cooperation (FOCAC)
by Ian Taylor (University of St. Andrews)

For further information regarding the series, please contact:

Craig Fowlie, Senior Publisher, Politics & International Studies
Taylor & Francis
2 Park Square, Milton Park, Abingdon
Oxford OX14 4RN, UK

+44 (0)207 842 2057 Tel
+44 (0)207 842 2302 Fax

Craig.Fowlie@tandf.co.uk
www.routledge.com

The United Nations and Human Rights

A guide for a new era

Second edition

Julie A. Mertus

Routledge
Taylor & Francis Group

LONDON AND NEW YORK

First published 2005
Second edition published 2009
by Routledge
2 Park Square, Milton Park, Abingdon, Oxon OX14 4RN

Simultaneously published in the USA and Canada
by Routledge
711 Third Avenue, New York, NY 10017

Routledge is an imprint of the Taylor & Francis Group, an informa business

Typeset in Times New Roman by
Taylor & Francis Books

British Library Cataloguing in Publication Data
A catalogue record for this book is available from the British Library

Library of Congress Cataloging in Publication Data
Mertus, Julie, 1963–
    The United Nations and human rights : a guide for a new era / Julie A.
    Mertus. – 2nd ed.
        p. cm. – (Global institutions)
    Includes bibliographical references and index.
    1. Human rights. 2. United Nations. 3. United Nations. General
    Assembly. Universal Declaration of Human Rights. I. Title.
    JC571.M4447 2009
341.4′8–dc22   2008047758

ISBN 978-0-415-49132-7 (hbk)
ISBN 978-0-415-49140-2 (pbk)
ISBN 978-0-203-87801-9 (ebk)

This book is dedicated to Janet, Lynne, and Daniel

Contents

List of illustrations   xii
Foreword to the second edition   xiv
Acknowledgments   xvii
List of abbreviations   xviii

1   A guide to the new UN human rights practice   1

2   The Office of the High Commissioner for Human Rights   8

3   UN Charter-based bodies (and other non-treaty bodies)   37

4   UN treaty bodies   64

5   The Security Council   98

6   The International Labour Organization and the UN
    Global Compact   124

7   Conclusion: looking backward, going forward   148

Postscript to the second edition   152
Appendix: selected directory of UN human rights bodies   155
Notes   167
Selected bibliography   184
Index   193

Illustrations

Figures

2.1   OHCHR's organizational chart   15
6.1   The main bodies of the ILO   126
6.2   The ILO's regular system of supervision   135

Tables

2.1   Forms of technical assistance   17
3.1   Human rights provisions in the UN Charter for Human
       Rights   38
3.2   Thematic procedures of the UN Commission on Human
       Rights   58
4.1   UN treaty bodies and their parent treaties   66
5.1   Security Council responses to human rights   102
5.2   Summary of opinions on humanitarian intervention/
       responsibility to protect   109

Boxes

2.1   UN Expert on Internally Displaced Persons concerned
       about the situation in Georgia   20
2.2   OHCHR field presences   23
2.3   High Commissioners for Human Rights, 1994–2008   31
3.1   Main themes addressed by the Human Rights Council   52
3.2   Using the 1503 procedure   56
3.3   How to bring information to the attention of the Special
       Rapporteurs   60

4.1	Illustration of dialogue process between Committee monitoring Children's Rights Convention and States Parties	67
4.2	Examples of state reports and NGO shadow reports	69
4.3	Illustration of how treaty reporting works	71
4.4	Model complaint form	74
4.5	Illustration of National Plan of Action	79
4.6	Illustration of treaty reservations	89
4.7	Illustration of strategies devised to encourage reporting by States Parties	95
5.1	Examples of UN peace operations	110
5.2	UN Security Council and children and armed conflict	120
6.1	Criteria for NGO participation	127
6.2	ILO standard-setting mechanisms	132
6.3	The Article 26 Procedure in action—the case of Burma	137
6.4	Goals of Global Compact entities	144

Foreword to the second edition

First published in 2005, Julie Mertus' volume was the first in a dynamic series on "global institutions," which now includes more than 30 published titles and another 30 commissioned, and it is also the first to go into a second edition. The series strives (and, based on the volumes published to date, succeeds) to provide readers with definitive guides to the most visible aspects of what many of us know as "global governance." Remarkable as it may seem, there exist relatively few books that offer in-depth treatments of prominent global bodies, processes, and associated issues, much less an entire series of concise and complementary volumes. Those that do exist are either out of date, inaccessible to the non-specialist reader, or seek to develop a specialized understanding of particular aspects of an institution or process rather than offer an overall account of its functioning. Similarly, existing books have often been written in highly technical language or have been crafted "in-house" and are notoriously self-serving and narrow.

The advent of electronic media has undoubtedly helped research and teaching by making data and primary documents of international organizations more widely available, but it has also complicated matters. The growing reliance on the Internet and other electronic methods of finding information about key international organizations and processes has served, ironically, to limit the educational and analytical materials to which most readers have ready access—namely, books. Public relations documents, raw data, and loosely refereed web sites do not make for intelligent analysis. Official publications compete with a vast amount of electronically available information, much of which is suspect because of its ideological or self-promoting slant. Paradoxically, a growing range of purportedly independent web sites offering analyses of the activities of particular organizations has emerged, but one inadvertent consequence has been to frustrate access to basic, authoritative, readable, critical, and well-researched texts. The market for such has actually been reduced by the ready availability of varying quality electronic materials.

For those of us who teach, research, and practice in the area, such limited access to information has been particularly frustrating. We were delighted when Routledge saw the value of a series that bucks this trend and provides key reference points to the most significant global institutions and issues. They are betting that serious students and professionals will want serious analyses. We have assembled a first-rate line-up of authors to address that market. Our intention, then, is to provide one-stop shopping for all readers—students (both undergraduate and postgraduate), negotiators, diplomats, practitioners from nongovernmental and intergovernmental organizations, and interested parties alike—seeking information about the most prominent institutional aspects of global governance.

UN human rights machinery

Today as we write these lines virtually on the 60th anniversary of the Universal Declaration of Human Rights in December 1948, human rights are far more central to the discourse of international public policy and scholarship, and national, regional, and international mechanisms have evolved dramatically since the signing. Four years ago, we asked Julie Mertus—associate professor in the School of International Service at the American University in Washington, D.C.—to undertake the daunting task of making sense of what Eleanor Roosevelt once predicted: that human rights NGOs would serve as a "curious grapevine" that would spread information about human rights violations to the world community. Julie's best work always mixes both micro and macro perspectives on the law and practice of human rights that reflect serious scholarship, practical exposure in the field to problems, and a passion for the issues.

This second edition was motivated by the overwhelmingly positive response to the first edition and the fact that since it was first published there have been numerous important developments in the field of human rights. For example, readers loved the first edition but wished it could have included information on the UN Human Rights Council (which replaced the Commission on Human Rights in June 2006) and more in-depth treatment of the Global Compact. Julie has responded to that feedback with this concise volume, which reaches a broad audience with many useful descriptions, lists of resources, and numerous concrete examples that draw especially on the vital question of the human rights of children. Together with two new books in the series on contemporary human rights ideas and preventive human rights strategies[1] and a host of others on the related fields of humanitarian action,[2] this second edition offers readers a complete guide to the most important human rights issues and institutional arrangements especially within the UN system. In order to keep the length of the volume consistent with others in the series, all but the most essential appendices from the first edition have been omitted. The timeline for human rights can now be found at www.american.edu/humanrights.

As always, we look forward to comments from first-time or veteran readers of the Global Institutions Series.

Thomas G. Weiss, The CUNY Graduate Center, New York, USA
Rorden Wilkinson, University of Manchester, UK
March 2009

Acknowledgments

Many thanks to Thomas Weiss and Rorden Wilkinson for conceiving of this series of readily accessible texts on international organizations. I appreciate their comments and suggestions, as well as those of Effie MacLachlan and other readers, and the fine editorial assistance at Taylor & Francis.

This book benefited greatly from the input of many scholars and practitioners. Stephanie Kleine-Ahlbrandt, Margaret Bedggood, Janet Lord, Madeleine Rees, Markus G. Schmidt, and Kirsten Young invested considerable time in reading and commenting on the text. In addition, many individuals agreed to be interviewed and/or contributed to the text in other ways, including Jo Becker, Fanny Benedetti-Howell, Mark Bromley, Brian Burdekin, Scott Campbell, Zakiya Carr Johnson, Sandra Coliver, Vienna Colucci, Jane Connors, Jack Donnelly, Richard Falk, Katherine Guernsey, Neil Hicks, Margaret Huang, Elena Ipolliti, Ann Jordan, Scott Long, Larry Minear, Michael O'Flaherty, Cynthia Price Cohen, Jennifer Rasmusen, Dinah Shelton, Chandra Sriram, James Turpin, Stephanie Willman-Bordat, and Richard Wilson.

I am also indebted to the support of the School of International Service, American University and the hard work of my research assistants, without whom this work would never have seen the light of day: Molly Doran, Eve Bratman, Jill Gerschutz, and QueTran Nguyen.

Abbreviations

BiH	Bosnia and Herzegovina
CAT	Committee Against Torture
CEDAW	Committee on the Elimination of Discrimination Against Women
CERD	Committee on the Elimination of All Forms of Racial Discrimination
CESCR	Committee on Economic, Social and Cultural Rights
CFA	Committee on Freedom of Association
CHR	Commission on Human Rights
CIS	Commonwealth of Independent States
CoE	Council of Europe
CRC	Committee on the Rights of the Child
CRMW	Committee on the Protection of the Rights of All Migrant Workers and Members of Their Families
CSW	Commission on the Status of Women
DAW	Division for the Advancement of Women
DDR	Disarmament, Demobilization, and Rehabilitation
DPnet	Development Policy Network
ECHR	European Convention on Human Rights
ECOSOC	Economic and Social Council
EU	European Union
FAO	Food and Agriculture Organization of the United Nations
FFCC	Fact-Finding and Conciliation Commission on Freedom of Association
FRY	Federal Republic of Yugoslavia
GA	General Assembly
GATT	General Agreement on Tariffs and Trade
GC	Global Compact
GDP	Gross domestic product

HRC	Human Rights Committee, also known as the Committee on Civil and Political Rights
HRFOR	Human Rights Field Operation in Rwanda
ICC	International Criminal Court
ICCPR	International Covenant on Civil and Political Rights
ICESCR	International Covenant on Economic, Social and Cultural Rights
ICISS	International Commission on Intervention and State Sovereignty
ICJ	International Court of Justice
ICTR	International Criminal Tribunal for Rwanda
ICTY	International Criminal Tribunal for the Former Yugoslavia
IE	Independent Expert
ILA	International Law Association
ILO	International Labour Organization
IMF	International Monetary Fund
IPEC	International Programme on the Elimination of Child Labour
LMG	Like-Minded Group
NAFTA	North American Free Trade Agreement
NGO	Non-governmental organization
NHRI	National human rights institution
OAS	Organization of American States
OAU	Organization of African Unity
OECD	Organisation for Economic Co-operation and Development
OHCHR	Office of the High Commissioner for Human Rights
OIOS	Office of Internal Oversight Services of the United Nations Secretariat
OSCE	Organization for Security and Co-operation in Europe
P-5	Permanent five members of the Security Council
PRSP	Poverty Reduction Strategy Paper
RMAP	Rights-based Municipal Assessment Project
RTD	Right to Development
SC	Security Council
SG	Secretary-General
SIDA	Swedish International Development Agency
SR	Special Rapporteur
SRep	Special Representative
TBP	Time-Bound Program
TCNs	Troop-Contributing Nations
UDHR	Universal Declaration of Human Rights

UN	United Nations
UNAMIR	United Nations Assistance Mission for Rwanda
UNCTAD	United Nations Conference on Trade and Development
UNDP	United Nations Development Programme
UNEF	United Nations Emergency Force
UNESCO	United Nations Educational, Scientific and Cultural Organization
UNFPA	United Nations Population Fund
UNHCHR	United Nations High Commissioner for Human Rights
UNHCR	United Nations High Commissioner for Refugees
UNICEF	United Nations Children's Fund
UNIFEM	United Nations Development Fund for Women
UNMIBH	United Nations Mission in Bosnia and Herzegovina
WG	Working Group
WHO	World Health Organization
WIPO	World Intellectual Property Organization
WTO	World Trade Organization

1 A guide to the new UN human rights practice

This book owes a great debt to human rights scholars and practitioners who have written earlier guides to the UN human rights system. Without their contributions to the field this book could not have been written. This account, however, departs considerably from traditional approaches to the study of the UN human rights system, both in content and in methodology. It includes many topics and actors not often considered in an introductory guide, and offers familiar topics under a new organizational structure. This book proceeds from a new orientation to the UN to human rights practice more generally. Why the difference? The evolving content of human rights, the growing diversity of actors of the UN human rights system and the changing nature of human rights practice reflect a shift in the way in which the UN human rights system has tended to address human rights challenges.

What is the new UN human rights practice?

Nearly all guides to UN human rights practice focus on the work of UN treaty and Charter-based bodies and procedures. According to these models, monitoring and reporting of violations of civil and political rights occupy the central field of advocacy practice for the international human rights movement. New issue areas do arise, but they "are either ushered into the methodological fold of the mainstream movement, or face obstacles to their integration."[1]

This book presents a much more varied and expansive view of UN human rights practice that more accurately reflects the reality of post-Cold War activity. Human rights complaint procedures and reporting under the treaty and Charter-based bodies remain important for human rights enforcement. Marginalized groups seeking the imprimatur of legitimacy within the mainstream human rights community continue to push for new treaties reflecting their concerns. In many respects, UN standard-setting remains a crucial concern, especially for those who have not yet had input into the process. To a large extent, however, the UN human rights system has in fact moved from standard-setting to implementation of human rights policies through institutionalization and enforcement. Many of these new measures are controversial and will continue to be contested as the precise content of UN human rights practice evolves over time.

In addition to making treaties more effective, UN human rights practice today is taking on a broader mandate. Human rights practice is likely to address human rights education programs for police officers and soldiers, projects to combat trafficking in women, efforts to limit the use of child soldiers, electoral assistance, and other field-oriented, in-country endeavors. Contemporary UN human rights practice speaks to concerns once deemed to be the province of other fields, such as development, humanitarian and refugee affairs, trade, labor or security. In exceptional cases, the UN also has indicated a willingness to sanction the use of military force to address human rights violations. Vigorous human rights enforcement would not have been possible during the Cold War.

Efforts to promote human rights-based advancement of economic and social development have also received particular attention in the post-September 11 climate. In the past, development organizations often sacrificed human rights in the name of development, in an "instrumentalist *quid-pro-quo* that saw human rights as a deferrable luxury of rich countries."[2] Today, however, many development organizations—including the United Nations Development Programme (UNDP)—have publicly embraced the integration of human rights in their work, often with the explicit goal of addressing the underlying tensions that provide fertile ground for terrorist acts.[3] At the same time, some states have reacted to September 11 by retrenching and regressing on human rights, violating the civil liberties of their citizens of Middle Eastern ancestry, torturing Afghan and Iraqi prisoners under the purported cloak of human rights, and threatening journalists with arrest should they not reveal their sources in cases that would ordinarily attract little attention.

These developments have been accompanied by new attempts to hold non-state actors, including paramilitary troops, NATO forces and transnational corporations, accountable for human rights abuses. The foundational international instruments of the international human rights framework, namely the Universal Declaration of Human Rights,[4] the International Covenant on Civil and Political Rights,[5] and the International Covenant on Economic, Social and Cultural Rights,[6] focus on the need to protect individuals from abuse by state authorities. Moreover, although these documents ostensibly place all civil and political rights (such as the right to a fair trial and freedom from torture) on an equal footing with economic, social and cultural rights (such as the right to education or health care), greater attention has been paid by most Western governments and NGOs to civil and political rights. This orientation has been reconsidered in recent years with an increasing realization that non-state actors, groups and organizations can also be responsible for atrocities and that economic wrongs may be as grave and as in need of redress as civil and political abuses committed by state actors.

Drawing on these developments, the organization and composition of this book reflect a broader and deeper human rights practice than guides to the UN have traditionally offered. It begins its discussion of the UN human rights system with a review of the work of the Office of the High Commissioner for Human Rights (OHCHR), the focal point for all UN human rights activities since its establishment in 1993. The High Commissioner's extensive involvement in technical assistance projects in country and field offices reflects a shift in UN human rights practice from monitoring of violations to the building of institutions and capacities to facilitate compliance. This book does contain separate chapters on contemporary practices of the OHCHR Charter and treaty-based bodies, but, breaking with tradition, the text begins with an extended treatment of the OHCHR. This reflects the OHCHR's central and ever-expanding coordinating and operational role in the UN system. Unlike many introductory guides to the UN human rights system, this book also includes information on UN affiliated and associated organizations (such as the UNDP, and the United Nations High Commissioner for Human Rights (UNHCHR)) and separate chapters on the human rights practice of the Security Council and the International Labour Organization (ILO). While this text does not aim to address every new human rights practice area, it provides a more comprehensive overview of the field for practitioners and students wishing to assess the human rights system today.

Where does UN human rights work happen?

The answer to this question used to be easy. Simply put, UN human rights practice used to happen where the name plate on the door said "human rights." So, human rights were almost entirely contained within a limited set of specific human rights bodies. This is no longer the case. Today, virtually all United Nations bodies and specialized agencies, including the World Bank and the International Monetary Fund, are undertaking efforts to incorporate the promotion or protection of human rights into their programs and activities. To be sure, these endeavors invite criticism. For starters, many of the employees of these organizations that are confronting new human rights mandates have limited training on human rights. Nonetheless, one could argue, by bringing their own experiences and perspectives to bear on human rights problems, they offer the possibility for new solutions. This book provides examples of how human rights are currently becoming diffused throughout the UN system. Pockets still exist in which human rights can be ignored, but progress has been made nonetheless.

Even as it focuses on the international system, this book recognizes that the international human rights system addresses behavior that occurs at the national level. As human rights activist Scott Long observes:

> Some people speak of "international human rights" as though it were a single word, as though the rights cannot be talked about separately from the international framework. But rights do not begin at the international level. They begin with local problems and local lives, with individuals who realize their dignity has been injured, and strive to imagine remedies and solutions.[7]

Not only are violations experienced locally, but durable solutions to long-term human rights abuses can only be found at the local level as well. The international human rights system would fail without domestic implementation of human rights.[8] As Secretary-General Kofi Annan observed, "Since respect for human rights is central to the legitimacy of the State order, human rights should be nurtured locally by branches of government, national human rights institutions and civil society."[9] In light of the increased attention devoted to human rights at local levels, this book includes information on the involvement of UN human rights bodies in the establishment and strengthening of national human rights institutions, the creation of national action plans, and civil society capacity-building.

Who are the actors?

The variety of actors involved in UN human rights practice has expanded tremendously. States still remain central to the human rights system. Without state commitment to the domestic implementation of human rights, the system will fail. Today more than ever, states both invoke human rights concerns to justify foreign policy decisions and defend their own domestic policies on human rights grounds. However, public authority on human rights practice has now shifted beyond the state to intergovernmental and non-governmental organizations. This book captures this trend by incorporating information on NGOs (a heterogeneous group) throughout the text (instead of pushing it into a separate chapter as in many books) and by including more information on the diversity of UN actors addressing human rights concerns.

The strategies and tactics of human rights NGOs have changed dramatically in recent years. Mainstream Western human rights organizations have tended to work through a particular methodology according to which human rights violations are named and perpetrators publicly identified, so as to become shamed into compliance. This methodology employs public campaigning involving such techniques as letter writing and public acts of condemnation. The efficacy of this approach has developed as the technical expertise of the "watchers" has improved and as communications technology has advanced. Additionally, NGOs have adopted new techniques that have proven to be extremely effective at influencing government leaders and UN officials. In contrast to the technique of public shaming, these new efforts often involve private meetings and cooperative information sharing, the provision of concrete policy proposals, and offers of technical assistance.

Moreover, included on the agenda of many of the newer human rights organizations is a broader array of human rights issues, including economic, social, and cultural rights. The traditional model of investigation and public exposure of misconduct that is effective in cases involving state responsibility for violation of civil and political rights will probably not be as effective in cases involving economic and social rights where there is unlikely to be "relative clarity about violation, violator and remedy."[10] The violations of economic, social, and cultural rights are difficult to address, both because of their often diffuse nature, and because affected populations often experience communal violations, rather than individual abuses of rights.

The new human rights advocacy reaches beyond the state as duty-bearer and violator of human rights, targeting also international financial institutions (IFIs), transnational corporations, trade regimes and other institutions. Among other methods, "new rights advocates" tackle issues of social justice and call into question the international practices that weaken states' capacity to meet social and economic rights. As Paul Nelson and Ellen Dorsey have explained, "this approach often seeks to weaken, not draw on, the influence of international organizations and powerful governments, and tends to involve NGOs in more complex relationships with poor country governments, relations that are sometimes adversarial, sometimes supportive."[11] Not all of these new efforts concern the UN human rights machinery and thus, while acknowledged, are not explored in this book.

Another development in human rights practice concerns the extensive involvement of human rights organizations in technical assistance projects in country and field offices. This trend reflects a general shift in international human rights practice from the monitoring of violations to the building of institutions and capacities to facilitate compliance. Especially in the post-September 11 climate, there is more urgency than ever to include victims in human rights program design and implementation. In traditional accounts of human rights, victims are passive recipients of the wisdom and good work of human rights NGOs and benevolent diplomats. The new focus on field-oriented, in-country human rights programs, however, must rely on human rights victims becoming active, empowered participants in human rights practice. National systems that are imported from outside, with little local input, are designed for failure. This book argues that a more participatory approach will necessarily be a more effective means of promoting and protecting human rights.

Organization and goals of this book

This book is part of a series on international organizations designed to be a resource for practitioner and student alike. All of the books in the series seek to provide comprehensive and current information, while also remaining clear and concise. From interviews with both international relations and law students and human rights practitioners in preparation for this book, the need to include specific, interesting examples of UN human rights practice became clear. However, given the space limitations, not every detail of every procedure could be reviewed, nor could every UN body or UN affiliate addressing human rights issues be covered. Students did not want to be bogged down in procedural detail, but at the same time they hoped for a book that could help them imagine a potential role for themselves in the UN human rights system.

To make the human rights process more tangible, this book includes primary documents, such as complaint forms and UN reports and the text provides specific illustrative case examples. Ultimately, the book seeks to provide meaningful engagement with the UN human rights system as it operates in practice. Historical and political content is provided throughout, but readers seeking further information are advised to consult the readings and Web resources listed in the Selected Bibliography, and the directory of UN bodies and affiliated organizations in the Appendix. Having read the text, students and practitioners will be better prepared to use these resources.

In sum, the book is designed to do the following:

- provide a comprehensive and current overview of the UN human rights system, yet not overwhelm with detail;
- explore the role played by a greater diversity of actors and institutions in this system;
- address the role of NGOs in human rights promotion and protection;
- introduce the relevant debates on reform and funding issues; and
- include concise, user-friendly resources for further research and practice.

Never before has the UN human rights system offered so many access points for new advocacy and human rights activities. The system is now a dynamic space where an array of actors can use a range of tools to address human wrongs and advance human rights. To be sure, many aspects of the system are susceptible to political manipulation, ineffective, unresponsive or otherwise in need of reform. Yet the system has in fact worked well in many cases, offering protection for individuals and groups and redress for wrongs. The act of participating in the international human rights system has also proven to be an effective tool of conflict prevention and conflict transformation. Involvement in the UN system increases citizen participation in problem-solving and provides a civil mechanism for translating, reflecting, and challenging claims to power.[12] By addressing malfunctioning relationships and structural problems that lie at the root of conflict, participation in UN human rights structures helps to promote a more just and peaceful future.

2 The Office of the High Commissioner for Human Rights

When the United Nations General Assembly agreed to the establishment of the Office of the High Commissioner for Human Rights (OHCHR) in December 1993, many human rights advocates were sure that "a new era of commitment to ensuring human rights had arrived."[1] Decades of human rights standard-setting had at last given way to a new age of human rights implementation and enforcement. As Felice Gaer recalls, "During the Cold War years—when Soviet bloc countries routinely challenged the relevance of individual rights—the discussion of specific violations by countries remained a largely taboo topic within UN human rights bodies."[2] When the Cold War ended, anything seemed possible. All hopes were pinned on the OHCHR and expectations were high that the UN human rights system would mature and its effectiveness would significantly be enhanced.

Ever since the office's founding, then, a heavy burden has been placed on the OHCHR. New challenges are constantly being presented to the High Commissioner charged with leading the office. With the increased awareness of human rights issues and the growing tendency of states to invoke human rights as integral to foreign policy decisions, the expectations upon the UN human rights system have increased dramatically in recent years. Demands on the Office of the High Commissioner for Human Rights further increased as a result of the direction given by the UN Secretary-General, Kofi Annan, as part of his "Agenda for Further Change."[3]

The Secretary-General's report, submitted to the 57th session of the General Assembly in September 2002, highlighted the importance of the United Nations' work on human rights and the need to build upon achievements while simultaneously strengthening the human rights structures of the organization. Among other measures, the report required the High Commissioner to undertake two enormous tasks: mainstreaming human rights into the work of all UN activities and agencies,[4] and developing and implementing a plan to strengthen human rights-related United Nations actions at the country level.

The discussion of the OHCHR in this chapter is divided into four parts. First, the chapter describes the origins of the office, highlights the expectations of the main actors advocating for the office's creation, and identifies the High Commissioner's mandate. Second, it outlines the key activities of the OHCHR, and to illustrate the OHCHR's work in the field, it uses a case study of Bosnia. The third part of this chapter then turns to the OHCHR's support of key implementing partners at the national level and in particular, National Human Rights Institutions (NHRIs). Finally, the chapter concludes with a brief review of the work of the individual commissions to date.

Origins and organization

Genesis of an idea

The idea that human rights enforcement would be facilitated by placing broad authority in a single individual can be traced as far back as 1947. At the time of the drafting of the Universal Declaration of Human Rights, Professor René Cassin suggested the establishment of a post of Attorney-General for Human Rights who could assist aggrieved individuals and groups in proceedings before a new international human rights tribunal.[5] Cassin's proposal was flatly dismissed as unworkable. Subsequent proposals for a human rights commissioner abandoned the idea of a human rights tribunal but instead stressed the general need to create institutions for human rights enforcement. Remembering the lessons of the Holocaust, Jewish organizations were among those taking the lead in pressing for strong international human rights enforcement mechanisms. In 1949, the Consultative Council of Jewish Organizations, an organization that took a significant role in the process because it hoped to prevent another Holocaust, referred to the Cassin proposal in urging the Commission to create an office for a human rights commissioner, even in the absence of an international human rights court.

In 1950 and 1951, Uruguay submitted proposals to the General Assembly for establishing a human rights attorney-general that would provide a means of implementing the International Covenant on Civil and Political Rights, which was being drafted at that time.[6] The concept was for an attorney-general for human rights to receive and review petitions from individuals and groups and to present complaints on their behalf. Although this proposal was more successful at garnering attention, it also failed to attract substantial support.

Another proposal began circulating in the early 1960s when, in a speech at Columbia University, Jacob Blaustein outlined his proposal for a high commissioner who could coordinate and facilitate human rights investigations, albeit without the power of an attorney-general. In 1964, non-governmental organizations (NGOs) gathered in a series of three meetings to consider proposals for the creation of the new post: first, in Paris under the auspices of the World Veterans Association; second, in London under the auspices of Amnesty International; and third, in Geneva under the auspices of the International Commission of Jurists. With strong input from the NGOs in attendance, Costa Rica introduced a draft proposal to the UN Commission on Human Rights in 1965 which provided for the establishment of a High Commissioner for Human Rights.

The Costa Rican plan succeeded. Following the completion of the working group's study, the Commission adopted the Costa Rican proposal. The Commission directed the Economic and Social Council to submit its draft resolution to create a United Nations High Commissioner's Office for Human Rights to the General Assembly. Over the objections of socialist states, in 1967, the Economic and Social Council recommended that the General Assembly establish the post of High Commissioner, but each year the Assembly postponed a decision regarding the recommendation and the proposal was perpetually sidelined. Although it was discussed intermittently during the 1970s, the idea of creating a High Commissioner for Human Rights was unable to achieve consensus during the entire Cold War.

Human rights standard-setting and institution-building did progress, however, during the Cold War. Eager to signal their allegiance to human rights, states signed treaty after treaty, and through the procedures of the UN, agreed to a host of new treaty-based human rights committees, working groups and special rapporteurs. These human rights institutions and mechanisms proved effective in setting minimum standards on human rights and in drawing public attention to abuses. Most importantly, throughout the Cold War, international human rights institutions and mechanisms served to provide a focal point around which concerned citizens could organize. Through these structures, information on human rights standards became more accessible, and following this, NGOs and networks of activists made use of the new opportunities for advocacy and for making human rights claims heard. Ultimately, the burgeoning of international human rights organizations and laws provided the framework for advocacy networks to begin identifying human rights abusers and shaming them into addressing their abuses. Benefiting from an information and communication revolution that facilitated the growth of advocacy networks and improved the sophistication and quality of their advocacy, human rights NGOs grew in their influence and their efficacy. They began to demand better enforcement mechanisms from within the same structures that had given them this legitimacy.

The human rights landscape looked very different at the beginning of the 1990s than it did at the end of the 1970s, with more advocates and institutions addressing more issues in more places. Yet even as human rights NGOs grew in number and human rights institutions proliferated, the number of claims of human rights violations increased and the record of enforcement grew ever more dismal. Each year, the UN continued to receive an increasing number of complaints relating to serious human rights violations. In its report to the 1993 World Conference on Human Rights, Amnesty International stated that the UN Working Group on Enforced or Involuntary Disappearances had received 17,000 reports of "disappearances" in 1991. At the end of 1992, even the UN Secretary-General conceded that the UN had decidedly failed to put an end to massive human rights violations.[7] Nearly 50,000 complaints had been received by the Working Group on Enforced or Involuntary Disappearances and transmitted to governments by 2001.[8]

Many of the political struggles that emerged in the wake of the Cold War resulted in new campaigns of repression and new wars in which civilian populations were the targets. To some extent, the United Nations committed itself as never before to protecting civilians, dispatching peacekeeping and peace-monitoring missions in the former Yugoslavia, Cambodia, El Salvador, Guatemala, and Haiti.[9] But these efforts, emanating from UN headquarters in New York and far away from the UN's human rights mechanisms in Geneva (then centered around the UN Centre for Human Rights), were deeply criticized. The personnel assigned to the missions often lacked training in human rights and their missions were ineffective in protecting international human rights treaty standards. The continuing marginalization and isolation of the United Nations' human rights program proved troublesome: "Denounced by diplomats and bureaucrats as 'political,' the human rights program was considered by some countries as a threat to development assistance, and by others, to the resolution of long-standing armed conflicts."[10]

Contribution of world conferences

As a solution to the growing human rights enforcement gap, the idea of a UN High Commissioner for Human Rights re-emerged as an attractive prospect. Many human rights NGOs claim credit for having resurrected the idea. According to one of the most persuasive accounts, the campaign for a new office can be traced to a 1992 meeting of the Dutch section of Amnesty International. Andrew Clapham recounts that "the idea was [then] promoted by Amnesty International at the Tunis regional preparatory meeting to the World Conference [on Human Rights] in December 1992 and became the centre-piece of its proposals to the World Conference."[11] At the time, the idea was for a new orga- nizational body to be headed by a high-level UN official to respond promptly to serious violations of human rights.

On the eve of the World Conference, the UN Secretary-General voiced his opposition to the plan. He agreed that both "the principles and practice of human rights are under stress." He suggested, however, that the solution lay in "quiet diplomacy," not in "[p]roposals for new bureaucracies" which "may only arouse discontent and resistance at a time when liberality and leeway are called for."[12] The NGOs flatly rejected this reasoning. Using the preparatory processes for the World Conference and the World Conference itself to voice dissent, the NGOs urged that years of quiet diplomacy had failed and that the new post had the potential of increasing participation in and satisfaction with the UN human rights system.

Ultimately, support for the OHCHR proved to be extremely broad and strong. The NGO and government representatives supporting the proposal succeeded in obtaining the following endorsement for the creation of the office in the Declaration and Platform for Action that emerged from that World Conference on Human Rights:

> An Office of a High Commissioner for Human Rights should be established as a new high-level independent authority within the United Nations system, with the capacity to act rapidly in emergency situations of human rights violations and to ensure the coordina- tion of human rights activities within the United Nations system.[13]

Although not a legally binding treaty, the Vienna Declaration was agreed to by the 171 state representatives in attendance at the meeting and, as evidence of international consensus on the matter, it carried great weight as an indication of state consensus on human rights and developing state practice.

Mandate and organization

The creation of the new office was made official six months after the Vienna Declaration was passed. In December 1993, the UN General

Assembly passed Resolution 48/141, establishing the Office of the High Commissioner for Human Rights as the umbrella and coordinating body for all of the UN human rights machinery. Based at the Palais Wilson in Geneva, Switzerland, with an office at United Nations head-quarters in New York, the High Commissioner for Human Rights was tasked with leading this office. A ranking Under-Secretary-General of the United Nations, the High Commissioner carries great authority. Because human rights is considered a "cross-cutting issue," the High Commissioner is a member of all four executive committees of the United Nations: Peace and Security, Economic and Social Affairs, Development Cooperation, and Humanitarian Affairs.

The mandate of the High Commissioner encompasses the following:

- promote and protect the effective enjoyment of civil, cultural, economic, political and social rights, including the right to development;
- provide advisory services, technical and financial assistance to states that request them;
- coordinate United Nations education and public information programs in the field of human rights;
- help remove the obstacles to the full realization of human rights and prevent the continuation of human rights violations throughout the world;
- engage in a dialogue with governments in order to secure respect for human rights;
- enhance international cooperation for the promotion and protection of human rights;
- coordinate human rights promotion and protection activities throughout the United Nations system; and
- rationalize, adapt, strengthen and streamline the United Nations machinery in the field of human rights in order to improve its efficiency and effectiveness.[14]

In carrying out its mission, the OHCHR is charged with giving priority to "the most pressing human rights violations, both chronic and acute," focusing on "at risk" and "vulnerable" populations; and paying "equal attention to the realization of all rights, including the 'right to development.'"[15]

Of all the political debates that arose over the creation of the OHCHR, none was more significant than that over the decision to give the right to development prominence in the new office's mandate.[16] The USA had a long track record of opposing economic rights, but in particular the right to development. As Stephen Marks explains, the

USA has been "frustrated by what it perceives as the determination of countries in the Non-Aligned Movement (NAM) to force their interpretation of this right on what is essentially the group of donor states."[17] It was over the objections of the United States that the UN General Assembly in 1986 proclaimed development as a human right. At that time, the United States cast the only vote against the Declaration on the Right to Development (eight other countries abstained).[18] The U.S. position remained unchanged even after the 1993 Vienna Declaration and Programme of Action called the right to development "a universal and inalienable right and an integral part of fundamental human rights."[19] Likewise, the U.S. position did not budge after the General Assembly required the High Commissioner to establish "a new branch whose primary responsibilities would include the promotion and protection of the right to development."[20]

The work of the OHCHR has grown exponentially. In 2008, the OHCHR employed over 850 staff in its New York and Geneva offices, and in 11 countries and 7 regional offices around the world. This number includes some 240 international human rights offices serving on UN peace missions.[21] The mandate of the office is to promote universal ratification and implementation of human rights instruments; assist in the development of new norms; support human rights organs and treaty-monitoring bodies; respond to human rights violations; produce manuals, handbooks and training materials; and develop technical cooperation programs. The day-to-day work of the OHCHR is divided into an Executive Office, an Administrative Branch and External Relations Branch, and four additional functional branches (see Figure 2.1).

- *The Research and Right to Development Branch* is involved in all activities related to the promotion and protection of the right to development, and is also responsible for carrying out research projects on the protection of human rights.
- *The Treaties and Commission Branch* serves as a secretariat to the six treaty bodies, the voluntary funds, and to the Commission on Human Rights and its subsidiary bodies.
- *The Capacity Building and Field Operations Branch* coordinates all advisory services and technical cooperation projects and the human rights field offices worldwide.
- *The Special Procedures Branch* provides support to the Special Rapporteurs of the Commission on Human Rights and services other special procedures.

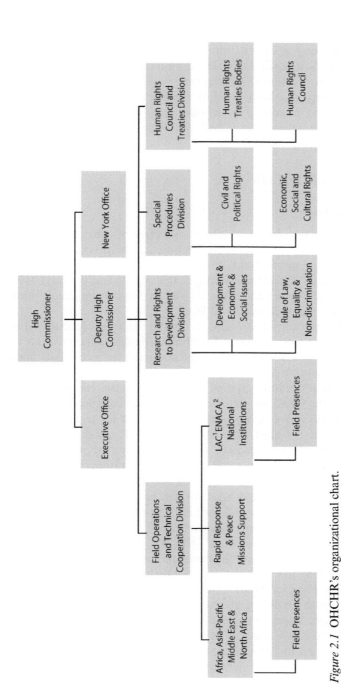

Figure 2.1 OHCHR's organizational chart.
Source: Adapted from High Commissioner's Strategic Management Plan 2008–2009, www.ohchr.org/Documents/Press/SMP2008-9.pdf

Notes:
1 Latin America and the Caribbean
2 Europe, North America and Central Asia

OHCHR's spending is divided into 11 main activities. In descending order, the four most costly OHCHR expenditures are field operations and technical cooperation (12.7 percent), research and right to development (11.2 percent), human rights treaties (8.4 percent), and program support and management services (7.4 percent). The OHCHR maintains that the latter category "allowed the office to direct resources to projects with the greatest needs."[22]

Key activities of OHCHR

Technical assistance

The term "technical assistance" refers to a variety of activities, in which OHCHR human rights specialists offer practical help with the implementation of international human rights standards (see Table 2.1). For years, a wide range of actors have sought the expertise of the OHCHR, including both UN bodies and states, as well as non-governmental actors at international, regional, and local levels.

One of the important innovations stemming from the creation of the Office of the High Commissioner for Human Rights is the creation of a streamlined process for requesting and receiving technical assistance in the field of human rights. Instead of involving other parts of the UN (as the previous procedure required), the whole matter remains within the purview of the OHCHR. The technical assistance procedure can be broken down into a five-step process: (1) a request for technical assistance is made to the OHCHR; (2) the OHCHR conducts a needs assessment (based on such factors as the availability of other international governmental and non-governmental organizations to undertake the task and the comparative advantage the OHCHR brings to the project); (3) should there be a need for the project that the OHCHR can address, a project is formulated; (4) the project is implemented; and (5) the project is independently evaluated.[23]

Even before the establishment of OHCHR, the UN placed special emphasis on advising states on the domestic implementation of human rights. Since 1955, the United Nations Technical Cooperation Programme in the Field of Human Rights has been assisting states, at their request, in the building and strengthening of national structures that have a direct impact on the overall observance of human rights and the maintenance of the rule of law. The creation of the OHCHR has led to an expansion of activities at national levels, providing assistance in training law enforcement officials, revising national legislation or reforming the justice system to incorporate international human

Table 2.1 Forms of technical assistance

Category of assistance	Activities
Administration of justice	Training courses for judges, lawyers, prosecutors and prison officials, as well as law enforcement officers.
Constitutional and legislative reform	Advisory services provided by experts, organization of conferences, provision of human rights information and documentation, assistance in drafting laws, or support for public information campaigns to ensure the involvement of all sectors of society in law-making.
National parliaments	Advisory services on ratification of international human rights instruments, the provision of information on comparative national human rights legislation, the role of parliamentary human rights committees.
The armed forces	Training activities for military officers in international human rights and humanitarian norms.
Electoral assistance	Preparation of guidelines for analysis of electoral laws and procedures, publication of a handbook on human rights and elections, and public information relating to human rights and elections.
Treaty reporting	Training activities for government officials in preparing state reports.
Non-governmental organizations and civil society	Assistance to non-governmental organizations in the context of its country activities, by including them in seminars and training courses and supporting appropriate projects they have developed.
Training materials	Development of a series of training manuals and handbooks, for use by both instructors and participants. See: www.unhchr.ch/html/menu6/2/training.htm.
Human rights education	Work to promote human rights education by: • developing human rights education and training materials; • supporting national efforts for human rights education, in the context of its Technical Cooperation program; • facilitating information-sharing, through international and regional seminars and workshops and the development of educational resources; • supporting local efforts for human rights education through the Assisting Communities Together project, which provides financial assistance to human rights grass-roots initiatives.
National Plans of Action	Advising states in the drawing-up of national action plans identifying what steps needed to improve promotion and protection of human rights.

rights standards, and creating strong national structures capable of supporting a human rights-respecting democracy.[24]

Assistance has taken the form of expert advisory services, training courses, workshops and seminars, fellowships, grants, provision of information and documentation, and assessment of domestic human rights needs. Technical cooperation often takes place in countries where the OHCHR has a country office or field presence, but it also can be provided as a stand-alone service.

While technical cooperation activities are not a substitute for the important monitoring and investigating aspects of the United Nations human rights program, they can be seen as an integral part of it. The Secretary-General, as well as the Commission on Human Rights, has repeatedly emphasized that a government's responsibility to account for the human rights situation in its own territory does not decrease simply because the OHCHR has stepped in to provide technical assistance. Additionally, governments do not become exempt from their monitoring duties if they are engaged in various other United Nations procedures. Rather, technical cooperation activities are meant to support and strengthen state monitoring and investigation. In fact, as the International Council on Human Rights Policy has noted, when technical assistance is done properly, it entails fundamental structural change and thus is even more demanding—and more intrusive—than monitoring and reporting.[25]

Country offices/regional offices

The OHCHR has found it necessary to expand its work from merely providing project-specific assistance and advice to actually creating offices in those countries where an intensive, long-term presence is both appropriate and requested. In contrast to technical assistance, which is project-oriented, country offices are geographically based endeavors. The hope is that the OHCHR staff who live in-country are likely to be more effective as they are able to understand both the mandates and the practical abilities of their organization, in addition to the cultural, political, and legal contexts of the countries in which they are working.[26]

The presence of an OHCHR office can also improve the confidence and skills of local staff by providing a measure of much-needed safety and protection. This enables the OHCHR and local partner organizations to engage civil society and enhance political participation, thus facilitating an end to conflict situations and human rights abuses. Finally, an OHCHR office as a permanent presence can help increase the accountability of governments by acting as a long-term watchdog, ensuring that human rights abuses are addressed openly and honestly—thus increasing opportunities for new democracies to develop.

In 2008, OHCHR had country offices in Angola, Bolivia, Cambodia, Colombia, Guatemala, Mexico, Nepal, Togo, and Uganda, as well as stand-alone offices in the occupied Palestinian territories and Kosovo (offices in Kosovo were phased out when Kosovo became an independent country on 17 February 2008).[27] The legal basis for the operation of field offices is a negotiated agreement with the respective government, based on the High Commissioner's mandate. Country offices vary in size, depending on the phase of deployment and the nature of the work undertaken.

In addition to creating numerous country offices, OHCHR has found regional offices to be of great utility for effective human rights monitoring and promotion. Through regional "hubs" OHCHR staff developed regional strategies, targeting regional organizations and utilizing, where available, regional systems and mechanisms. In 2008, OHCHR had regional offices in Addis Ababa (East Africa), Bangkok (Southeast Asia), Beirut (Middle East), Bishkek (Central Asia), Dakar (West Africa), Panama (Latin American, with a small liaison office in Santiago, Chile, where the former South America Regional Office was located), Pretoria (Southern Africa), and Suva (Pacific). Further plans for extended regional work included opening additional offices covering Southwest Asia and North Africa.[28] Like country offices, regional offices vary in size; their activities, analyses, conclusions and recommendations are integrated in the High Commissioner's annual report.

To support staff both in the field and back home in New York and Geneva, OHCHR increasingly calls on the geographic and subject matter expertise of staff who can be deployed as Human Rights Advisers to support UN Country Teams. As of December 2007, OHCHR had Advisers in Ecuador, Guyana, Indonesia, Kyrgyzstan, Maldives, Pakistan, Rwanda, Somalia, Sri Lanka, and the South Caucasus (Azerbaijan and Georgia); and national staff in Country Teams in FRY Macedonia, Serbia, and Russia. These experts can also use special press releases and urgent reports to try to influence the UN to take actions on particularly pressing issues. Box 2.1 presents one such example.

Other forms of field presence

Along with its country and regional offices, OHCHR staff have made their presence in the field effective through working in close collaboration with the Department of Peacekeeping Operations (DPKO), the Department of Political Affairs (DPA), and other actors involved in peace operations. Their main task is "to ensure that human rights

Box 2.1   UN Expert on Internally Displaced Persons concerned about the situation in Georgia

14 August 2008

Geneva: The Representative of the Secretary General on the Human Rights of Internally Displaced Persons, Walter Kalin, is deeply concerned about the growing number of civilians displaced in Georgia, estimated at close to 100,000, the continuing dangers to which many of them are still exposed and the difficulties in providing them with shelter, medical care and food. He is also alarmed about reports that humanitarian access is still blocked and by allegations of widespread looting of property left behind by the displaced.

Kalin urges all parties to the conflict to ensure that persons who wish to do so can leave areas affected by violence, that property left behind be protected, and that unimpeded access for humanitarian organizations to conflict areas be granted so they may reach internally displaced persons and other civilians at risk without further delay. He welcomes aid already provided to Georgia to meet the huge humanitarian needs of the displaced but in light of the extensive needs encourages international organizations, non-governmental organizations and donors to immediately come together to provide support for the efforts of the Georgian Government to alleviate the suffering of its population.

The expert reminds both the Russian Federation and the Georgian Government of their obligation to respect the rights of internally displaced persons and provide protection and assistance to them. He also urges the two governments to adhere to the provisions in the UN Guiding Principles on Internal Displacement, which the 2005 World Summit Outcome Document declared "an important international framework for the protection of internally displaced persons."

The Representative welcomes the signing of a ceasefire and calls on the Governments of Georgia and the Russian Federation to refrain from all actions that would cause further displacement. He also urges both governments to include in the envisaged peace plan provisions allowing the displaced to voluntarily return to their homes in safety and dignity and to have their property returned to them and compensations paid for damages. Those who cannot or

Box continued on next page.

do not want to return should be given the opportunity to integrate elsewhere in the country.

For further information or interview requests, please contact M. Duchatellier +41 22 917 9369 or mduchatellier@ohchr.org.

Source: www.unhchr.ch/huricane/huricane.nsf/view01/BBC1AEDBF2EB0231C 12574A5004972A3?opendocument (14 September 2008)

components of UN peace missions are adequately guided and supported," by "monitoring the human rights situation, issuing public reports, and assisting in building national capacities to address human rights issues."[29]

The heads of human rights components of peace missions are selected by OHCHR, and they report to both the Special Representative of the Secretary-General heading the mission and to the High Commissioner. As of August 2008, human rights components of UN peace missions were deployed, or about to be deployed, in Afghanistan, Burundi, the Central African Republic, Chad, Côte d'Ivoire, the Democratic Republic of the Congo, Ethiopia/Eritrea, Georgia/Abkhazia, Guinea-Bissau, Haiti, Iraq, Liberia, Sierra Leone, Somalia, Sudan, and Timor-Leste.

Rwanda provides a good example of the difficulties facing human rights workers in conflict areas. The first large-scale field presence was the Human Rights Field Operation in Rwanda (HRFOR), set up during the chaotic aftermath of the 1994 genocide. Deployed following the genocide in 1994, and ending its term in July 1998, HRFOR's goal was not only to meet "the most immediate and pressing needs, but also to put in place medium- and long-term initiatives to promote sustained assistance to the people of Rwanda with respect to human rights protection and promotion."[30]

According to the agreement reached between the OHCHR and the government of Rwanda, HRFOR had four separate units for these functions, in addition to a headquarters. The Operations and Documentation Unit compiled reports and analyzed the human rights situation based on the information garnered by the field monitors. The Legal Unit focused on projects related to the administration of justice, including monitoring of the genocide trials. In particular, the Legal Unit assisted the Prosecutor's Office, trained the gendarmerie and the communal police, and worked with human rights organizations to increase their capacity in the same areas. The Education and Promotion Unit worked to improve the situations of the most vulnerable groups in

Rwandan society, including women and children. Last, the Security and Communications Unit provided for the security of HRFOR staff through liaison work with the Rwandan authorities and by training personnel in safety techniques.

The most striking feature of field presences is their ability to monitor human rights where—and often when—abuses are happening. In Rwanda, the intensive presence of the HRFOR monitors was intended to function as a confidence-building measure; the goal was to produce a climate and an infrastructure capable of accounting for the past, building for the future, and strengthening civil society so that the political solutions absent in the early 1990s are available to the population when the tensions of conflict next begin to rise. Although its early work came too late to prevent conflict, HRFOR helped contribute to the resolution of the horrific violence of 1994 and to the creation of a functioning democracy. It thereby contributed to long-term structural prevention of conditions like those present before the genocide in 1994.

The initial deployments in Rwanda were severely constrained by financial resource problems, and HRFOR came to be seen as part of the United Nations Assistance Mission for Rwanda (UNAMIR) band-aid operation, unable to staunch the extremes of the genocide. Although HRFOR's mission was not able to stop the genocide, one must view the international community's efforts in Rwanda as a whole. It was only later, once some semblance of order was established in the country, that HRFOR's efforts began to pay off through capacity-building and infrastructural development.[31]

As a response to the failures in Rwanda and elsewhere, OHCHR created the Rapid Response Unit, composed of teams with complementary skills who were ready and able to deploy on very short notice. These well equipped and logistically supported units give OHCHR the ability to respond more proactively to tension spots before they erupt in full-scale conflict. The goal is to address deteriorating human rights matters at the root of many violent conflicts. As part of its support to peace missions, Rapid Response Units have developed training materials for peacekeeping units. Since their inception in 2006, the Rapid Response Units have included: Timor-Leste, Western Sahara, Liberia, Lebanon, and Beit-Hanoun (Occupied Palestine).[32]

Bosnia and Herzegovina: the OHCHR field office at work

After years of work on a wide range of human rights issues, the OHCHR closed its Office in Bosnia and Herzegovina in June 2007. The metamorphosis of the office and the imprint it left behind is

Box 2.2 OHCHR field presences

Country Offices: OHCHR staff engage in human rights protection and promotion activities with host government approval.

UN Peace Missions: OHCHR staff seek to integrate human rights in all components of UN Peace Missions with four priorities: "ensuring justice and accountability in peace processes; preventing and redressing human rights violations; building capacities and strengthening national institutions; and mainstreaming human rights in all UN programmes." (See www.ohchr.org/EN/Countries/Pages/WorkInField.aspx for more information.)

Regional Offices: Regional OHCHR staff are able to work on regional strategies and to utilize regional human rights systems and mechanisms for human rights protection and promotion.

Human Rights Country Advisers: OHCHR staff with special expertise are also deployed as Human Rights Advisers to support UN Country Teams' plans for strengthening nations' capacities and institutions in promoting and protecting human rights.

Rapid Response to Emerging Rights Crises: OHCHR's Rapid Response Unit also supports the work of OHCHR by swiftly deploying personnel to the field, responding to imminent crises and rapidly deteriorating human rights situations across the globe.

instructive. The office evolved in four stages: (1) from a monitoring and reporting body which, beginning in 1994, serviced the mandate of the Special Rapporteur (SR) appointed by the Commission on Human Rights,[33] to (2) a peace supporting role under the 1995 Dayton General Framework Agreement for Peace[34] (while also continuing to support the SR until 2002); to (3) an organization with a formal cooperation agreement with the UN Mission in Bosnia (UNMIBH),[35] extremely active on gender issues and on the training of police officers; to (4) a post-UNMIBH organization (The European Union Police Mission took over from UNMIBH in January 2003)[36] working on five areas of action, namely non-discrimination and women's rights; transitional justice; anti-trafficking; treaty body reporting; and protection of economic and social rights of vulnerable groups. Under the direction of Chief of Mission Madeleine Rees,[37] the office concentrated on gender, discrimination, the protection of minorities and the rule of law with an emphasis on social and economic rights. This led to involvement in some of the most contentious areas of protection, particularly relating to gender-based violence including the trafficking of women and children and the due process rights of those suspected of terrorism.

The OHCHR viewed its role in Bosnia and Herzegovina as serving "as a catalyst in respect of the promotion and protection of human rights and the rule of law, with a particular focus on those aspects not directly addressed through the mandates of others, and ... ensur[ing that] human rights promotion and protection becomes nationally sustainable."[38] The office described its approach as:

- identifying the situation on the ground in critical human rights areas of concern;
- analyzing the legislative and policy framework relating to the issue in light of relevant human rights standards; and
- working toward human rights compliance, including legislative and policy reform, and implementation.

The specific activities of the field office included: (1) treaty body reporting; (2) the Rights-based Municipal Assessment Programme; (3) the design of a Poverty Reduction Strategy Plan; (4) addressing the problem of gender-based violence and the trafficking in persons; (5) protection of the rights of those socially excluded as a result of conflict, such as families of missing persons, camp survivors and victims of torture, civilian war-disabled, and witnesses to war crimes. In addition, the Bosnia field office was unique in explicitly making gender a cross-cutting issue throughout all of its activities.

The treaty body reporting activity focused on strengthening the competency of Bosnian civil society to monitor the government's role in meeting its reporting obligations to the UN treaty bodies (see Chapter 4). BiH was remiss in all of its reporting obligations, but since 2001 has tried to make up for its failings by working closely with UNICEF to produce reports on compliance with the specific provisions of the treaty bodies. The OHCHR was, for the first time, able to bring representatives of government to meet with NGOs to discuss and to listen to their views on the issues to be reported upon. This was profoundly effective in relation to the Committee Against Torture (CAT).

The Rights-based Municipal Assessment Programme (RMAP) refers to an effort to undertake rights-based assessments of selected municipalities throughout BiH with the aim of subsequently addressing those issues identified so that there can be real and participatory development. A rights-based approach to development is a conceptual framework for the process of human development that is normatively based on international human rights standards and operationally directed to promoting and protecting human rights. Craig Mokhiber explains:

> Essentially, a rights-based approach integrates the norms, standards, and principles of the international human rights system into the plans, policies and processes of development. The norms and standards are those contained in the wealth of international treaties and declarations, and in the authoritative interpretations of the bodies established to monitor treaty implementation. The principles include those of participation, accountability, non-discrimination, empowerment and direct (and express) linkage to the international human rights instruments and standards themselves.[39]

The very existence of RMAPs is evidence that even as the right to development remains controversial, the human rights framework is entering the practical realm of development implementation and planning.

According to Rees,[40] the goal of RMAPs, which are being undertaken in partnership with the United Nations Development Programme, is to train local stakeholders in rights-based analysis of development needs. A further objective of the project, Rees adds, is to generate increased participation of stakeholders. This work is based on the premise that human rights, including the right to development, are interrelated and indivisible. Human rights cannot be measured solely by gross domestic product (GDP), but must be measured by assessing a broad spectrum of indicators. Through rights-based assessments, the RMAP provides reports including analyses, baselines, and indicators specifically relevant to the municipality, against which progress can be measured and targeted programming can be designed and implemented.

As a condition of receiving funding, the World Bank required Bosnia to create a Poverty Reduction Strategy Plan (PRSP). In helping Bosnia and Herzegovina meet its obligations for developing a PRSP, the OHCHR has introduced a rights-based approach to development. Unlike typical development approaches which emphasize economic efficiency, a rights-based approach seeks to foster the understanding of the human rights dimension of poverty. This approach pushes the OHCHR to focus on the process, to emphasize broad participation and identify gaps in human rights protection that either lead to poverty or are results of poverty, whether directly or indirectly. The OHCHR brought groups which had been excluded into the process, including trade unions, the families of missing persons, women's groups, and others. This involved field testing the guidelines of the OHCHR on human rights approaches to poverty reduction to help identify the causes of poverty within these groups, and the steps which would be needed to address them. The aim was that this should then become part of the strategy of the government to address poverty at macro and micro levels.

The OHCHR also spent considerable resources on the issue of trafficking in persons. Beginning in 1998, NGOs working in the border areas with Serbia and members of the International Police Task Force began reporting instances of women being trafficked into Bosnia and Herzegovina to work in the sex industry, primarily for the international workers ready to pay well for their "services." In the year 2000 alone, thousands of women passed through Bosnia and Herzegovina for this purpose.[41] To combat trafficking comprehensively, the OHCHR addresses its causes and consequences, emphasizing the rights of the victim, state responsibility, and appropriate law enforcement. Efforts to ensure coordination and collaboration have sought an integrated approach by working with the government, the NGOs and the international community to address the cycle of trafficking from prevention to reintegration. The main focus, given urgent circumstances, had to be on the immediate protection of victims, hence the need to build NGO capacity to run shelters, to train police and to reform legislation so that women were not prosecuted for status offences or prostitution, and ultimately to ensure their legal status in BiH for a sufficient period of time to enable recovery and an informed choice as to their next move. While the framework for this has been largely achieved, BiH is now a country of origin and the emphasis must now be on prevention, which in turn is linked to an appropriate poverty reduction strategy.

In addition to integrating gender throughout all of its endeavors, the OHCHR presence in Bosnia supported gender centers throughout Bosnia and Herzegovina. It also aimed to mainstream gender issues throughout the operations of other international organizations at work in Bosnia. An extensive independent review of OHCHR technical assistance programs throughout the world notes that the OHCHR in Bosnia was, at least at that time, the only OHCHR country office where activities were equally targeting men and women in design and implementation and ensuring participation of women and their inclusion among the beneficiaries.[42]

OHCHR support of national human rights institutions (NHRIs)

National human rights institutions (NHRIs) are, as the name suggests, national-level human rights bodies engaged in human rights monitoring and protection activities. NHRIs are quite unique organizations. What makes them different from other institutions in civil society is that they are most often established by law and resourced by government. At the same time, what makes NHRIs different from other governmental institutions is that, although the state may hold the purse strings, NHRIs are independent of the state and, in fact, part of their purpose is to investigate alleged abuses committed by their governments. While the United Nations toyed for a long time with the idea of establishing national institutions to protect human rights, the involvement of the UN in the formation of national human rights institutions (NHRIs) is a relatively new phenomenon.[43]

The Secretary-General of the United Nations placed a priority on the development by the United Nations of the capacity of NHRIs in his report of 9 September 2002. He noted that "the capacity of the United Nations to help individual countries to build strong human rights institutions will be strengthened." He further noted:

> Building strong human rights institutions at the country level is what in the long run will ensure that human rights are protected and advanced in a sustained manner. The emplacement or enhancement of a national protection system in each country, reflecting international human rights norms, should therefore be a principal objective of the Organisation. These activities are especially important in countries emerging from conflict.[44]

As the centrality of national human rights mechanisms in democracy-building and conflict prevention has become more clear, the United Nations has in turn become more invested in encouraging the development of such institutions and seeking to provide guidelines for how they should operate. The number of NHRIs has skyrocketed from 36 in 1993[45] to nearly 120 in 2008.[46]

The majority of existing national human rights institutions can be grouped together in three broad categories:[47]

1 "ombudsmen"—appointed by the parliament; the mandate of ombudsmen is to protect the rights of aggrieved individuals. Some countries have maintained the name "ombudsman," while other countries have used different titles that are expressive of the duties of

the institution, such as Parliamentary Commissioner for Administration (United Kingdom, Sri Lanka), Public Protector (South Africa), *Protecteur du Citoyen* (Protector of the Citizen, Quebec, Canada), *Volksanwaltschaft* (People's Advocate, Austria), and *Difensore Civico* (Civic Defender, Italian regions and provinces);

2   "human rights commissions," which function independently from other organs of government, but may be required to report to the legislature on a regular basis (for example, in Canada, Australia, New Zealand, India, Sri Lanka, Uganda, and South Africa);

3   hybrid institutions that expressly have been given or that in practice undertake two roles: to protect and promote human rights and monitor government administration (for example, in Poland (Commissioner for Civil Rights Protection, 1987), Croatia (National Ombudsman, 1992), Slovenia (Human Rights Ombudsman, 1995), Bosnia and Herzegovina (Federation Ombudsmen, Bosnia and Herzegovina Human Rights Ombudsman, 1995), Hungary (Parliamentary Commissioner for Civil Rights, Parliamentary Commissioner for the Protection of National and Ethnic Minority Rights, 1995), Russia (Plenipotentiary for Human Rights, 1997), Romania (Advocate of the People, 1997), Moldova (Parliamentary Advocates), Georgia (Public Defender, 1995, started operations in 1998), and Albania (People's Advocate, 1998, appointed in 2000)).

The overall goal of OHCHR involvement in national mechanisms is to sponsor the creation of human rights institutions that would serve as impartial, independent, and autonomous entities to enforce national and international human rights norms.[48] NHRIs can further this goal only if their establishment meets certain standards and principles governing their existence and performance.[49] It is the OHCHR's job, in issuing technical assistance, to promote compliance with international norms on national human rights institutions.

Beginning in 1991, states have sought guidance in the "Paris Principles" (named after a Paris meeting of existing national institutions) which define the minimum attributes of a national human rights institution as including adequate powers of investigation and a great degree of independence, as well as accessibility, accountability and pluralistic participation. National institutions that conform with the Paris Principles are invited to join the International Coordinating Committee of National Institutions, a group endorsed by a resolution of the UN Human Rights Commission which often works in partnership with the OHCHR. Since the adoption of the Paris Principles, an even more ambitious set of standards has emerged—the *National Human Rights*

Institutions: Best Practice.[50] The emergence of this publication by the Commonwealth Secretariat perhaps indicates that the progressive development of national human rights procedures and institutions will continue.

The OHCHR operates two assistance procedures to help countries establish human rights institutions. The first procedure, the technical assistance program, integrates support for national institutions with other forms of UN assistance. The second procedure involves the OHCHR gathering information from and working through the Special Adviser to the High Commissioner for the Establishment and Strengthening of National Institutions for Human Rights. Special Advisers have enabled the UN to acquire a wealth of comparative knowledge, which has been used effectively in many countries. The OHCHR has supported the establishment and operation of human rights commissions, ombudsmen, and other hybrid intuitions in many countries, including Fiji, Ghana, Guatemala, Indonesia, Latvia, Mexico, Moldova, Rwanda, South Africa, Sri Lanka, Tajikistan, Uganda, and Uzbekistan. Other countries have received assistance through the United Nations Development Programme, rather than through the OHCHR directly.[51]

The OHCHR has supported many superb broad-based regional human rights organizations. The Asia Pacific Forum of National Institutions is among the most effective. Composed of twelve full and two associate members, the Forum opens up important new avenues for strengthening human rights observance and advancing human rights protection for the peoples of the region in a constructive and cooperative environment.[52]

From a practical standpoint, there are valid justifications for the OHCHR involvement in national human rights mechanisms.[53] The primary responsibility for human rights rests with the state and, thus, efforts designed to enhance state capacity to respond to human rights abuses at the national level are imperative. To some extent, national human rights institutions can serve as local counterparts to international human rights bodies.[54] Moreover, national human rights are thought to be more effective than international mechanisms in promoting a human rights culture. The OHCHR explains:

> Human rights involve relationships among individuals, and between individuals and the State. Therefore, the practical task of protecting and promoting human rights is primarily a national one, for which each State must be responsible. At the national level, rights can be best protected through adequate legislation, an independent judiciary, the enactment and enforcement of individual safeguards

and remedies, and the establishment of democratic institutions. In addition, the most effective education and information campaigns are likely to be those which are designed and carried out at the national or local level and which take the local cultural and traditional context into account.[55]

Furthermore, the relationship between international and national law most often requires some kind of national action.[56] When states ratify a human rights instrument, they usually either incorporate its provisions directly into their domestic legislation or undertake other measures to comply with their obligations. The involvement of UN human rights experts in assisting in the drafting of legislation in line with universal human rights standards is thought to further this process.

OHCHR work on national institutions, however, has not been free from criticisms. One line of criticism focuses on the activities and methodology of the OHCHR. "Because one individual holds the position of Special Advisor, and because the Special Advisor's advice is often generic, it is difficult to obtain country-specific advice," notes one observer.[57] This is completely untrue, according to OHCHR employees who point to folders upon folders of country-specific information. "The advice is complete and accurate," says Stephenie Kleine-Ahlbrandt, a long-term consultant to the High Commission. "The real problem is the lack of political will to respond."[58]

Another line of criticism points to the OHCHR's practice of doing its best to assist all countries who seek help, regardless of their human rights record. In such cases, international support may be seen as legitimizing weak human rights commissions that operate to cover up serious governmental abuses. According to Human Rights Watch, many national commissions "see [their] role as being a mouthpiece to defend repressive government policies or to deny the existence of abuses."

A study on the effectiveness of national human rights institutions by the International Human Rights Council (Geneva) suggested that while many national institutions have won widespread respect from the public they are intended to serve, many more were regarded as illegitimate. To improve public acceptance, the OHCHR could do more to support locally conceived ways of operation—instead of offering heavy-handed suggestions that may seem remote and resisted by their intended public. The report advised OHCHR to:

- beware of prioritizing particular modes for the development of national institutions that may not be appropriate for the country concerned;

- beware of prioritizing national institutions at the expense of other important developments needed to protect and promote human rights—strengthening the judiciary, for example ...;
- consult civil society human rights activists ...[59]

For its part, the OHCHR has defended national human rights institutions against critics, asserting that there will never be a quick-fix for states which consistently abuse human rights:

> [National human rights machinery] cannot be expected to solve those problems which governments and the international community have been unable effectively to address. Neither are they set up to replace the human rights organs of the United Nations or non-governmental organizations working in the same area. Their role is clearly complementary, and a strengthening of such institutions can only enhance the effectiveness of both national and international systems for protection and promotion of human rights.[60]

The OHCHR and its supporters contend that national human rights institutions are essential to bringing the human rights message clearly to individuals regarding their specific circumstances, while international mechanisms can offer best practices guidance and research findings.

Preliminary evaluation of the individual High Commissioners

Observers have been generally critical of the first UN High Commissioner for Human Rights, Ambassador José Ayala-Lasso, who served from 1994 to 1997. The Ecuadorian diplomat began his tenure one day before the outbreak of genocidal killing in Rwanda. Although Mr. Ayala-Lasso did call for the convening of an emergency session of the Commission

---

Box 2.3   High Commissioners for Human Rights, 1994–2008

Ms. Navanethem Pillay, 2008–
Mrs. Louise Arbour, Canada, 2004–8
Mr. Sergio Vieira de Mello, Brazil, 2002–3
Ms. Mary Robinson, Ireland, 1997–2002
Mr. José Ayala-Lasso, Ecuador, 1994–97

on Human Rights to address the Rwanda crisis,[61] his many critics assert that he could have used his office more effectively to create momentum for a stronger and quicker international response.[62] As the first High Commissioner, Ayala-Lasso found himself continually justifying the moral authority of human rights.[63] Southern governments and many Southern human rights activists praised Ayala-Lasso for offering them more technical support for human rights programs. Northern governments and many Northern human rights activists, however, criticized the same technical assistance programs, which they interpreted as praising governments' human rights efforts "while downplaying their violations."[64] Disappointingly, Ayala-Lasso's term did little to bridge the widening gap between the North and the South in terms of their differing perspectives on human rights practices.

The second High Commissioner, the former president of Ireland, Mary Robinson (1997–2002) more successfully used human rights as an effective bridge between North and South. After being named to the post, she promised to "stand up to bullies" and to narrow the gap between civil and political rights, on the one hand, and economic and social rights, on the other.[65] "Part of [the integrity of the human rights message] is to know what we mean by the agenda of human rights," she urged, "it's not just civil and political rights, it also includes economic, social and cultural rights—the right to food, to education, to health."[66] Ms. Robinson declared that extreme poverty is the worst violation of human rights, as it prevents the achievement of other rights.[67] In a speech in 1998, she implored:

> Freedom of speech and belief are enshrined but also freedom from fear and want. Fair trial and the right to participatory democracy and representative Government sit shoulder to shoulder with the right to work, to equal pay for equal work, and the right to education. Both sets of rights are proclaimed as "the highest aspiration of the common people." ... We must be honest, however, and recognize that there has been an imbalance in the promotion at the international level of economic, social and cultural rights and the right to development.[68]

During her tenure, Ms. Robinson continually used her post of High Commissioner for advocacy. She pressed to see that trafficking in persons would be addressed as a human rights issue, for example. Also, early in her tenure she condemned the governments of Algeria and Democratic Republic of the Congo for human rights abuses. Additionally, she brought the UN closer to national institutions by establishing regional OHCHR representatives at UN Economic Commissions and sub-regional institutions.[69] Ms. Robinson spoke out against human rights abuses committed by Russian forces against local civilians in Chechnya and by U.S. prison guards against Afghan prisoners imprisoned in Guantánamo Bay in Cuba. Under her direction, the available resources for the OHCHR increased by approximately 33 percent.[70]

Given her strong track record, the UN Secretary-General persuaded Ms. Robinson to extend her term another year. But, angered by her stance on Afghanistan (where she was critical of U.S. actions), the USA opposed her candidacy, as did Russia for her position on Chechnya.[71] Over the strenuous objection of human rights advocates, Ms. Robinson did not receive enough votes to remain in office.

The third High Commissioner, Sergio Vieira de Mello (2002–3), was a prominent, long-time UN employee. He stressed in his initial speeches that human rights was now "fully at the centre of intergovernmental debate" and that strengthening the "rule of law" was the key goal of his term of office.[72] The Brazilian diplomat brought to the post a strong record of success in working human rights into UN programs, having served as chief UN official in Kosovo following the NATO bombing campaign and head of the UN East Timor Transitional Administration. As transitional administrator in East Timor, he received praise for adopting a philosophy of involving the East Timorese as much as possible in these decisions and deferring as many fundamental decisions as possible to an elected East Timorese government.[73]

In 2003, after only a short time in office as High Commissioner— only eight months—Mr. Vieira de Mello took a leave of absence in order to serve as the UN representative in post-war Iraq. The decision of the USA and its allies to recruit Vieira de Mello for the position and his decision to accept set off an outcry in the human rights community. The UN could hardly claim to prioritize human rights if it allowed the highest-ranking UN human rights position to remain vacant.

Mr. Vieira de Mello never returned to his position as he had planned. Tragically, he was at his desk at work on 19 August 2003 when a suicide bomber slammed a truck into UN headquarters in Iraq, killing Mr. Vieira de Mello and 16 others.[74] Mr. Vieira de Mello's death drew new attention to the work of the UN and its ability to address the human rights abuses that create the conditions for violent conflict.

The connection between human rights and conflict was indeed one item on top of the agenda for the next High Commissioner, Louise Arbour, a member of the Supreme Court of Canada who had also served as chief prosecutor for the International Criminal Tribunal for the former Yugoslavia and Rwanda. In her speech before the 81st session of the Human Rights Committee, held the week after she took office in July 2004, Ms. Arbour explicitly linked breach of human rights obligations in Afghanistan and Iraq to the continued violence there. In her words:

> These examples show us that the prevention of, and solution to, conflicts depend on the implementation of fundamental human right standards. Respect for human rights and human security are inextricably linked. Rights are invariably violated in situations of violence; history is replete with examples of this terrible linkage and, all too sadly, this is still the situation in the world today. Conflict not only has an immediate devastating impact on the rights of those caught up in its unfolding; it also has a malevolent, lingering presence, hindering progress in all spheres of life, civil, political, as well as cultural, economic and social.[75]

Judge Arbour had a reputation for taking on difficult organizational challenges, and human rights advocates hoped that she would indeed prove to be an effective ally in their efforts to open and reform the UN human rights system. In her 22 July introductory press briefing, she highlighted "extreme poverty" as "the most widespread denial of human rights [which] is at the root of many conflicts and abuses."[76] While she acknowledged the need for "legitimate and robust responses to terrorism ... within legal constraints," she urged that "the war on terrorism should not obscure all other pressing social problems. There are very few burning issues today that don't have a human rights component."[77] As for her strategy for tackling the challenges ahead, she said, "I intend to focus on the most vulnerable—the very poor, the imprisoned, the disenfranchised, the targets of intolerance and hatred, and I intend to come to their assistance through the most effective legal means at my disposal."[78]

After a stormy first term as High Commissioner, Mrs. Arbour announced that she would not seek re-election. Like her predecessors, Arbour had been a frequent target of vehement attacks from a broad range of countries. For conservatives, she was too aggressive in her human rights investigations and, for liberals, she did not go far enough.[79] Arbour maintained that although she was stung by the criticism, her decision to step down was not due to pressure from her critics, but rather was prompted by a decision to spend more time with her family.[80] Many human rights advocates praised her work and urged the UN to provide better support for the office, including filling the position of Deputy High Commissioner, a post that had long been unfilled.

On 28 July 2008, the General Assembly approved of Navanethem Pillay as the fifth UN High Commissioner for Human Rights.[81] A Harvard-trained South African national, Ms. Pillay has strong academic training, years of experience as a judge, and longstanding commitment to human rights. Before she became a professor, in the 1960s and 1970s she acted as a defense attorney for anti-apartheid activists, exposing torture, and helping establish key rights for prisoners on Robben Island. In 1995, after the end of apartheid, Ms. Pillay was appointed a judge on the South African High Court, and in the same year was chosen to be a judge on the International Criminal Tribunal for Rwanda, where she served a total of eight years, the last four (1999–2003) as president. She played a critical role in the ICTR's groundbreaking jurisprudence on rape as genocide, as well as on issues of freedom of speech and hate propaganda. In 2003, she was appointed as a judge on the International Criminal Court in the Hague, where she remained until being appointed to the UN's top human rights post in August 2008.

Ms. Pillay's appointment as High Commissioner came at a challenging time, with the OHCHR under fire for rapid ad hoc growth, both in terms of activities and staff, with few quantifiable results. Ms. Pillay used her first meeting with the media to draw attention to the plight of those worldwide—including some 1 million children—who are deprived of their liberty and are being held in prisons and other places of detention, often illegally.[82] She specifically drew attention to three controversial issues: the Myanmar government's recent release of seven political prisoners, the case of Aung San Suu Kyi, the pro-democracy leader and Nobel laureate who has been under house arrest for the past 12 years, and to the USA's use of detention cells in Guantánamo Bay. If her first news conference is any indication, Ms. Pillay will tackle the hardest and most controversial issues directly and without hesitation.

Concluding thoughts

In the final analysis, there is no doubt that the OHCHR's efforts have helped the UN move beyond human rights standard-setting. The process of mainstreaming, monitoring and implementing human rights norms through its programs, funding and field presences has contributed significantly toward the growth of a strong international system of human rights. The incremental and ad hoc growth of the OHCHR can also be viewed as a process of addressing new needs as they arise and as organizational capacities grow. The office is very much beholden to the financial constraints and mandate constraints provided by the nations participating in the UN system. While changes in leadership of the OHCHR do have profound impacts upon the functioning of the office, in general, the organizational role of the OHCHR has consistently increased the relevance of human rights issues within the United Nations and improved human rights practices at the regional, national, and local levels. One significant aspect of the OHCHR's leadership concerns the supportive role it plays for UN Charter-based and treaty-based bodies, a topic to which we now turn.

3   UN Charter-based bodies (and other non-treaty bodies)

The drafters of the UN Charter knew that they were writing the constitutive document of an important organization, one which they hoped would save the world from future world wars. Yet they never imagined that they were creating an international system of human rights. To be sure, human rights provisions were scattered throughout the Charter. But these rather scattered references (see Table 3.1) were never intended to serve as a *system* for human rights protection. Even the vague provisions on human rights which were included in the Charter had a tough time squeaking in over the objection of the Soviet Union. The consensus among states in attendance at the founding of the UN meeting in San Francisco, however, favored making reference to human rights without defining the concepts used or listing in any detail specific human rights obligations.

Article 1 of the UN Charter makes clear that one of the aims of the UN is to achieve international cooperation by "promoting and encouraging respect for human rights and for fundamental freedoms for all without distinction as to race, sex, language or religion." The remaining human rights provisions of the Charter establish a nascent infrastructure and goals for human rights enforcement. Significantly, Article 55 identifies three purposes which the states of the United Nations vow to promote: "(a) higher standards of living, full employment, and conditions of economic and social progress and development; (b) solutions of international economic, social, health, and related problems; and international cultural and educational cooperation; and (c) universal respect for, and observance of, human rights and fundamental freedoms for all without distinction as to race, sex, language, or religion." By agreeing to the Charter, Article 56 of the Charter elaborates, "All Members pledge themselves to take joint and separate action in cooperation with the Organization for the achievement of the [three] purposes set forth in Article 55."

Table 3.1 Human rights provisions in the UN Charter for Human Rights

Article	Provision
Article 1	UN aims towards—"promoting and encouraging respect for human rights and for fundamental freedoms for all without distinction as to race, sex, language or religion."
Article 13(1)	General Assembly will—"initiate studies and make recommendations for the purpose of … promoting international cooperation in the economic, social, cultural, educational, and health fields, and assisting in the realization of human rights and fundamental freedoms for all without distinction as to race, sex, language, or religion."
Article 55	Member states pledge to promote: • higher standards of living, full employment, and conditions of economic and social progress and development; • solutions of international economic, social, health, and related problems; and international cultural and educational cooperation; and • universal respect for, and observance of, human rights and fundamental freedoms for all without distinction as to race, sex, language, or religion.
Article 56	"All Members pledge themselves to take joint and separate action in co-operation with the Organization for the achievement of the [three] purposes set forth in Article 55."
Article 62	Authorization for the Economic and Social Council to—"make or initiate studies and reports" and—"make recommendations for the purpose of promoting respect for, and observance of, human rights and fundamental freedoms for all."
Article 68	Authorization for the UN Economic and Social Council (ECOSOC) to set up commissions for—"the promotion of human rights."
Article 76	UN trusteeships will incorporate human rights.

A question remained, however, as to whether another important UN Charter article—Article 2(7), prohibiting the UN from intervening in matters essentially within the domestic jurisdiction of a state—excluded human rights issues from the agenda of the organization. Indeed, governments have continually invoked article 2(7) to shield themselves from scrutiny of human rights abuses in their own country. Nonetheless, human rights conditions have become recognized as core indicators of the maintenance of international peace and security. Over the years, the UN Charter human rights provisions have been interpreted and applied to create an expansive system of UN human rights protection, offering many opportunities for states and advocates to raise their concerns. These human rights bodies which draw their authority and existence from the UN Charter are referred to as "Charter-based bodies." This chapter's discussion of Charter-based human rights bodies begins with an overview of the main Charter-based bodies addressing human rights concerns. (The Security Council does not appear in this section because it is discussed separately in Chapter 5; the OHCHR is discussed in Chapter 2.) It then focuses in more detail on the operation of Charter-based bodies, highlighting in particular the Human Rights Council ("the Council") and thematic mechanisms. The chapter concludes with a note on the accreditation process for NGOs seeking to take part in these procedures.

Overview of Charter-based bodies

The General Assembly

The General Assembly's competence to address human rights issues is broad, since Article 10 of the UN Charter allows it to "discuss any questions or any matters within the scope of the present Charter" and to make "recommendations" to the member states on these subjects. Furthermore, Article 13(1) of the UN Charter specifically authorizes the General Assembly to "initiate studies and make recommendations for the purpose of ... promoting international cooperation in the economic, social, cultural, educational, and health fields, and assisting in the realization of human rights and fundamental freedoms for all without distinction as to race, sex, language, or religion."

Making good use of this broad mandate, the General Assembly has authorized studies and issued recommendations on a variety of human rights issues, often in response to the concerns of NGOs. Resolution 49/184 (1994), for example, established a UN Decade for Human Rights Education, and Resolution 56/115 (2001) announced a comprehensive world program of action on human rights and disability. Among the most significant of any General Assembly resolutions were the 1948 declaration proclaiming the Universal Declaration of Human Rights, the 1956 declaration affirming that genocide is a crime against international law, and the declaration identifying "the principles of international law" with regard to war crimes and crimes against humanity, which were included in the Charter and Judgment of the International Military Tribunal at Nuremberg in 1945.[1]

A General Assembly recommendation can effectively draw attention to an issue, and may shame states into taking action. Although they are not legally binding on states, General Assembly resolutions may wield considerable influence. In some cases, a human rights issue will begin its journey through the international human rights system as a non-binding General Assembly resolution and eventually form the basis of a binding treaty. The Declaration on the Rights of the Child of 1959 is but one case in point. A General Assembly resolution, or some of its provisions, may also acquire the status of customary international law over time. The impact of a General Assembly recommendation also may be particularly strong in the case of a text adopted unanimously and when a state is specifically named as committing egregious human wrongs. At any given time, the General Assembly may meet to discuss a specific country. Afghanistan, to take one example, was the subject of Resolution 56/176 (2001).

Two of the six Main Committees of the General Assembly participate in the drafting of international instruments concerning human rights: the Social, Humanitarian and Cultural Committee (Third Committee) and the Legal Committee (Sixth Committee). These committees, which are known as "committees of the whole" because all UN members are entitled to be represented on them, often add comments and changes to proposed human rights documents before they are submitted to the plenary General Assembly for approval.[2]

All of the treaty bodies and the Economic and Social Council submit human rights reports to the General Assembly. Upon considering a case, the General Assembly has the power to authorize the creation of a special rapporteur to study and report on the issue further. Member states also may draw publicity to a particular human rights situation by raising it in public debate on the floor of the General Assembly. Each year, roughly 20 percent of General Assembly resolutions relate to human rights.

The influence of the General Assembly on human rights can also be seen in its sponsorship of world conferences, such as the World Conference against Racism, Racial Discrimination, Xenophobia and Related Intolerance (held in Durban, South Africa from 31 August to 7 September 2001).[3] Each conference produces a "declaration and platform for action" which, although not a binding treaty, serves to provide evidence of the understanding and commitment of states to international human rights standards. The conferences have proven to be not only sites for norm development but avenues for ongoing human rights education and catalysts for human rights organizing. Many of the conferences called for by the General Assembly have follow-up meetings and additional specific monitoring measures. In 2006, for example, the United Nations General Assembly decided to convene in 2009 a review conference on the implementation of the Durban Declaration and Programme of Action (charging the Human Rights Council with responsibility for preparing this event).[4]

Critics of the General Assembly point out that in such a large, openly politicized body, "human rights are more susceptible to being subordinated to non-human rights considerations ... [and] voting, including 'bloc voting,' has led to 'selective targeting' of some States, sometimes exaggerating their violations, and overlooking some of the other States, including some that are guilty of gross violations."[5] In contrast, politics is thought to play less of a role in international bodies composed of independent experts, as well as in smaller bodies composed of government representatives. Creating an independent human rights body is incredibly difficult, however, as demonstrated by the experience of the Human Rights Council.

The Human Rights Council

Establishment and mandate

The Human Rights Council, initially established in 1946 as the Commission on Human Rights, was created by a UN General Assembly vote in March 2006.[6] News of the new Council was released with great fanfare. Then-UN High Commissioner for Human Rights Louise Arbour, heralded the new body as representing the "dawn of a new era" in promoting human rights in the United Nations.[7] UN General Assembly President Jan Eliasson, who oversaw the reform negotiations, called the council "a new beginning for the promotion and protection of human rights" and declared that the council would be "principled, effective and fair."[8] As Human Rights Watch observed, the United Nations Human Rights Council was former Secretary-General Kofi Annan's dream child: a new, stronger institution to replace the much-maligned Commission on Human Rights, where human rights would be treated as the UN's "third pillar" along with security and development.[9]

For nearly six decades, the Commission on Human Rights had been the central UN human rights body charged with reviewing the human rights record of individual countries around the world. Over time, however, the Commission came under intense criticism for its politicized membership, which included countries with horrendous human rights records; its ineffective procedures which lumbered at a slow pace and were utterly unable to address urgent human rights crises; and its selective, politicized decision making. The Commission's disrepute eventually eclipsed all of its earlier successes and became so great that even former UN Secretary-General Kofi Annan acknowledged, "We have reached a point at which the Commission's declining credibility has cast a shadow on the reputation of the United Nations system as a whole, and where piecemeal reforms will not be enough."[10] The Secretary-General urged that the 53-member Commission be replaced by a smaller Human Rights Council, a body of experts chosen for their commitment to human rights.[11] The new Council, a permanent body, possibly on par with the Security Council, would be capable of meeting whenever necessary throughout the year.

Reformists thus sought to create a smaller body, with greater stature in the UN system, either a principal organ of the UN or a subsidiary body of the General Assembly. Many human rights supporters backed a plan for Council members to be elected by a two-thirds majority of the General Assembly members present and voting, with membership criteria, would be based on human rights performance, and with a strict prohibition on electing nations to the council that are under UN Security Council sanction for human rights abuses. Under this proposal, the elected body would either be a standing body or, at the very least, have the ability to meet often and to respond more effectively to immediate human rights concerns.

Very few of these goals were even partially addressed by the new Human Rights Council. The General Assembly negotiations produced a 47-member council that is only marginally smaller than the commission. The seats in the Council are distributed among the UN's regional groups as follows: 13 for Africa, 13 for Asia, 6 for Eastern Europe, 8 for Latin America and the Caribbean, and 7 for Western Europe and others. Members are approved by a simple majority vote for election, based on regional affiliation, rather than the two-thirds requirement originally proposed.[12]

The resolution that created the Council established no hard criteria for membership other than quotas for each of the regional groups in the UN and a requirement that council members be elected by a simple majority of the General Assembly (currently 97 of 192 votes). The resolution simply instructed UN member states that "when electing members of the council, Member States shall take into account the contribution of candidates to the promotion and protection of human rights." Under this language, no state, no matter how poor its human rights record, is barred from membership.[13] Even states under Security Council sanction for human rights abuses are not excluded. Candidates are also asked to submit "voluntary pledges and commitments" on their qualifications for the council based on their past and future adherence to and observance of human rights standards.

On the more positive side, the goal of elevating the status of the main human rights organ of the UN was addressed by the new institution. The Council does have the status of a subsidiary body of the General Assembly. Another positive development is that the Council did establish a policy of universal periodic review, guaranteeing that all countries would be reviewed, starting with the membership of the Council. This new review procedure is designed to ensure that all states are treated equally and are subject to a review of their human rights record. Not only are members of the Council subjected to periodic review, but under the new procedures Council members are amongst those first to be placed under scrutiny.

The broad mandate of the Council, which it inherited from the CHR, calls on mandate holders to examine, monitor, advise and publicly report on human rights situations in specific countries or territories, known as country mandates, or on major phenomena of human rights violations worldwide, known as thematic mandates. In addition, various activities can be undertaken by "special procedures," including responding to individual complaints, conducting studies, providing advice on technical cooperation at the country level, and engaging in general promotional activities. Special Procedures allow the Council to receive information on specific allegations of human rights violations and send urgent appeals or letters of appeal to governments asking for clarification. The Council may also carry out country visits to investigate the situation of human rights at the national level.

The Complaint Procedure of the Council was established to address consistent patterns of gross and reliably attested violations of all human rights and all fundamental freedoms occurring in any part of the world and under any circumstances. It is comprised of two distinct working groups—the Working Group on Communications and the Working Group on Situations. They bring to the attention of the Council consistent patterns of gross and reliably attested violations of human rights and fundamental freedoms. The Working Group on Situations (WGS), a five-country body, examines the particular situations referred to it by the Working Group on Communications under the 1503 Procedure and makes recommendations to the Council.[14]

Criticism of the Council

Although the universal review of the human rights practices in all countries was a welcome improvement over the HRC's more politicized, selective approach, the procedures for the review adopted by the Council were very weak and "virtually assure a milquetoast outcome."[15] As an analyst for the Heritage Foundation explained:

> For instance, the review for every country, whether Sweden or Sudan, is limited to three hours every four years, and the review

will be a country-led process in which input from non-governmental organizations is slight. In other words, a genocide or massive political crackdown could occur in Burma, China, Sudan, Venezuela, or some other country, and the Council could wait four years or more before examining whether a country has addressed the human rights concerns raised during the review.[16]

The first reports produced under the universal periodic review procedure were indeed troubling. The language of the reports was watered-down, as if the council was "more intent on not offending the country under review than it was on addressing human rights abuses."[17] The timidity of some governments in reviewing others can be seen in the marked contrast in the strength of criticism faced by some countries under review, with, for instance, the Czech Republic facing detailed questioning regarding the treatment of Roma, while Tunisia and Algeria were delicately questioned on their records. Fellow African states avoided talking about rights violations and instead used the opportunity to congratulate both countries for their achievements.[18] When it came its turn to question countries, Algeria returned the favor:

> The Algerian ambassador trod softly with regard to both Tunisia and Bahrain, noting the difficulties the Tunisian government faced protecting human rights while combating terrorism and asking only if Tunisia believed it would be "a good idea to have a seminar" on that subject, while congratulating Bahrain for the progress it has made with regard to protection of women's rights. In contrast, Algeria gave a strong, detailed statement when the United Kingdom was reviewed, raising concerns over its rate of incarceration of children, the violation of the UK's commitments under the Convention Against Torture, excessive use of pre-trial detention, and the lack of protection for asylum seekers and migrants.[19]

Another area that has come under scrutiny is the Council's attitude toward its "Special Procedures," the system that involves some 41 independent human rights experts and working groups focusing either on particular themes, like violence against women and arbitrary detention, or on human rights situations in specific countries, including Burma and Sudan. At first, the Council hinted that it might do away with the entire system, but then the Council announced that a new selection and retention process might compromise the independent nature of the process. This new process gives the Council's regional groups a role in selecting experts from a published roster of qualified candidates and subjects all experts to a new "code of conduct" that leaves their independent role intact, but is overly intrusive regarding their working methods, according to one of the world's leading human rights organizations, Human Rights Watch.[20] In its first year of operation, the Council bowed to political pressure by eliminating two country experts immediately, those for Belarus and Cuba.

Human Rights Watch also noted the disproportionate attention devoted to Israel:

> The agenda established for the work of the council sets broad outlines, giving the council little guidance on addressing its growing backlog. The notable deviation from the agenda's broad-brush approach is a specific item on the "human rights situation in Palestine and other occupied Arab territories," continuing the practice of the council's predecessor, the UN Commission on Human Rights. While the deteriorating human rights situation in the Occupied Palestinian Territories certainly warrants the council's attention, the council's decision to single that situation out for separate treatment on the agenda is a textbook example of selectivity and politicization, which the resolution that established the council calls for it to avoid.[21]

The council has the potential to be far more effective than the commission—if governments that care about human rights do all they can to make it so. The council's failings can be blamed not only on the minority of members with troubling records, but also the poor performance of a broader group of states with a professed commitment to human rights.[22]

In its first four regular sessions and four special sessions, the Council failed to address ongoing repression in some of the most acutely troubled human rights scenarios, such as Belarus, China, Cuba, North Korea, and Zimbabwe, and many other dire human rights situations around the world. Nor did the Council censure the government of Sudan for its role in the genocide in Darfur. Instead, it adopted three mild decisions expressing "concern" regarding the human rights and humanitarian situation in Darfur and dispatched a High-Level Mission to assess the human rights situation in Darfur and the needs of the Sudan in this regard.[23]

As the USA attempted to exercise influence from the sidelines, in 2006 the General Assembly elected notorious human rights abusers Algeria, China, Cuba, Pakistan, Russia, and Saudi Arabia to the Council.[24] The second council election, held on 17 May 2007, gave seats to Angola, Egypt, Qatar, and Bolivia, and, in response, U.S. criticism of the Council grew.[25] In the summer of 2008, the United States announced that it was giving up on the Council: "it would only participate in debates at the council when absolutely necessary and it feels compelled to do so by 'matters of deep national interest.'" Although not a member of the Human Rights Council, the United States had participated as an observer at the council since its inception.[26]

The Sub-Commission

The Sub-Commission on the Promotion and Protection of Human Rights is the main subsidiary body of the Human Rights Council. It is composed of 26 elected human rights experts whose mandate is to conduct studies on discriminatory practices and make recommendations to ensure that racial, national, religious and linguistic minorities are protected by law.

A number of working groups within the Council investigate the following:

- Minorities
- Transnational corporations
- Administration of justice
- Anti-terrorism
- Contemporary forms of slavery
- Indigenous populations
- Communication
- Social forum.

The 26 members of the Sub-Commission are elected by the Council from a list created by UN member states. While this process can be politicized, members of the Sub-Commission serve in their personal capacities and are chosen because of their human rights expertise, thus adding to their credibility as a legitimate research arm of the Council.

The Economic and Social Council (ECOSOC)

Like the General Assembly, the Economic and Social Council (ECOSOC) has considerable competency to address human rights issues. Article 62 grants the ECOSOC the authority to "make or initiate studies and reports" and "make recommendations for the purpose of promoting respect for, and observance of, human rights and fundamental freedoms for all." ECOSOC has used its Article 62 authority to address a variety of human rights concerns, "including genocide, prevention of statelessness, discrimination, protection of minorities, the organization of the 1948 Conference on Freedom of Information, the establishment of the Yearbook on Human Rights and, in cooperation with the International Labour Organization (ILO), the protection of the right to form trade unions and the prevention of forced labour."[27]

Article 68 of the Charter further authorizes ECOSOC to set up commissions for "the promotion of human rights." As explained further below, it was pursuant to Article 68 that ECOSOC established the Commission on Human Rights and created an intergovernmental commission that would report directly to it on issues concerning the status and rights of women.

ECOSOC operates through nine functional committees, five regional commissions and several additional sub-organs. Many of these are engaged in human rights-related activities. The Commission on the Status of Women provides one good example.[28]

The Commission on the Status of Women

The Commission on the Status of Women (CSW) was established by resolution by ECOSOC in 1946. CSW is charged with preparing recommendations and reports to the Council on promoting women's rights in political, economic, civil, social, and educational fields. The CSW also makes recommendations to the Council on urgent problems requiring immediate attention in the field of women's rights. The mandate of the CSW has been expanded several times. Instead of addressing specific cases of violations of women's rights, the CSW has tended to focus its activities on the coordination of and follow-up to UN world conferences and other promotional activities.[29]

After the 1995 Fourth World Conference on Women, the General Assembly mandated the CSW to integrate into its program a follow-up process to the Conference. This has involved regularly reviewing the critical areas of concern in the Platform for Action and drawing on the Platform and follow-up activities to promote the mainstreaming of a gender perspective in United Nations activities.

CSW, which began with 15 members, now consists of 45 members elected by the Economic and Social Council for a period of four years. Members, who are appointed by governments, are elected on the following formula: 13 from African states; 11 from Asian states; 4 from Eastern European states; 9 from Latin American and Caribbean states; and 8 from Western European and other states. CSW meets annually at the United Nations headquarters in New York for a period of ten working days.

The Division for the Advancement of Women (DAW), located within the UN Secretariat, is partially responsible for servicing CSW.[30]

Additional non-treaty bodies concerned with human rights

Several other parts of the UN system address human rights. To provide an overview of the breadth of human rights activity within the UN, this section outlines the human rights mandates of four such organizations: the International Court of Justice; the United Nations High Commissioner for Refugees; the United Nations Children's Fund; and the United Nations Development Programme.

The International Court of Justice[31]

The International Court of Justice (ICJ), made up of 15 independent judges elected by the General Assembly and the Security Council, is the principal judicial organ of the United Nations. Established under the authority of the UN Charter in 1946, the ICJ replaced the Permanent Court of International Justice, which had been established in 1921 and the Permanent Court of Arbitration, formed in 1899. The Statute of the ICJ (annexed to the UN Charter) provides for both judicial opinions and mediations and arbitrations.

According to Article 34, paragraph 1, of the Statute of the Court, "only States may be parties in cases before the Court." Individuals, juridical persons and international or non-governmental organizations may not be parties in litigation before the Court. The ICJ may, however, address human rights issues by interpreting human rights conventions incumbent upon states or by evaluating state conduct implicating human rights concerns. Thus, the ICJ has the authority to make two kinds of decisions: (i) binding rulings that apply when all states involved in a case agree at the outset to accept its jurisdiction ("contentious cases"); and (ii) advisory opinions that do not settle a particular case, but rather determine a legal issue that may be of relevance in many current and future cases; and dispute resolution and mediation opinions.

The ICJ's Advisory Opinion on the Continued Presence of South Africa in Namibia (South West Africa)[32] illustrates the way in which the jurisprudence of the ICJ may create pressure to change state behaviors. This 1971 decision ruled not only that South Africa's occupation of Namibia was illegal, but also that all UN member states had the duty to avoid recognizing or supporting the illegal behavior of the occupying force. The political implications of this opinion were monumental as it paved the way for the arms embargo and other restrictions imposed on Pretoria. In this way, human rights are both addressed and enforced through such judicial proceedings.

The United Nations High Commissioner for Refugees

The UN General Assembly established the office of the United Nations High Commissioner for Refugees (UNHCR) on 14 December 1950. The agency's original mandate was only for three years, but as the number of refugees has increased exponentially, its mandate is now almost automatically extended every five years. Today, the organization's staff of more than 6,200 people assists refugees in 115 countries throughout the world. The UNHCR's programs are approved by an executive committee of 64 member states which meets annually in Geneva. A second working group, or "Standing Committee," meets several times a year. Additionally, the High Commissioner consistently reports on the UNHCR's activities to the General Assembly through the Economic and Social Council. There have been nine High Commissioners since the agency's inception.

The UNHCR mandate is to provide international protection to refugees and others of concern to the UNHCR, and to seek durable solutions to their plight. Activities in fulfillment of this mandate include provision of material assistance, legal advice and assistance, and cooperation with other agencies. UNHCR staff do human rights work through defending the rights of refugees by providing them with protection and assistance.

The UNHCR considers international protection to be the "cornerstone" of its work—the main goal of the organization is to maintain the protection of refugees' basic human rights and to ensure that no one will be returned to countries where they will be persecuted. The UNHCR promotes international refugee agreements and monitors government compliance with refugee laws and works to find long-term solutions to refugee problems. The UNHCR has projects in locations ranging from urban areas to rural refugee camps. The work of the UNHCR on establishing guidelines for protection of refugee women and on other protection issues has made strong contributions to the progressive development of international human rights and humanitarian norms.

The United Nations Children's Fund (formerly known as the United Nations International Children's Emergency Fund)

The United Nations Children's Fund (UNICEF) was started by the United Nations in December 1946 in order to bring humanitarian aid to European children affected by the Second World War. In 1953, the

General Assembly voted to extend the organization's mandate and UNICEF became a permanent part of the United Nations. UNICEF has had numerous successes in a wide variety of issues, from education to health care to helping children in areas of armed conflict. While UNICEF world headquarters is in New York, the organization does work in 157 countries worldwide. It has eight regional offices and 126 country offices, as well as a research center in Florence, a supply operation in Copenhagen, and offices in Tokyo and Brussels.

In 1989, the UN General Assembly adopted the Convention on the Rights of the Child, which formally entered into force in September 1990. This was the first Convention that charged a specific UN organization—UNICEF—with overseeing its implementation. Article 45 of the Convention assigns UNICEF with the legal duty to promote and protect child rights. As such, UNICEF provides expert advice on the implementation of the Convention, assists in consideration of states' reports, and submits its own reports regarding children's rights worldwide. While UNICEF was an extremely important organization prior to 1989, the role of UNICEF in the Convention on the Rights of the Child brought children's rights into the broader field of human rights in an unprecedented way.

Just as UNICEF has played a role in the interpretation of the Children's Convention, the Children's Convention has influenced UNICEF's interpretation of its own mandate. Despite some initial resistance within the organization, today UNICEF adopts a rights-based approach to programming. This is reflected in all of UNICEF's operations worldwide, and is a strong example of how the broader commitment made by the United Nations to mainstream human rights is implemented.[33]

The United Nations Development Programme

The United Nations Development Programme (UNDP) administers and coordinates most of the technical assistance provided through the UN system. Formed by General Assembly resolution, the current Mission Statement "is to help countries in their efforts to achieve sustainable human development by assisting them to build their capacity to design and carry out development programmes in poverty eradication, employment creation and sustainable livelihoods, the empowerment of women and the protection and regeneration of the environment, giving first priority to poverty eradication." Poverty reduction is the overarching goal of the UNDP. It also focuses on democracy and democratic governance, the environment and energy policy, crisis prevention, and HIV/AIDS.

Human rights often figure into UNDP programming, often under "good governance" programs, but in other areas as well. The OHCHR and other UN human rights bodies frequently have contact with UNDP. For example, the Human Rights Committee (established to monitor the International Covenant on Civil and Political Rights; see Chapter 4) has been "mandated to cooperate with UNDP in the development of human rights indicators for common country assessments."[34] The field offices of OHCHR at times work in conjunction with HCR in implementing technical and economic assistance projects. As the Bosnia case study in Chapter 2 demonstrated, UNDP works closely with the OHCHR to ensure a "rights-based approach to development,"[35] highlighting the crucial linkages between poverty, economics, and human rights.

As the field of technical assistance has expanded, so has UNDP. The UNDP now has more than 130 country offices throughout the world, and has a presence in more than 166 countries.[36]

Operation of Charter-based bodies

Standard-setting activities

One of the most important tasks entrusted to the UN Human Rights Commission was the elaboration of human rights standards. Eleanor Roosevelt, the CHR representative from the United States, served as the chairperson of the CHR when it first met in early 1947.[37] She was accompanied by several other distinguished diplomats and intellectuals, including Charles Malik, a Lebanese existentialist philosopher and spokesperson for the Arab League; René Cassin, the French legal scholar, who had lost 29 relatives in the Holocaust; and Pen-Chung Chang, the Chinese Confucian philosopher/diplomat, who served as vice-chairman.[38] The initial task of the new organization was to make reports and draft proposals for an "International Bill of Rights." Debate over the Bill of Rights centered on the legal character of the document, in particular whether it should be drafted as a legally binding treaty or as a non-binding declaration. The Commission chose the latter option, and drafted a non-binding document which the General Assembly adopted as the Universal Declaration of Human Rights (UDHR) in 1948. In adopting the UDHR, the General Assembly simultaneously directed ECOSOC to mandate the CHR to prepare a draft treaty on human rights.[39]

The plan at the time was to make the Declaration the first of three parts to the International Bill of Rights. A second binding document would spell out the rights identified in the UDHR, and a third document was to provide for measures of implementation. This plan was blocked by disputes over the role of international bodies in implementation. While some states pushed for strong international oversight, others insisted that human rights should remain primarily a matter of state authority. States also were split over the indivisibility of human rights, with some states arguing for the primacy of social and economic rights and others stressing instead civil and political rights. As a compromise, the CHR decided to place these two groupings of rights into two different treaties, the International Covenant on Civil and Political Rights (ICCPR), and the International Covenant on Economic, Social, and Cultural Rights (ICESCR). In 1954, ECOSOC submitted the CHR's draft documents to the General Assembly for review. These treaties, as substantially amended by the General Assembly's Third Committee, were not adopted by the General Assembly until 1966. They did not receive enough state signatures to enter into force until 1976.

In addition to the International Bill of Rights, the CHR developed standards on a wide range of issues. The treaties that the CHR helped create on these topics are legally binding for the States Parties (states that sign and ratify the treaty). Each treaty establishes an "international enforcement system designed to ensure that States Parties comply with their obligations."[40] (Chapter 4 examines the international enforcement system created by the seven main treaty bodies.) This enforcement system has been inherited by the Human Rights Council.

Box 3.1   Main themes addressed by the Human Rights Council

- the right to self-determination;
- racism;
- the right to development;
- the question of the violation of human rights in the occupied Arab territories, including Palestine;
- the question of the violation of human rights and fundamental freedoms in any part of the world;
- economic, social and cultural rights;
- civil and political rights, including the questions of torture and detention, disappearances and summary executions, freedom

Box continued on next page.

of expression, the independence of the judiciary, impunity and religious intolerance;

- the human rights of women, children, migrant workers, minorities and displaced persons;
- indigenous issues;
- the promotion and protection of human rights, including the work of the Sub-Commission, treaty bodies and national institutions;
- advisory services and technical cooperation in the field of human rights.

Source: Thomas Buergenthal, Dinah Shelton, and David Stewart, *International Human Rights in a Nutshell* (St. Paul, Minn.: West Group, 2002).

Protection activities: 1235 and 1503 procedures

For the first two and a half decades of its existence, the Commission on Human Rights narrowly interpreted its own mandate and focused principally on promotional activities and standard-setting through the preparation of draft human rights instruments. As soon as it was established, the UN was flooded with communications from individuals and groups seeking UN intervention for alleged violations of human rights. Yet in 1947, the CHR ruled that it had "no power to take any action in regard to any complaints concerning human rights."[41] Interpreting the word "promoting" in the Charter's human rights provisions as something less than "protecting," the CHR refrained from establishing any monitoring and human rights enforcement mechanisms. ECOSOC confirmed this decision in 1947, through passing Resolution 75(V).[42]

Thus, in its early years, the CHR utilized communications with offending states only as a means of identifying general trends without responding directly to the violations at issue. The breakthrough did not come until the 1960s, when public pressure on the United Nations to respond to apartheid and gross human rights abuses in southern Africa allowed the CHR to create its first monitoring body, the Ad Hoc Working Group on Southern Africa.[43] The opportunity provided the foundation for pushing ECOSOC in other human rights directions: ECOSOC agreed in 1967 to allow the CHR and Sub-Commission to examine gross violations of human rights that come to its attention (ECOSOC resolution 1235)[44] and in 1970 to establish a Commission procedure for the consideration of complaints of gross and systematic violations of human rights (ECOSOC resolution 1503).

The "1235 procedure" mandated the CHR and Sub-Commission to thoroughly study situations where human rights were consistently violated, and particularly drew attention to apartheid in South Africa and racial discrimination in Southern Rhodesia. Initially, many states attempted to restrict the reach of the 1235 procedure to cases similar to the two examples provided in the declaration: apartheid and extreme racial discrimination. These efforts failed, however, and 1235 was read to apply to *any* violation of human rights and fundamental freedoms. "At that time," Nigel Rodley observes, "NGOs were not allowed to make written or oral interventions or circulate written statements complaining about human rights violations in UN Member States."[45] Thus, "it came as something of a shock" when the Sub-Commission used its authority under 1235 to establish a Committee of Experts to investigate the human rights situation not only in Southern Rhodesia but also in Greece. "This initiative goaded the CHR into developing a procedure under which information from non-governmental sources could be considered in a less directly threatening manner." The result was the "1503 procedure."[46]

The 1503 procedure allowed the CHR to process individual complaints that help identify those that "appear to reveal a consistent pattern of gross and reliably attested violations of human rights and fundamental freedoms" and pass them on to the relevant human rights bodies. The oldest human rights complaint mechanism in the United Nations system, the mechanism was exercised only in the case of large-scale or systematic denials of human rights. Overall, an average of 50,000 complaints were received annually. Only a tiny fraction of these complaints were ever investigated. The majority of these cases concern patterns of human rights violations involving torture, arbitrary detention, summary or arbitrary executions, and disappearance.

The procedure for Resolution 1503, as modified in 2000 by ECOSOC resolution 2000/3, can be summarized as a four-step process. First, communications are to be received by the Office of the UN High Commissioner for Human Rights. The initial screening of those complaints takes place at the OHCHR, where staff eliminate untimely and manifestly ill-founded claims. Second, the complaints that pass this first hurdle are examined by the Working Group on Communications of the Sub-Commission which conducts its own evaluation. Third, if this body identified reasonable indication of a consistent pattern of gross violations of human rights in a given country, it forwards its recommendations to the Working Group on Situations of the CHR. The Working Group on Situations then evaluates the claims and makes recommendations to the full Commission. Finally, the CHR undertakes its own evaluation in light of the recommendations.

When the CHR takes up consideration of a country situation, the government in question is invited to participate in a discussion of the human rights situation in private session. Resolution 2000/3 gave the CHR a repertoire of responses to these cases, including appointing an independent expert to make direct contact with the government and the people concerned, keeping the case under consideration, transferring the case to the public procedures,[47] or dismissing the situation altogether.

The new procedure considerably opened the 1503 process to public scrutiny. Under the modified form found in Resolution 2000/3, the CHR announced the names of the states under consideration and indicated the ones that have been dropped from consideration. ECOSOC also had the ability to publicize cases. As the UN website makes clear: "If a pattern of abuses in a particular country remains unresolved in the early stages of the process, it can be brought to the attention of the world community through the Economic and Social Council."[48] Furthermore, under the new procedures, the text of any final decision on the merits of a case or of a decision of inadmissibility was to be posted on the OHCHR's website.[49]

These improvements in the 1503 procedure, although considerable, did not resolve other complaints about the process. The 1503 procedure was still criticized for its slowness, complexity, and vulnerability to political influence. In addition, the procedure was only capable of considering an extremely limited number of complaints. Nonetheless, for the few advocates fortunate to be selected for review, the 1503 procedure provided a useful technique for placing increasing pressure on offending governments while encouraging them to engage in a constructive exchange of views to improve the situation.

Today, individuals wishing to use the 1503 procedure can direct communications to the UN High Commissioner for Human Rights in Geneva. Communications must include specific mention of the rights violated and descriptive facts, such as names, dates and places, and should include evidence, such as testimony. They should demonstrate exhaustion or unavailability of domestic proceedings (e.g. because domestic courts do not have the ability to hear the particular kind of complaint or to entertain cases by the particular type of complainant). Additionally, complaints should be made within a reasonable amount of time after national procedures have been exhausted. Anonymous, overtly political, or verbally abusive complaints are not considered. To ensure that complaints are considered, they should be submitted at least two months prior to the annual meetings of the Sub-Commission. The steps for using the 1503 procedure are summarized in Box 3.2.

Box 3.2   Using the 1503 procedure

1 Draft a cover letter:
   • refer to ECOSOC resolutions 728F and/or 1503;
   • summarize the allegations;
   • include a statement of purpose (e.g. seeking UN action to bring an end to the violations of human rights disclosed in this communication).
2 Describe the pattern of gross human rights violations:
   • include dates, names, and places;
   • note the relevant treaty articles violated;
   • show that domestic proceedings have either failed, endured unreasonably long, or failed to address the abuses;
   • sign and date all communications.
3 Include annexes with relevant evidence, especially direct testimony.
4 Send six copies to: UN High Commissioner for Human Rights, OHCHR-UNOG CH-1211, Geneva 10, Switzerland. Hotline fax for urgent cases: (41) 22 917 9003.
5 If no action is taken in the session, it is useful to update the complaint and resend the following year.

Source: Kate Thompson and Camille Giffard, *Reporting Killings as Human Rights Violations Handbook* (Colchester, UK: University of Essex Human Rights Centre, 2002). Available online at www.essex.ac.uk/reportingkillingshandbook/handbook/publishing_information.htm (2 September 2008).

Special procedures: working groups and thematic procedures

In addition to the 1503 procedure, the CHR (and, now, the Council) carried out its enforcement efforts through an ever-expanding array of special procedures. The term "special procedures" referred to the human rights mandate of either an individual, called "special rapporteur," "representative," or "independent expert," or a group of individuals called a "working group."

Rapporteurs may be focused on a particular country or theme. In general, thematic mechanisms are viewed by states as less threatening, because as they do not necessarily single out a particular country for criticism. Although the trend is to create more thematic mechanisms, the evidence seemed to indicate that the country-specific mechanisms have generally out-performed thematic mechanisms. Not surprisingly, states appeared to respond better to a report singling them out for criticism. In addition, country-based mechanisms had proven more useful for resolving individual cases. One explanation is that individual victims of human rights abuses had been better able to utilize country-based mechanisms in claiming their own rights because they had become more readily aware of them than of thematic mechanisms.[50] Another is that any mechanism worked better when there had been on-site visits and follow-up visits to ensure compliance, and that this occurred most often in the case of single-country investigations. Furthermore, when country-specific mechanisms were employed, it was more obvious when a particular state was being uncooperative.[51]

Some issues have both working groups and special rapporteurs focusing on their issue (i.e. trafficking[52] or the rights of indigenous peoples[53]). While many working groups and Special Rapporteurs/representatives carry out their work for a long period of time, with no set end in sight, others are envisioned to be more short-term in nature (e.g. the Special Rapporteur on the promotion and protection of human rights while countering terrorism). In addition, the appellation "independent expert" can be given to a less formal process involving an individual serving without compensation in his or her professional capacity (e.g. the Independent Expert on Human Rights and Extreme Poverty[54] and the Independent Experts).[55]

To date, the CHR (and, now, the Council) has created over 28 thematic procedures and over 25 country procedures (see Table 3.2). Thematic human rights investigators can also be appointed as special representatives of the Secretary-General (e.g. the "Special Representative of the Secretary-General on human rights and transnational corporations and other business enterprises"). Field missions are undertaken only at the invitation of a government; however, the special rapporteur could have worked to solicit an invitation from the country in question. Before a fact-finding mission took place, the government is asked to provide assurances that people interviewed will not be subjected to harassment or punishment and that the special rapporteur's staff will be permitted freedom of movement throughout the country, and confidential and unsupervised contacts.

Rapporteurs' dialogues

A rapporteur's dialogue with a particular government could have begun in one of two ways. If the rapporteur believed that the allegations she was investigating were credible, the rapporteur would either transmit an *urgent appeal* or raise the allegation in a *standard communication*. The

Table 3.2 Thematic procedures of the UN Commission on Human Rights

Selected thematic procedure	Framing the claim
Working Group (WG) on Arbitrary Detention	The detention must be arbitrary. The WG interprets this as meaning detention which (1) does not have a legal basis; (2) is a response to the exercise of fundamental rights, such as freedom of expression (e.g. the arrest of a journalist for the exercise of his profession); or (3) is rendered arbitrary because due process guarantees are not observed (e.g. if someone is not brought promptly before a judge). It is not enough to consider that the detention is "unfair."
WG on Enforced or Involuntary Disappearances	The WG acts only in clearly identified individual cases. If the person or organization submitting the information is not a relative but is acting directly or indirectly upon the family's request, she or he is required to maintain contact with the family at all times as any replies received are for the information of the relatives only.
Special Rapporteur (SR) on Torture	The SR examines allegations of torture and other cruel, inhuman and degrading acts and investigates legislative and administrative measures taken by countries to prevent torture and to remedy its consequences whenever it occurs. Another focus is on the ill-treatment of particular groups, especially children and women. The SR also responds to credible and reliable information of individual cases that comes before her /him.
SR on the Promotion and Protection of the Right to Freedom of Opinion and Expression	The SR's areas of interest include: persons exercising/promoting the exercise of the right, including professionals in the field of information; political opposition parties and trade union activists; the media (print and broadcast), including any threats to their independence; publishers and performers in other media; human rights defenders; obstacles to women's right to be heard; obstacles to access to information.
SR on the Independence of Judges and Lawyers	Information can be received about judges, lawyers and court officials. The SR is essentially concerned with safeguards and the proper functioning of the justice system.

Table continued on next page.

Table 3.2 (continued)

Selected thematic procedure	Framing the claim
SR on Human Rights Defenders	This is a relatively new mandate which aims to receive, examine, and respond to information on the situation and rights of those acting to promote human rights; to establish cooperation and conduct dialogue with governments; and to recommend strategies to better protect human rights defenders. All reliable information can be brought to the SR's attention and those submitting allegations are encouraged to provide information regarding their own human rights work.
SR on Violence Against Women	The SR examines cases of violence against women on account of their gender. Communications must show targeting because of her gender. A special feature of this mandate is that it looks at violence not only by the state but in the community and within the family.
SR on Trafficking in Persons, especially Women and Children	Considers individual complaints of violations committed against trafficked persons; undertakes country visits in order to study the situation in situ and formulate recommendations to prevent and or combat trafficking and protect the human rights of its victims.[1]
Special Representative of the Secretary-General on human rights and transnational corporations and other business enterprises	Charged with identifying and clarifying standards of corporate responsibility and accountability for transnational corporations and other business enterprises with regard to human rights.
SR on the promotion and protection of human rights while countering terrorism	Review of implementation of human rights standards on contemporary forms of slavery.[2]

Notes:
1 http://www2.ohchr.org/english/issues/trafficking/index.htm (8 September 2008).
2 http://www2.ohchr.org/english/issues/slavery/group.htm (8 September 2008).

urgent appeal procedure was designed to respond to information that an individual may be at imminent risk of being killed. Such appeals were non-accusatory in nature. The government was requested to ensure effective protection of those under threat or at risk of execution and to undertake full, independent and impartial investigation and adoption of all measures to prevent further violations of the right to life. In such an event, the rapporteur adopted no position as to whether or not the fear of death is justified.

Standard communications were transmitted to governments periodically and contained allegations concerning individual cases (individual allegations) in the form of case summaries. They requested progress reports on the investigation of these cases and any prosecutions or reparations that had resulted.

Extensive use of these fact-finding mechanisms had enabled individuals, NGOs, and others to report on situations pertinent to the country or theme in question and meet with individuals or working groups during on-site visits. Both NGOs and the CHR benefited from this approach. Participation in the fact-finding of the special procedures helped NGOs to organize and develop expertise on issues. The Commission, in turn, benefited from the improved information received as the result of NGO cooperation.

Box 3.3   How to bring information to the attention of the Special Rapporteurs

[Fact Sheet no. 4; designed for Special Rapporteurs on Torture and on Violence Against Women, but adaptable to other special rapporteurs]

The following information regarding individual cases should be transmitted (if available):

(a) Full name of the victim;
(b) Date (at least the month and year) on which the incident(s) of torture occurred;
(c) Place where the person was seized (city, province, etc.) and location at which the torture was carried out (if known);
(d) Description of the alleged perpetrators of the violation (including position held and/or state affiliation);

Box continued on next page.

(e) Description of the form of torture used and any injury suffered or statement of reasons to believe that the person is at risk of torture;

(f) Identity of the person or organization submitting the report (name and address, which will be kept confidential).

The Special Rapporteur on violence against women needs the following information, if available:

(a) A summary of the main points of the case identifying the rights that have been or may be violated. If the state concerned has ratified human rights treaties, an indication of the provisions of the treaties believed to have been violated.

(b) If the submission concerns a law, practice or policy that affects women in general or women in a specific group, an explanation of how other women or a specific group of women are affected. A consistent pattern in individual cases can be used to demonstrate a general failure to prevent and respond to private abuses.

If the submission concerns violations by private individuals or groups (rather than government officials), the Special Rapporteur requires any information that might indicate that the Government failed to exercise due diligence to prevent, investigate, punish and ensure compensation for the violations, such as:

(a) Whether or not there is a law that addresses the violation;

(b) Any defects in existing laws such as inadequate remedies or definitions of rights;

(c) Refusal or failure by the authorities to register or investigate the case and other similar cases;

(d) Failure by the authorities to prosecute the case and other similar cases;

(e) Patterns of gender discrimination in the prosecution or sentencing of cases;

(f) Statistics and other data concerning the prevalence of the type of violation described in the submission.

Source: *Combating Torture*, Fact Sheet no. 4 (Rev. 1), www.unhchr.ch/html/menu6/2/fs4.htm (6 September 2008).

NGO participation in mechanisms

Only NGOs accredited with "consultative status" may take part in formal meetings of UN Charter-based bodies. Consultative status is granted by ECOSOC upon recommendation of the ECOSOC Committee on NGOs, which is composed of 19 member states. ECOSOC resolution 1996/31 (1996) outlines the eligibility requirements for consultative status.[56] To be eligible for consultative status, an NGO must have been in existence (officially registered with the appropriate government authorities as an NGO/non-profit organization) for at least two years, and must have an established headquarters, a democratically adopted constitution, authority to speak for its members, a representative structure, appropriate mechanisms of accountability, and democratic and transparent decision-making processes. The basic resources of the organization must be derived in the main part from contributions of the national affiliates or other components or from individual members. Organizations established by governments or intergovernmental agreements are not considered NGOs.

There are currently over 2,000 NGOs registered with the Economic and Social Council to lobby at the United Nations.[57] There are three categories of status: General consultative status, Special consultative status and Roster status:

- General consultative status is reserved for fairly large, established international NGOs with a broad geographical reach and interest in a large number of the fields of activity covered by the ECOSOC.
- Special consultative status is granted to NGOs which have a special competence in, and are concerned specifically with, only a few of the fields of activity covered by the ECOSOC.
- The Roster category is a "catch all" category. Organizations that apply for consultative status but do not fit in any of the other categories are usually included in the Roster. NGOs that have formal status with other UN bodies or specialized agencies (for example, the ILO, UNESCO, or WHO) can be included on the ECOSOC Roster.

Despite the fact that unaccredited NGOs are excluded from formal meetings, numerous unaccredited NGOs are often in attendance, participating in informal ways at the 60th session of the CHR. "The really important meetings are in the hallways and doorways anyway," explained one NGO veteran of Human Rights Commission annual meetings. "The parallel meetings are usually very informative," she added, "but now there are so many that it is difficult to attend all ... three in one day so attendance gets split."[58] "There's no question about whether to go or not," said another advocate who was undaunted by his NGO's unaccredited status. "Everyone shows up, so to maintain credibility you have to, too." For this advocate, "showing up" meant attending the informal meetings ("the informals"), not the formal session. "For the formal stuff, it is just so political that it is hard to be convinced by its credibility," said a woman who had experience at both informal and formal UN sessions. NGO staff described the Human Rights Commission meetings as "a time when ideas get generated and contacts made." Gay McDougall, Executive Director of Global Rights, has observed that the pattern of the UN relegating NGOs to the periphery of activity has become well established, "but it is now just as common for NGOs to function with remarkable flexibility from an outer ring of influence."[59]

Concluding thoughts

The most important and effective feature of the Charter-based bodies is their integrative and participatory processes. States, observer states, NGOs and national human rights institutions (NHRIs) can work through these bodies to address areas of concern. The give and take of negotiations not only leads to concrete human rights measures but, equally significant, it raises consciousness among all participants and generates impetus for further organizing. For Charter-based human rights bodies to achieve their purpose, however, it is important for states that have been integral to their creation to participate on a consistent basis. The failure of the United States to actively engage in the new Human Rights Council undermines not only that institution but the UN human rights system more generally. The treaty-based mechanisms provide a host of complementary and additional avenues for human rights promotion and protection and it is to their mechanisms that we now turn.

4 UN treaty bodies

The human rights treaty bodies run on a parallel track to the UN Charter-based mechanisms. Multilateral human rights treaties exist on a number of topics, from race discrimination to the rights of migrant workers. Instead of having one central oversight body for all of the treaties, each core human right treaty has its own compliance and oversight bodies embedded within its structure. Some of these treaty bodies allow individuals to raise concerns directly, while others grant access only to states. Human rights treaties have proliferated in recent years along with non-governmental organization involvement in treaty promotion and enforcement.

For human rights advocates, the advantage of a treaty setting forth obligations on a particular issue is that states will commit to specific obligations which directly address that issue. But treaties not only set standards for government conduct, they also educate the public and help create conditions for the voluntary compliance with standards.[1] States must also adopt internal legislation and policies to implement applicable human rights standards. In many countries, treaties form the foundation for national legal and policy changes. Where such treaty obligations are not met, human rights advocates have an important tool in the treaty with which to push for social and legal change on particular issues. For example, provisions of the Convention on the Rights of the Child highlight the practices of trafficking in children, economic exploitation and child labor, and forms of sexual exploitation and abuse.[2]

Critics of treaty bodies for human rights promotion and enforcement point to "treaty fatigue" and "treaty congestion." Treaty reporting and monitoring processes are often neither efficient nor effective. The national reporting mechanisms (requiring States Parties to report on their implementation of obligations) frequently receive reports that are inaccurate, incomplete, late, or not submitted at all. Even when adequate reports are received, under-resourced treaty-monitoring bodies may be forced into hasty and superficial reviews of the reports. The increase in the number of treaties with reporting requirements in the human rights treaty context (and international environmental realm) has led to concerns about the increasingly burdensome proliferation of reporting requirements, hence the term "treaty fatigue."

Proponents of treaties nonetheless respond that adjustments can be made in the reporting procedures so that the benefits of reporting mechanisms are maintained, without placing undue burden upon States Parties. As the human rights movement has turned from standard-setting to enforcement, the treaty creation process has slowed, but it has not stopped altogether. Negotiations over two new treaties—on the human rights of people with disabilities and on forced disappearance—have attracted considerable support throughout the United Nations structure and in many states. The Convention on the Rights of Persons with Disabilities and its Optional Protocol entered into force on 3 May 2008, thirty days after the deposit of the twentieth instrument of ratification or accession to the Convention. As of September 2008, language for a treaty on forced disappearances had emerged from a drafting committee with strong state support.[3]

This chapter introduces readers to the work of the main human rights treaty bodies (see Table 4.1). The chapter begins with a general introduction to the work of human rights treaty bodies, outlining procedures and methodologies that tend to characterize all treaty processes. The chapter then turns to the eight specific treaties, outlining their composition and mandates, and notes in particular whether individual complaint mechanisms are available. Finally, the chapter concludes with a brief discussion of treaty-body reform.

Overview of the work of human rights committees

Human rights treaty bodies create their own mechanisms for holding states accountable for their treaty commitments. Treaty bodies, or "committees", are composed of persons of "high moral character" who are generally experts in the issues covered by the treaty. They work as independent individuals, rather than representing the interests of their own home countries. The exact nature of their work varies, but human rights committees are generally involved in some, if not all, of the following functions: review of state reports; state-to-state, individual and other forms of communications; the issuance of "General Comments"; thematic discussions and other open fora; and establishing "National Plans of Action."

Table 4.1 UN treaty bodies and their parent treaties

Treaty body	Parent treaty	Date entered into force
Human Rights Committee	International Covenant on Civil and Political Rights (ICCPR)	1976
Committee on Economic, Social and Cultural Rights	International Convention on Economic, Social and Cultural Rights (ICESCR)	1976
Committee on the Elimination of Racial Discrimination	Convention on the Elimination of All Forms of Racial Discrimination (CERD)	1969
Committee on the Elimination of Discrimination Against Women	Convention on the Elimination of Discrimination Against Women (CEDAW)	1981
Committee Against Torture	Convention Against Torture and Other Cruel, Inhuman, or Degrading Treatment or Punishment (CAT)	1987
Committee on the Rights of the Child	Convention on the Rights of the Child (CRC)	1990
Committee on the Rights of All Migrant Workers and Members of their Families	International Convention on the Protection of Rights of All Migrant Workers and Members of their Families	1993
Committee on the Rights of Persons with Disabilities	Convention on the Rights of Persons with Disabilities	2007
Committee on Enforced Disappearances	Convention for the Protection of All Persons from Enforced Disappearance	

State reporting

Under all human rights treaties, States Parties are required to submit periodic reports on their own behavior under the treaty. In agreeing to a treaty, countries may single out a few provisions to which it does not agree because of a conflict with domestic law (unless specifically prohibited by the treaty)—these are called reservations, understandings and declarations (RUDs). Reservations note exceptions to specific provisions of a treaty; understandings provide clarifying interpretations where treaty language is arguably ambiguous; and declarations set specific terms for ratification.

State Parties are required to submit their reports under each treaty that they have signed and ratified, as a process of self-evaluation. For example, under Article 40 of the International Covenant on Civil and Political Rights (ICCPR), States Parties must submit reports every five years on the measures they have adopted which give effect to the rights recognized in the Covenant and on the progress made in the enjoyment of those rights. The reports are subsequently examined by the Human Rights Committee (the body charged with overseeing the ICCPR) in public meetings, through a dialogue with representatives of each State Party whose report is under consideration. The manner in which dialogue is conducted before the Committee monitoring the Convention on the Rights of Children is outlined in the document excerpted below (see Box 4.1).

Box 4.1 Illustration of dialogue process between Committee monitoring Children's Rights Convention and States Parties

[Excerpted from Overview of the Working Methods of the Committee on the Rights of the Child]

The State Party report will be discussed in open and public meetings of the Committee, during which both the State representatives and Committee members take the floor. Relevant United Nations bodies and agencies are represented. Summary records of the meetings are issued and the United Nations Department of Public Information is invited to cover the proceedings for the purpose of their Press Releases. Other journalists are free to attend, as are representatives of non-governmental organizations and any interested individuals.

With the factual situation largely clarified in writing, there should be room in the discussions to analyse "progress achieved" and "factors and difficulties encountered" in the implementation of the Convention. As the purpose of the whole process is constructive, sufficient time should be given to discussions about "implementation priorities" and "future goals." For these reasons the Committee welcomes the representation of the State Party to be a delegation with concrete involvement in strategic decisions relating to the rights of the child. When delegations are headed by someone with

Box continued on next page.

governmental responsibility, the discussions are likely to be more fruitful and have more impact on policy-making and implementation activities.

The Committee appoints two of its members to act as "country rapporteurs" to lead the discussions with the concerned State Party's delegation.

After a brief introductory statement by the head of delegation the interactive dialogue starts. The Chairperson of the Committee will request the country rapporteur(s) to provide a brief overview of the state of child rights in the concerned State Party. Thereafter the Chairperson will invite the Committee members to ask questions or make comments on the first cluster of rights, and the delegation may respond. The discussion moves step by step through the next group of issues identified in the reporting guidelines.

Towards the end of the discussion, the country rapporteurs summarize their observations on the report and the discussion itself and may also make suggestions and recommendations. Lastly, the State delegation is invited to make a final statement.

Source: "Overview of the Working Methods of the Committee on the Rights of the Child: Participation of Non-governmental Organizations and National Human Rights Institutions in the Activities of the Committee," www2.ohchr.org/english/bodies/crc/workingmethods.htm (2 September 2008).

Although only members of the Committee and representatives of the reporting State Party may take part in the official dialogue on the state reports, under some treaties (such as the Children's Convention) non-governmental organizations are encouraged to submit written information or reports to the Committee. Human rights advocates can review the state reports—which must be made public—and issue their own version of reality in a "shadow report" or "alternative report."

The general purpose of preparing a shadow report is to provide the Committee with an independent tool to assess and describe a government's accountability in fulfilling its obligations to promote and protect human rights, to monitor actions to honor commitments made in treaties or at world and regional conferences, and to put political pressure on States Parties through publicity and education. Shadow reports are particularly effective tools for committees because NGOs possess in-depth knowledge about their home countries that can be invaluable for busy committee members. Shadow reports can also help

NGOs to educate the public on particular issues, build coalitions, strengthen their own methods for holding governments accountable, and influence policy or law in their home countries. While NGO shadow reports cannot possibly focus on every theme covered by a particular treaty, they can focus on selected areas in order to provide committees with specific information on certain practices or issues that may require extra attention.[4]

On the final day of the session, the Committee adopts "concluding observations," summarizing its main concerns and making appropriate suggestions and recommendations to the State Party. Some Committees also have "follow-up" procedures designed to encourage States Parties to comply with the Committee's findings and with the obligations they assumed when they ratified the treaty. The Office of the High Commissioner for Human Rights (OHCHR) provides assistance with treaty follow-up to the ICCPR, after the Committee on Human Rights has made its "concluding observations." As part of this effort, the OHCHR has begun hosting a series of regional meetings for each treaty body. For example, in 2003 the OHCHR co-hosted a meeting with UNICEF and UNDP in Syria on the follow-up of the concluding observations of the CRC for Syria, Jordan and Lebanon. So far, UN staff and NGOs alike view the holding of regional meetings as a successful innovation. Nonetheless, some of the treaty bodies still cannot undertake follow-up because of workload, and the effectiveness of the follow-up procedures remains an area of concern.[5]

Box 4.2   Examples of state reports and NGO shadow reports

The following is an excerpt from Japan's State Party Report (Second Periodic Report, submitted November 2001)

Family trials

129. Article 1 of the Law for Determination of Family Affairs and Article 1 of the Rules for Determination of Family Affairs stipulate that the best interests of each child are to be considered. Determination of family affairs proceedings are conducted according to these provisions, thus it can be said that the child's best interests are taken into consideration.

Box continued on next page.

Juvenile trials

130. Article 1 of the Juvenile Law and Article 1 of the Rules of Juvenile Proceedings stipulate that the best interests of each child are to be considered. Juvenile proceedings are conducted according to these provisions, thus it can be said that the child's best interests are taken into consideration.

Correctional institutions

131. As stated above, Article 1 of the Juvenile Law stipulates that the child's best interests are to be considered. Treatment of juveniles in correctional institutions is as follows:

(a) In juvenile classification homes, it is prescribed in Article 2 of the Juvenile Classification Homes Treatment Regulations that juveniles shall be placed in a nice quiet environment so that they can attend their hearings, feeling secure. Article 1 of the Juvenile Training School Treatment Regulations stipulates that in juvenile training schools, juveniles shall be treated with due consideration for the state of their mental and physical development, in a lively environment, aiming at their sound development;
(b) In juvenile prisons, school education and vocational training are provided according to the mental and physical condition of the detained juveniles, paying attention to their sound development. Juveniles are treated with due consideration for their best interests.

The following is an excerpt from an NGO shadow report from Japan that roughly corresponds, and also responds, to the State Report from Japan

Little progress has been achieved in strengthening the right of the child to express their views freely in all matters concerning them and to have them taken into consideration. There are still many areas where this right is not provided in legislation; the Government Report mostly refers to guidance of desirable practices, which are neither legal entitlements nor what is actually practiced. Even when the need to allow children to express their views is recognized, there is no requirement to give "due weight" to their views and no guidelines have been offered for this purpose.

Source: Japanese Committee for NGO Reporting on the Convention on the Rights of the Child, submitted in advance of the State Party Report in July 2003.

The reporting process is a core part of the human rights treaty review system. The reporting process can be an important impetus for review and action at the domestic level as well as at the international level. At its best, the process creates opportunities for governments, NGOs and other members of civil society, including, for example, the media, to have a constructive dialogue regarding national priorities, successes, best practices, and challenges in meeting convention obligations. The lively nature of the dialogue is illustrated by the excerpt from a press report on the presentation of Guyana before the CRC, in Box 4.3.

Box 4.3 Illustration of how treaty reporting works

[Excerpt from Press Report, Committee on Rights of Child Reviews Initial Report of Guyana, *14 January 2004]*

The Committee on the Rights of the Child today considered the initial report of Guyana on how that country was giving effect to the provisions of the Convention on the Rights of the Child.

[Presentation of Country Report]

Discussion

GHALIA MOHD BIN HAMID AL-THANI, the Committee Expert who served as country rapporteur to the report of Guyana, said that the State Party had not yet ratified either of the two Optional Protocols to the Convention or The Hague conventions relating to the rights of the child. Although the report was submitted after a nine-year delay, it dealt with many of the problems frankly. She wanted to know how the report had been prepared, and if nongovernmental organizations and children themselves had been involved in its preparation.

Ms. Al-Thani asked the delegation how the provisions of the Convention were disseminated. Was it translated into various vernaculars, and were training sessions and seminars provided? She asked if appropriate measures had been taken in the field of data collection on children, which was lacking in the report.

Box continued on next page.

Another Expert asked about the roles of the various institutions dealing with children and if their work was overlapping. She also asked about the functions of the forthcoming constitutional commission on the rights of the child. Had the Government evaluated the achievements made following the implementation of the five-year national plan of action for children? What measures had been taken to harmonize the provisions of the Convention and children's bills?

An Expert said that the State Party did not have a general rule on attainment of majority age. The end of compulsory schooling was fixed at 15 but children under 14 were employed. The age for sexual consent for girls was maintained at 13 years; what would happen if such an act took place with a girl under 13?

Turning to indigenous children, another Expert asked if Amerindians and other indigenous children were discriminated against in terms of access to health services, education and other basic needs.

Referring to the burden of the external debt of the State Party, an Expert asked if the Government had, within its national plan of action, made attempts to reform its budget structure in order to guarantee adequate allocation to health and education.

[...]

An Expert said that Guyana's rule of law had been weakened because of the prevailing problems the country was facing. The administration of justice was also on the verge of being dysfunctional, resulting in negative consequences on the juvenile justice system. The delegation was asked to provide further information on those issues.

Responding, the delegation said that the Ministry of Foreign Affairs, in consultation with other ministries, was actually preparing the ground for the ratification of a number of treaties. The country, since it became independent, had been carrying out legislative reforms on various issues.

[...]

The Committee Experts continued raising further questions on such issues as the situation of disabled children; the non-distribution of

Box continued on next page.

anti-retroviral medication to child victims of HIV/AIDS; the rate of illiteracy among the population; the situation of breastfeeding; the quality of education and the rate of dropouts; the training of teachers and upgrading their capacity to teach; the low school enrolment of boys in some areas; violence among the youth; the situation of street children and placement institutions, among other things.

Responding, the delegation of Guyana said that the HIV/AIDS pandemic was not a problem among the Amerindian indigenous peoples. It was rare to find an Amerindian who was HIV-positive.

Source: *Committee on Rights of Child Reviews Initial Report of Guyana*, 14 January 2004, www.unog.ch/news2/documents/newsen/crc04004e.htm (2 September 2008).

Communications

In addition to reporting, procedures allowing for interstate communications, individual and group communications, and procedures of inquiry are likewise important and highly significant additional components of an effective implementation system.

- *Interstate communications*: A standard procedure allows treaty bodies to receive communications from a State Party regarding violations of convention obligations by another State Party. Interstate complaints procedures are not presently invoked as a matter of practice in the international context, however, because states are reluctant to use the procedure.
- *Individual communications*: Treaty bodies are sometimes given the authority to receive communications (also known as "complaints") from individuals and groups (NGOs) regarding States Parties violations of the convention. A number of international human rights treaties now allow for such a procedure, either within the framework of the convention, or as a result of an additional agreement establishing such a procedure (through an "optional protocol," that is a separately negotiated treaty adding to the enforcement component of the original treaty). A model complaint form is reproduced in Box 4.4.

Box 4.4   Model complaint form

For communications under:

- Optional Protocol to the International Covenant on Civil and Political Rights
- Convention against Torture, or
- International Convention on the Elimination of Racial Discrimination

Please indicate which of the above procedures you are invoking:

_____

Date: _____

I. Information on the complainant:

Name: _____   First name(s): _____
Nationality: _____   Date and place of birth: _____
Address for correspondence on this complaint: _____

Submitting the communication:
- ☐ on the author's own behalf
- ☐ on behalf of another person

[If the complaint is being submitted on behalf of another person:]

Please provide the following personal details of that other person
Name: _____   First name(s): _____
Nationality: _____   Date and place of birth: _____
Address for correspondence on this complaint: _____

If you are acting with the knowledge and consent of that person, please provide that person's authorization for you to bring this complaint _____

or

If you are not so authorized, please explain the nature of your relationship with that person and detail why you consider it appropriate to bring this complaint on his or her behalf: _____

Box continued on next page.

II. State concerned/Articles violated

Name of the State that is either a party to the Optional Protocol (in the case of a complaint to the Human Rights Committee) or has made the relevant declaration (in the case of complaints to the Committee against Torture or the Committee on the Elimination of Racial Discrimination): _____

Articles of the Covenant or Convention alleged to have been violated:
_____

III. Exhaustion of domestic remedies/Application to other international procedures

Steps taken by or on behalf of the alleged victims to obtain redress within the State concerned for the alleged violation—detail which procedures have been pursued, including recourse to the courts and other public authorities, which claims you have made, at which times, and with which outcomes: _____

If you have not exhausted these remedies on the basis that their application would be unduly prolonged, that they would not be effective, that they are not available to you, or for any other reason, please explain your reasons in detail: _____

Have you submitted the same matter for examination under another procedure of international investigation or settlement (e.g. the Inter-American Commission on Human Rights, the European Court of Human Rights, or the African Commission on Human and Peoples' Rights)? If so, detail which procedure(s) have been, or are being, pursued, which claims you have made, at which times, and with which outcomes: _____

IV. Facts of the complaint

Detail, in chronological order, the facts and circumstances of the alleged violations. Include all matters which may be relevant to the assessment and consideration of your particular case. Please explain how you consider that the facts and circumstances described violate your rights. _____

Box continued on next page.

Author's signature: _____

V. Checklist of supporting documentation (copies, not originals, to be enclosed with your complaint):

☐ Written authorization to act (if you are bringing the complaint on behalf of another person and are not otherwise justifying the absence of specific authorization).

☐ Decisions of domestic courts and authorities on your claim (a copy of the relevant national legislation is also helpful).

☐ Complaints to and decisions by any other procedure of international investigation or settlement.

☐ Any documentation or other corroborating evidence you possess that substantiates your description in Part IV of the facts of your claim and/or your argument that the facts described amount to a violation of your rights.

Source: Model Complaint Form, www.unhchr.ch/html/menu6/2/annex1.pdf (8 September 2008). See also Office of the High Commissioner for Human Rights, www.unhchr.ch/html/menu6/2/fs7.htm (8 September 2008).

One important requirement for the consideration of a communication by a treaty body is known as the "exhaustion requirement." This provides that the Committee shall not consider any communication unless all available domestic remedies have been exhausted, provided that the application of such remedies is not unreasonably prolonged or is unlikely to bring effective relief. Communications also cannot be under consideration by another international procedure. Another common procedural requirement is that communications must not be anonymous. Communications cannot be considered unless they come from a person or persons subject to the jurisdiction of a state that is a party to the Optional Protocol.

In most cases, the treaty bodies require that communications should be sent by the individual who claims that his or her rights have been violated by the state. However, when it appears that the alleged victim is unable to submit the communication, the Committee may consider a communication from another person who must prove that he or she is acting on behalf of the alleged victim. It is also common for the Committee considering the case to ask the alleged victim or the state concerned for additional information or comments and to set a time limit for a response. The individual complainant generally will be provided with an opportunity to respond to state submissions. A large percentage of individual communications are dismissed at earlier stages, based on failures to exhaust state remedies and on failure to provide adequate information.[6]

Procedure of inquiry

A procedure of inquiry is an additional mechanism allowing treaty bodies to initiate investigations into treaty violations. The procedure is triggered in cases where a particular human rights committee receives information relating to "grave and systematic violations" of the convention. The Committee is empowered to invite the cooperation of the State Party in question to submit its observations. Thereafter, the Committee reviews the information submitted by the State Party and other reliable information submitted by other parties. The Committee may choose to authorize one or more of its members to conduct an inquiry and report "urgently" to the Committee. Such an inquiry may include a visit to the territory of the State Party, subject to that state's consent. The findings of any such inquiry are sent to the State Party, along with Committee views, recommendations and comments. The State Party is given an opportunity to respond within six months. The procedure is confidential; accordingly, the proceedings are entirely closed and the written findings are not made public. Follow-up procedures in relation to communications or inquiry mechanisms enhance compliance with recommendations and other measures.

General comments

In developing the meaning of specific human rights norms, many Committees also rely heavily on procedures known as general recommendations or general comments. These are published interpretations of the content of human rights provisions. Often, NGOs have input into the creation of these important documents, both through invited participation in thematic discussions and other meetings with Committees, and through writing their own parallel documents.

The general comments and recommendations of all human rights treaty bodies are compiled and published on the website of the OHCHR. Recommendations often provide guidance to states on the content of their reports. While some recommendations interpret existing provisions of a treaty, others address new topics. The main value of recommendations is that they contribute to the interpretation of the human rights conventions and in so doing influence the progressive development of human rights treaty obligations.

Thematic discussions

Treaty bodies typically offer several additional avenues for NGOs, UN specialized agencies and other organizations to have influence on the development and implementation of human rights norms. These may take the form of thematic discussions, held on a regular basis or called to address a particular concern. In the case of the Committee on the Rights of the Child, a theme is chosen for "Days of Discussion," an event which occurs annually coinciding with the annual meeting of the Committee. The CRC's Days of Discussion on Children with Disabilities provides a good illustration as to the link between the treaty system and activism and coalition-building, and the crucial role of fora like the Days of Discussion in this process.[7]

Held in 1997, the aim of the Days of Discussion on Children with Disabilities was to raise awareness and understanding of the situation of disabled children and the nature of rights violations they experience, and to identify strategies for more effective protection of their rights. The meeting led to a decision to establish a working group, Rights for Disabled Children, to follow up the commitments made by various states. Chaired by Bengt Lindqvist, the former UN Special Rapporteur for Disability, the group's membership includes several prominent NGOs, including Disabled People's International, World Blind Union, World Federation of the Deaf, Inclusion International and Save the Children Alliance. A member of the Committee on the Rights of the Child is nominated to attend the meetings as an observer. The NGO Disability Awareness in Action acts as the administrator for the group, and funding has been provided by the Swedish International Development Cooperation Agency (SIDA).[8]

Rights for Disabled Children undertook a series of country studies in different regions of the world in order to do the following:

- identify the extent of continuing violations of their rights;
- examine the impact of the Convention on the Rights of the Child in addressing the situation of disabled children;
- examine strategies being developed to address those violations;
- examine the extent to which the voices of disabled children are being heard;
- explore the role being played by disabled people's organizations and their effectiveness in promoting change;

- highlight and disseminate examples of positive practice in respect of legislation, policy, and implementation of the rights of disabled children.[9]

The study was highly participatory and NGOs within each country were given the opportunity to comment on and correct draft reports which were then published and available for use as a tool for advocacy.

National plans of action

States Parties to a multilateral treaty often are encouraged by treaty bodies to develop national plans of action for the implementation of treaty commitments. National plans of action can be effective instruments for assessing the degree of compliance with convention obligations according to defined indicators that address the full set of convention obligations. In some instances, however, national plans of action in a particular context have had little or only minor connection to a convention. Accordingly, treaty bodies have found it important to provide explicit guidance to states. An excerpt from Canada's National Plan of Action for implementation of the Children's Convention appears in Box 4.5.

Box 4.5 Illustration of National Plan of Action

[Excerpt from A Canada Fit for Children, *April 2004]*

B. Goals, Strategies and Actions for Canada

1. Supporting Families and Strengthening Communities

[...]

Priorities for action

(A) CHILD- AND FAMILY-FRIENDLY POLICIES

66. Policies within the workplace, the community and the larger social environment structure our daily lives as citizens. Understanding the way in which children and families are affected by the

Box continued on next page.

policies we design and implement is crucial. Policies that are child- and family-friendly are defined by their ability to support children and families where they live, learn, play and work. Such policies provide opportunities for social inclusion and participation in community life.

[...]

(C) POVERTY

[...]

71. While significant efforts have been made to address poverty in Canada, we need to continue to work to ensure that all children have a good start in life. Income security and the health and well-being of children are central to the kind of society we want. We must never lose sight of the goals of supporting families in their efforts to secure work, find affordable housing, access health care and pursue learning opportunities ...

(D) SEPARATION AND DIVORCE

73. Families that are breaking up require special supports. Separation and divorce are stressful transitions that can have a profound effect on the health and well-being of children ...

(E) SOCIAL INCLUSION AND DIVERSITY: BUILDING COMMUNITY

77. Respect for diversity and active civic participation are core Canadian values. Yet some children, young people and adults, such as members of ethnic and racialized groups and various religious faiths, those with disabilities, immigrants and refugee children, Aboriginal peoples, children who are living on the streets, members of official language minority communities, or people living in the North or other remote areas, may experience barriers to full participation in society. Barriers may also exist based on gender or sexual orientation. These barriers can prevent parents, families and legal guardians from providing a balanced, integrated life for their children. Barriers may also prevent children and young people from sharing their opinions and fully participating in the creation of a Canada that responds equitably to all ...

Box continued on next page.

(F) ABORIGINAL CHILDREN

80. Although there have been improvements in the health and wellbeing of Aboriginal children in Canada over the years, it is clear that significant challenges remain. Improving the situation of Aboriginal children consistently ranked among the highest priorities Canadians identified as this national plan of action was being prepared. Many Aboriginal children live in poverty and have poor physical and mental health. As a group, they are over-represented in the child welfare and youth justice systems. Far too many Aboriginal children living on reserve are in substandard and crowded housing and have difficulties accessing health, social and educational services; and their parents have higher unemployment rates. Inuit children living in Canada's northern communities experience many problems including high suicide rates ...

(G) INCLUSION AND SUPPORT OF CHILDREN WITH DISABILITIES

83. Canadians believe that children with disabilities should have equity of access to programs and services that allow them to reach their full potential and participate as they wish in society, along with other Canadian children and young people. Canadians also recognize the particular challenges faced by parents of children with disabilities and the extra supports they may require.

84. To reach this goal we in Canada must ensure that children with disabilities are presented with a wide range of opportunities for participation in society. We will support measures that allow for the inclusion of children with disabilities so they can interact alongside their peers and increase access to integrated, quality learning and recreational programs ...

[The remaining provisions concern promoting healthy lives, protection from harm, promoting education and learning, and building momentum.]

Source: *A Canada Fit for Children: Canada's Plan for Action in Response to the May 2002 UN Special Session on Children*, April 2004, www.hrsdc.gc.ca/en/cs/sp/sdc/socpol/publications/2002-002483/canadafite.pdf (2 September 2008).

Overview of specific treaty bodies

Human Rights Committee

The International Covenant on Civil and Political Rights (ICCPR) was adopted by the General Assembly on 16 December 1966 and entered into force on 23 March 1976. The Human Rights Committee ("the Committee") was established pursuant to Article 28 of the Convention in order to oversee the implementation of the ICCPR. The 18-member Committee convenes three times a year for sessions of three weeks' duration, typically in March at United Nations headquarters in New York and in July and November at the United Nations office in Geneva. After submitting an initial report, States Parties to the ICCPR must submit reports on their compliance with treaty obligations every five years.

Each session of the Committee is preceded by two simultaneous pre-session working groups. One working group is entrusted with the task of making recommendations to the Committee regarding communications received under the Optional Protocol (see below). The other working group is mandated to prepare concise lists of issues concerning state reports due for examination by the Committee at the next session. The Committee operates independently of ECOSOC oversight, although it is required to submit to the General Assembly an annual report on its activities. In addition to the reporting procedure, Article 41 of the Covenant provides for the Committee to consider interstate complaints.[10]

The substantive rights protected within the ICCPR include: self-determination; legal redress; equality; life; liberty; freedom of movement; fair, public, and speedy trial of criminal charges; privacy; freedom of expression, thought, conscience, and religion; peaceful assembly; freedom of association (including trade union rights and political parties); family; and participation in public affairs.

Are individual communications permitted?

Yes. The first Optional Protocol to the Convention established a mechanism to review individual complaints regarding violations of the treaty. (The second Optional Protocol, which entered into force on 11 July 1991, legally abolishes the death penalty.)

The first Optional Protocol allows the Committee to consider any alleged violation of any of the rights set forth in the Convention against an individual—provided that the state in question has agreed separately to the Optional Protocol. The Committee seeks to place individuals who complain and states that are alleged to have violated their rights on an equal footing throughout its proceedings and to provide each with an opportunity to comment on the other's arguments. The findings of the Committee, namely its views on communications that have been declared admissible and examined on their merits and its decisions declaring other communications inadmissible, are always made public immediately after the session at which the findings are adopted. They are reproduced in the Committee's annual report to the General Assembly and are available online. The Committee works by consensus, but individual members can append their opinions to the views it expresses on the merits of a case or to its decisions to declare communications inadmissible. In urgent cases requiring immediate action, for example, a threatened expulsion or imposition of the death penalty, the Committee may address urgent requests to the states involved without prejudging the merits of complaints.

Individuals have used the complaints procedure under the Optional Protocol extensively, and the findings of the Committee have proven to be influential. Over 104 different states have been named in communications to the Committee.[11] Several countries have changed their laws as a result of decisions by the Committee on individual complaints under the Optional Protocol. In a number of cases, prisoners have been released and compensation paid to victims of human rights violations. Although Committee decisions are not binding on other jurisdictions, other human rights juridical and fact-finding bodies (such as the European Court of Human Rights) have looked to Committee decisions for guidance in making their own judgments.

Committee on Economic, Social and Cultural Rights

The International Covenant on Economic, Social and Cultural Rights (ICESCR) entered into force in 1976. Unique amongst the treaties, the enforcement body of the ICESCR was established through a resolution of the Economic and Social Council (ECOSOC), rather than through the treaty itself. Unlike the ICCPR, the ICESCR does not operate independently of UN oversight; rather, it is required to assist ECOSOC in fulfilling its role.[12] When the treaty first entered into force, ECOSOC established a working group for implementation, in particular to assist with the consideration of state reports. In 1985, ECOSOC renamed the working group the Committee on Economic, Social and Cultural Rights, to be comprised of 18 independent experts. The Committee on Economic, Social and Cultural Rights meets three times a year in Geneva.

Some of the specific rights included in the ICESCR include the right to gain a living by work, to enjoy trade union rights, to receive social security, to have protection for the family, to possess adequate housing and clothing, to be free from hunger, to receive health care and to obtain free public education, and to participate in cultural life, creative activity, and scientific research.

Are individual communications permitted?

No. There is no individual complaint procedure under ICESCR. A draft optional protocol which would allow such complaints was adopted at the 15th session of the Committee on Economic, Social and Cultural Rights, held in Geneva in 1996, but it has yet to attract sufficiently broad support for its adoption.[13] A newly convened working group of the UN Commission on Human Rights met in early 2004 to debate the feasibility of an optional protocol to the ICESCR that would provide for the adjudication of individual and group complaints against states under that Covenant. Proponents of a complaints mechanism argued that the absence of strong enforcement mechanisms in the ICESCR has marginalized economic, social, and cultural rights and stymied their full realization. Opponents contend that, given their aspirational nature,[14] economic, social, and cultural rights are not "justiciable," that is not subject to the possibility of formal third-party adjudication, with remedies for findings of non-compliance. Participating states were in sharp disagreement over the viability of the proposal, however, and the session ended with the issue still open.[15]

The Committee on the Elimination of Racial Discrimination

The International Convention on the Elimination of All Forms of Racial Discrimination ("the Race Discrimination Convention") entered into force in 1969. It established a Committee on the Elimination of All Forms of Racial Discrimination (CERD) of 18 experts, selected by States Parties. CERD meets in two-week sessions, twice a year in Geneva.

The Race Discrimination Convention defines discrimination in Article 1.1 as:

> Any distinction, exclusion, restriction or preference based on race, colour, descent, national or ethnic origin with the purpose or effect of nullifying or impairing the recognition, enjoyment or exercise, on an equal footing, of human rights in any field of public life, including political, economic, social or cultural life.

The rights enshrined in Article 5 of the Race Discrimination Convention include:

> [the] right to equality before the law without distinction as to race, color, or national or ethnic origin and to equality in the enjoyment of ... the right to equal treatment before tribunals and all other organs administering justice; the right to security of the person and the protection by the states against violence or bodily harm, whether inflicted by government officials or others; the right to vote and stand for election; and the right of access to any place or service intended for use by the general public.

Other civil, political, economic, social and cultural rights are also specifically enumerated by the treaty. The Committee publishes its interpretation of the content of human rights provisions, known as "general recommendations" (or "general comments"), and organizes thematic discussions.

In addition to its monitoring procedure and acceptance of interstate and individual complaints, enforcement of CERD is aided by preventive measures which include "early-warning" measures aimed at preventing the escalation of existing situations, and urgent procedures to respond to problems requiring immediate attention to prevent or limit the scale or number of serious violations of the Convention.[16]

Are individual communications permitted?

Yes. Article 14 of the Race Discrimination Convention establishes a procedure that makes it possible for individual complaints to be brought to CERD, provided that the State Party in question has made a declaration recognizing the competence of CERD to receive such complaints. States that have made the declaration may also, pursuant to the Race Discrimination Convention, establish or indicate a national body competent to receive petitions from individuals or groups who claim to be victims of violations of their rights and who have exhausted other local remedies. In this case, only if petitioners fail to obtain satisfaction from the body indicated may they bring the matter to CERD's attention.

The complaint procedure is largely secretive. CERD brings individual communications about alleged violations to the attention of the State Party in question, but does not—without its consent—reveal the identity of the individual or group claiming a violation. Should CERD consider the case, it transmits its conclusions and recommendations to the individual or group concerned and to the State Party.

Committee on the Elimination of Discrimination Against Women

The Convention on the Elimination of Discrimination Against Women ("the Women's Convention") entered into force in 1981. Article 17 of the Women's Convention establishes the Committee on the Elimination of Discrimination Against Women (CEDAW) to oversee the implementation of its provisions. CEDAW is composed of 23 experts who are elected by secret ballot from a list of persons "of high moral standing and competence in the field covered by the Convention" nominated by States Parties. In the election of persons to CEDAW, consideration is given to equitable geographical distribution and to the representation of different civilizations and legal systems. The members of CEDAW serve four-year terms. Although nominated by their own governments, members serve in their personal capacity and not as delegates or representatives of their countries of origin.

Under Article 20 of the Convention, CEDAW is to meet once a year for "a period of not more than two weeks." Under pressure from NGOs, this period has been expanded so that it now includes two sessions which are each two weeks long. CEDAW is serviced by the United Nations Division for the Advancement of Women, which moved from Vienna to New York in 1993. Although the only requirement is that they be "experts of high moral standing and competence in the field of women's rights," to date, all CEDAW members have been women.

Article 1 of the Women's Convention defines discrimination against women as:

> Any distinction, exclusion or restriction made on the basis of sex which has the effect or purpose of impairing or nullifying the recognition, enjoyment, or exercise by women, irrespective of their marital status, on a basis of equality of men and women, of human rights and fundamental freedoms in the political, economic, social, cultural, civil or any other field.

Among all the human rights treaties, CEDAW is second only to the Convention on the Rights of the Child in the number of nations that have ratified it, yet it is also the treaty with the greatest number of substantive reservations. In particular, states have made reservations to Articles 2, 5, 9, 15, and 16, which deal with eliminating discrimination, culture and tradition, nationality, legal capacity, and marriage and family relations.

Are individual communications permitted?

Yes. The Optional Protocol of the Women's Convention, which was opened for signature in 1999 and entered into force one year later, creates new communications and inquiry procedures for individuals and groups alleging discrimination.

- *The communications procedure* allows individual women or groups of individuals to submit individual complaints to CEDAW.
- *The inquiry procedure* enables CEDAW to initiate inquiries into situations of grave or systemic violations of women's rights in countries that have become States Parties to the Optional Protocol. CEDAW may only conduct inquiries in countries which are States Parties to both CEDAW and the Optional Protocol. Article 10 of the Optional Protocol provides an "opt-out clause" allowing states, upon ratification or accession to the Protocol, to declare that they do not accept the inquiry procedure.

Committee Against Torture

The Convention Against Torture and Other Cruel, Inhuman or Degrading Treatment or Punishment ("the Torture Convention") entered into force on 26 June 1987. The Torture Convention created the Committee Against Torture (CAT), a panel of 10 experts who are elected by the States Parties to the Torture Convention. CAT meets twice annually in Geneva.

Article 1(1) of the Torture Convention defines torture as:

> Any act by which severe pain or suffering, whether physical or mental, is intentionally inflicted on a person for such purposes as obtaining from him or a third person information or a confession, punishing him for an act that he or a third person has committed or is suspected of having committed, or intimidation of any kind, when such pain or suffering is inflicted by or at the instigation of or with the consent or acquiescence of a public official or other person acting in an official capacity.

The Torture Convention requires that States Parties incorporate the crime of torture in their domestic legal codes and punish accordingly any acts of torture committed by their own citizens. The Torture Convention makes no allowances for any exceptional circumstances, such as a state of war or political unrest, and requires States Parties to establish compensation and rehabilitation programs for victims of torture.

The Optional Protocol of the Torture Convention, adopted in 2002, aims specifically to prevent torture, as opposed to investigating incidences of torture after they have already occurred. The Protocol mandates that States Parties must establish "independent national preventative mechanisms for the prevention of torture at the domestic level." These preventative mechanisms, which must adequately represent all ethnic, cultural, and religious groups within the state (and which must have an equitable gender balance), have the power to investigate claims of torture, make recommendations to the relevant state authorities, and submit proposals concerning relevant domestic legislation. The Torture Convention Protocol grants these independent bodies the right to full access to information regarding torture, as well as protection from harassment by the state. To support the preventative mechanisms, the Protocol establishes a Sub-Committee on Prevention of Torture and Other Cruel, Inhuman or Degrading Treatment or Punishment, a subsidiary body of the Convention Against Torture. The Sub-Committee is charged with visiting States Parties to CAT, assisting them with the establishment of independent preventative mechanisms, and offering continuous training and technical assistance to the mechanisms.

Are individual communications permitted?

Yes. Individual complaints are permitted under the Torture Convention's Article 22. Article 22 of the Torture Convention contains an individual complaints procedure which enables individuals to submit a complaint to CAT if the State Party they believe violated their rights has made a declaration that it recognizes the competence of CAT to receive and consider such complaints. Over one-third of States Parties have done so, and the procedure has been used quite frequently by individuals, although not to the same extent as the Optional Protocol to the ICCPR.

The Committee on the Rights of the Child

The Convention on the Rights of the Child ("the Children's Convention") was adopted by the General Assembly in 1989 and was immediately signed by more nations in a shorter period of time than any other UN convention. It entered into force in 1990.[17] Pursuant to Article 43 of the Children's Convention, the Committee on the Rights of the Child (CRC) was formed to review States Parties' reports, which are due two years after entry into force, and every five years thereafter. The CRC meets in Geneva three times a year for three weeks each session, and consists of 18 experts of "high moral character." This committee's work on standard setting and human rights promotion also receives significant assistance through the publishing of its interpretation of the content of human rights provisions (known as general comments)[18] and through the organization of "days of general discussion," thematic meetings designed to promote deeper understanding of the convention.[19]

Children's rights have proven to be highly controversial. Although states are willing to ratify the Children's Convention, they do so with reservations. The Children's Convention has more reservations per signatory country than any other UN human rights convention. Sample reservations are given in Box 4.6.

Box 4.6 **Illustration of treaty reservations**

The following are some examples of reservations to the Children's Convention by a variety of States Parties:

- Afghanistan: "The Government of the Republic of Afghanistan reserves the right to express, upon ratifying the Convention, reservations on all provisions of the Convention that are incompatible with the laws of Islamic Shari'a and the local legislation in effect."
- Australia: "Australia accepts the general principles of article 37. In relation to the second sentence of paragraph (c), the obligation to separate children from adults in prison is accepted only to the extent that such imprisonment is considered by the responsible authorities to be feasible and consistent with the obligation that children be able to maintain contact with their families, having regard to the geography and demography of Australia. Australia, therefore, ratifies the Convention to the extent that it is unable to comply with the obligation imposed by article 37 (c)."
- China: "The People's Republic of China shall fulfill its obligations provided by article 6 of the Convention under the prerequisite that the Convention accords with the provisions of article 25 concerning family planning of the Constitution of the People's Republic of China and in conformity with the provisions of article 2 of the Law of Minor Children of the People's Republic of China."
- Uruguay: "The Government of Uruguay declares that, in the exercise of its sovereign will, it will not authorize any persons under its jurisdiction who have not attained the age of 18 years to take a direct part in hostilities and will not under any circumstances recruit persons who have not attained the age of 18 years."

Article 45 of the Children's Convention specifically provides for the participation of UN specialized agencies and other specialist organizations in the treaty-monitoring process. This highly unconventional provision states:

(a) The specialized agencies, the United Nations Children's Fund and other United Nations organs shall be entitled to be represented at the consideration of the implementation of such provisions of the present Convention as fall within the scope of their mandate. The Committee may invite the specialized agencies, the United Nations Children's Fund and other competent bodies as it may consider appropriate to provide expert advice on the implementation of the Convention in areas falling within the scope of their respective mandates. The Committee may invite the specialized agencies, the United Nations Children's Fund and other United Nations organs to submit reports on the implementation of the Convention in areas falling within the scope of their activities.

(b) The Committee shall transmit, as it may consider appropriate, to the specialized agencies, the United Nations Children's Fund and other competent bodies, any reports from States Parties that contain a request, or indicate a need, for technical advice or assistance, along with the Committee's observations and suggestions, if any, on these requests or indications.

(c) The Committee may recommend to the General Assembly to request the Secretary-General to undertake on its behalf studies on specific issues relating to the rights of the child.

(d) The Committee may make suggestions and general recommendations based on information received pursuant to articles 44 and 45 of the present Convention.

The CRC has a record of strong cooperation with UN agencies and bodies for the reporting process, organization of general discussion days, input in general comments, and assistance to informal field visits. The CRC often invites the specialized agencies, the United Nations Children's Fund and other competent bodies to provide it with expert advice. The CRC similarly encourages NGOs and national human rights institutions (NHRIs) to submit reports, documentation or other information in order to provide it with a comprehensive picture and expertise as to how the Children's Convention is being implemented in a particular country. The CRC issues written invitations to selected NGOs to participate in the pre-session working group tasked with making the agenda for the meeting. The pre-session working group is a meeting closed to the public, so no observers are allowed. NGOs, NHRIs and other competent bodies may request a private meeting with the CRC.

There are two Optional Protocols that were adopted after the wider adoption of the Children's Convention to supplement the rights protected therein. The Optional Protocol on the Sale of Children, Child Prostitution and Child Pornography, which entered into force on 18 January 2002, addresses the growing problem of sex trafficking, sexual exploitation and abuse, and outlines steps for the protection of child victims' rights during all phases of the criminal justice process. The Optional Protocol on the Involvement of Children in Armed Conflict, which entered into force on 12 February 2002, sets the minimum age limit for direct participation in conflict at 18, and limits recruitment to age 16.

Are individual communications permitted?

No. The CRC suggests that advocates bring complaints about children's human rights under other available individual complaint procedures as appropriate. For example, allegations of abuse of children in custody may be brought under the Torture Convention and allegations of discrimination against girls in schooling could possibly be heard under the Optional Protocol to the Women's Convention.

Committee on the Protection of the Rights of All Migrant Workers and Members of Their Families

On 1 July 2003, the International Convention on the Protection of the Rights of All Migrant Workers and Members of Their Families ("the Migrant Workers Convention") entered into force. The Convention is monitored by the Committee on the Protection of the Rights of All Migrant Workers and Members of Their Families (CRMW). The CRMW consists of 10 experts of high moral standing and acknowledged impartiality, serving in their personal capacity, elected by the States Parties in accordance with the procedure set forth in the Migrant Workers Convention. The first meeting of States Parties for the election of the members of the CRMW was held on 11 December 2003. The membership of the CRMW will increase from 10 to 14 experts once 41 ratifications of the treaty are registered.

The Migrant Workers Convention constitutes a comprehensive international treaty regarding the protection of migrant workers' rights. The Migrant Workers Convention aims to guarantee equality of treatment and the same working conditions for migrants and nationals. The Migrant Workers Convention addresses:

- preventing inhumane living and working conditions, physical and sexual abuse and degrading treatments;
- guaranteeing migrants' rights to freedom of thought, expression and religion;
- guaranteeing migrants' access to information on their rights;
- ensuring their right to legal equality, which implies that migrant workers are subject to correct procedures, have access to interpreting services and are not sentenced to disproportionate penalties such as expulsion;
- guaranteeing migrants' equal access to educational and social services; and
- ensuring that migrants have the right to participate in trade unions.

Are individual communications permitted?

Potentially. Under Article 77, a State Party may recognize the competence of the CRMW to receive and consider communications from or on behalf of individuals within that state's jurisdiction who claim that their rights under the Migrant Workers Convention have been violated. Such communications may be received only if they concern a State Party which has explicitly recognized the competence of the CRMW. This procedure requires 10 declarations by States Parties to enter into force. To date, no State Party has made the necessary declaration.[20]

Committee on the Rights of Persons with Disabilities

The Convention on the Rights of Persons with Disabilities (CRPD) entered into force in May 2008. The Committee on the Rights of Persons with Disabilities has three principal functions: (1) the review of periodic reports on implementation of CRPD and the constructive dialogue with States parties; (2) the receipt and examination of individual communications (complaints) under the Optional Protocol; and (3) the undertaking of inquiries in the case of reliable evidence of grave and systematic violations of the Convention (also under the Optional Protocol). In keeping with the practice of other treaty bodies, the Committee might decide to issue General Comments elaborating the meaning of the provisions of the Convention or cross-cutting themes, and might hold Days of General Discussion with States, civil society, United Nations entities and other international organizations.

In accordance with Article 34 of the Convention, the Committee shall, at the time of entry into force of the Convention, be composed of 12 experts. After an additional 60 ratifications or accessions to the Convention, the membership of the Committee shall increase by six, attaining a maximum number of 18 members. The Committee is to meet in Geneva two to three times a year.

The members of the Committee shall be elected by States Parties with consideration being given to the following priorities:

- equitable geographical distribution;
- representation of different forms of civilization;
- representation of the principal legal systems;
- balanced gender representation; and
- participation of experts with disabilities.[21]

Are individual communications permitted?

Yes, if the state has agreed to the Optional Protocol. The Optional Protocol to the Convention gives the Committee competence to examine individual complaints with regard to alleged violations of the Convention by States Parties to the Protocol.

Committee on Enforced or Involuntary Disappearance

As defined in the preamble of the Declaration on the Protection of All Persons from Enforced or Involuntary Disappearance, adopted by the General Assembly in its resolution 47/133 of 18 December 1992, enforced disappearances occur "when persons are arrested, detained or abducted against their will or otherwise deprived of their liberty by officials of different branches or levels of Government, or by organized groups or private individuals acting on behalf of, or with the support, direct or indirect, consent or acquiescence of the Government, followed by a refusal to disclose the fate or whereabouts of the persons concerned or a refusal to acknowledge the deprivation of their liberty, which places such persons outside the protection of the law."[22] Enforced disappearance when "committed as part of a widespread or systematic attack directed against any civilian population, with knowledge of the attack" has been defined as a crime against humanity in article 7 (1) (i) of the Rome Statute of the International Criminal Court.[23]

At the 58th Session of the Human Rights Commission, in 2002, it was decided to create an intersessional open-ended working group (ISWG) to elaborate a draft legally binding normative instrument for the protection of all persons from enforced disappearance. As of September 2008, the treaty had not yet been opened for signature.

Pressures for reform

A report of the International Law Association identifies numerous factors for evaluating human rights treaties:

> The extent to which states comply with their reporting obligations and submit reports; the amount of time the treaty bodies have to question state representatives; the amount of independent information on a state's human rights record available to the treaty body members; the accessibility of many aspects of the process to non-governmental organizations (NGOs) and individuals; the drafting of state reports, the dialogue, information flow to the treaty bodies; the ability of treaty bodies to follow up inadequate reports or oral replies; the quality of the treaty body's concluding observations; the extent to which the questioning and conclusions of the treaty bodies are followed by the media.[24]

The first factor, state compliance with reporting requirements, has proven to be most troublesome. Up to 80 percent of states which are party to the human rights treaties have overdue reports. Eighty-one states, or an average of 60 percent of States Parties to all the treaties, have five or more overdue reports. Many treaty bodies have taken steps to address delinquency in state reporting (see suggestions of CRC, below), but the problem continues. Additionally, the entire reporting system is burdened by a lack of time and resources. Committees meet for a limited amount of time each year, and thus have little time to spend on reviewing each report. The quality of state reporting is also jeopardized by resource constraints.[25]

No consensus has emerged, either among NGOs or states, on how to reform treaty processes. Reform is further complicated by procedural challenges and logistical difficulties. Every committee has its own rules of procedures and priorities, and there are further constraints imposed by the actual wording of the treaties which they are monitoring. All of these factors combine to make treaty reform highly complex. The following summarizes some of the main suggestions put forward:

• to ease duplication, the General Assembly should consolidate the reporting system so that each State Party submits only one comprehensive report, which should be disseminated to all committees;

- financial and technical support should be provided for NGO involvement in the preparation of reporting documents;
- governments should create their own permanent treaty mechanism, that is one that would exist at all times, not just during the treaty-monitoring season;
- treaty bodies should visit States Parties on fact-finding missions, paying special attention to those States Parties which have overdue reports;
- treaty bodies should publish a document on overdue reports, highlighting state by state the worst human rights abusers (some treaty bodies are already doing this and are proceeding to consider States Parties based on NGO reporting and other information, even in the absence of a state report);
- treaty bodies should be encouraged to offer "direct and forceful criticism" of the accuracy of state reports;
- treaty bodies should also set guidelines that indicate standards required both for state reports and for state representatives; and
- states should be required to resubmit unresponsive and unsatisfactory reports.[26]

Box 4.7   Illustration of strategies devised to encourage reporting by States Parties

[The following is excerpted from Overview of the Working Methods of the Committee on the Rights of the Child*]*

Convention makes reporting in time an obligation in itself. The Committee emphasizes the importance of timely reports. State parties encountering difficulties in preparing the reports, may request technical assistance from OHCHR or UNICEF.

At its twenty-ninth session (see CRC/C/114, paragraph 561), the Committee decided to send a letter to all States parties whose initial reports were due in 1992 and 1993, requesting them to submit that report within one year. In June 2003, similar letters were sent to three States parties whose initial reports were due in 1994 and never submitted. The Committee further decided to inform those States parties in the same letter that should they not report within one year, the Committee would consider the situation of child rights in

Box continued on next page.

the State in the absence of the initial report, as foreseen in the Committee's "Overview of the reporting procedures" (CRC/C/33, paras. 29–32) and in light of rule 67 of the Committee's provisional rules of procedure (CRC/C/4).

In addition to its guidelines for reporting (CRC/C/5 and CRC/C/58), the Committee also adopted recommendations that are relevant to States parties' reporting obligations. They provide guidance to States parties that [are] encountering problems in complying with the strict time frame for submission of reports established by the Convention in article 44, paragraph 1, or the consideration of whose reports has been delayed. These recommendations apply as an exceptional measure taken for one time only (see CRC/C/139).

Source: Committee on the Rights of the Child, *Overview of the Working Methods of the Committee on the Rights of the Child*, http://www2.ohchr.org/english/bodies/crc/workingmethods.htm (14 September 2008).

The OHCHR became active on the subject of reforming the existing human rights treaty bodies following initiatives on the subject undertaken by the UN Secretary-General. The Secretary-General's second report on the subject, *Strengthening of the United Nations: An Agenda for Further Change*, proposed, among other things, that the treaty bodies "should craft a more coordinated approach to their activities and standardize their varied reporting requirements" and that "each State should be allowed to produce a single report summarizing its adherence to the full range of international human rights treaties to which it is a party."[27] The Secretary-General requested that the OHCHR consult with the committees on new streamlined reporting procedures. One of the more controversial aspects of the various proposals concerned the concept of "summarizing" reporting, and the implication that a state could comply with reporting on its human rights obligations under all the treaties to which it was a party in a condensed, less detailed format. In order to address these concerns about watering down reporting obligations by proposing a summary or consolidated report, the OHCHR has produced draft guidelines on reporting, suggesting an expanded "core document" that could, in part, satisfy some core reporting obligations common to all human rights treaties, while maintaining the quality and content of reporting on issues particular to individual treaties.[28]

Concluding thoughts

The treaty bodies serve different functions: doing justice in individual cases, creating a deterrent and encouraging behavior modification, and interpreting and explaining human rights law beyond the individual case or particular set of state actors.[29] The effectiveness of the treaty bodies can ultimately be measured in relation to the different purposes they set out to achieve.[30] As a mechanism to protect human rights and establish universal standards and norms, human rights treaties have achieved much success. They have brought recognition to numerous human rights issues and serve as promises of "good behavior" from States Parties, creating mutual obligations and responsibilities. Individual wrongs have been remedied and national legislation changed as the result of the work of the treaty bodies. The treaty bodies also have produced a substantial amount of work which clarifies and elaborates the human rights laws of the treaties, which has served to broaden the scope and the application of the human rights treaties. As such, the treaty bodies play essential roles in implementing and following through on the commitments States Parties make upon ratifying human rights treaties.

Yet there remain a number of problems with the UN human rights treaty system. A central dilemma concerns the trade-offs inherent in pushing for universal acceptance and ratification of human rights treaties versus effective implementation. While it is a positive sign that more countries are ratifying human rights treaties, the true universality of human rights law is called into question when countries limit their treaty obligations through numerous reservations, understandings and declarations (RUDs). Another dilemma is posed by the complexity of the treaty reporting process that creates burdensome reporting requirements. While monitoring and reporting requirements will only serve their intended purpose by putting demands on states, the treaty bodies will be severely hampered in their effective operation as long as states have a strong argument that they are being overworked. State responsibility cannot be sacrificed in the name of alleviating state burdens. Yet as long as states fail to meet their reporting obligations, the legitimacy of the entire UN human rights system will be compromised.[31]

5 The Security Council

The United Nations Security Council has evolved considerably over time in relation to human rights. One of the six "principal organs" of the United Nations, the Security Council consists of five permanent members (China, France, Russia (formerly the Soviet Union), the United Kingdom and the United States ("P-5")) and 10 other members elected by the General Assembly for revolving two-year terms. The mandate of the Council has always been to safeguard international peace and security, but its interpretation of the nature of this mandate and the means necessary to carry it out have changed over the decades.

While other UN organs such as the General Assembly and the Economic and Social Council were expressly empowered in their original mandates to deal with human rights and fundamental freedoms, the Security Council was not. Rather, the Security Council was left free to interpret what it meant to promote international peace and security. In the early years and throughout much of the Cold War, the Security Council sought to isolate itself from human rights concerns and to close its decision-making processes to non-governmental organizations that might push human rights and humanitarian matters into international attention. The Security Council did its best to sidestep the few human rights issues that fell under its purview. Cloistered within intergovernmental machinery and Secretariat bureaucracy, the human rights agenda was designed to remain at a safe distance from the Council from the start.[1] Over time, however, this distance proved to be both impossible and unwise as the connection between ongoing human rights abuses and threats to international peace and security became increasingly clear.

The demands for UN involvement in peace-keeping and peace-building efforts in states torn by civil strife increased, and this work was intrinsically linked with human rights. To fulfill its mandate of safeguarding peace and security, the Security Council found it necessary to address the human rights issues at all stages of conflict. In the pre-conflict stage, human rights abuses are part of the root cause of conflicts turning violent. In the hot conflict stage, human rights abuses are integral to the strategy of warring factions or where they occur as a by-product of violence. In efforts to reach peace agreements, the Security Council found that it is essential that human rights are addressed so as to pacify and stabilize conflict areas, and in the post-agreement stages, human rights abuses must be incorporated so as to bring perpetrators to justice and to build institutions capable of handling conflict civilly. The agenda of the Council was suddenly full of human rights concerns.

This chapter is divided into five parts. First, it begins with the historical debate on the authority and political will of the Security Council to address human rights, with special attention given to the role of the Secretary-General. The second section turns to an exploration of Security Council measures to promote human rights, examining in particular humanitarian intervention and the concept of a "responsibility to protect." The third section discusses the responsibility of the UN for its own human rights violations. The fourth section introduces the most relevant debates over Security Council reform, and finally, the last section concludes with an illustration of the role of NGOs in human rights advocacy before the Security Council.

Human rights before the Security Council

Authority and will to address human rights

The authority of the Security Council to address human rights derives from its central role in maintaining international peace and security. The UN Charter endows the Security Council with primary responsibility for the maintenance of international peace and security. The Security Council has the responsibility to weigh the evidence in individual circumstances and identify threats to the peace, breaches of the peace, and acts of aggression.[2] Upon finding a threat to the peace, the Security Council is authorized to consider what kind of response is warranted under the circumstances. Under what is known as its "Chapter VI powers" (named after the relevant chapter in the UN Charter), the Council may recommend non-coercive measures to maintain the peace. Alternatively, under its "Chapter VII powers," the Council may make recommendations for the maintenance of international peace and security or take direct action under Articles 41 and 42, involving economic and military force.

In discharging its duties, the Security Council is to act on behalf of the membership "in accordance with the Purposes and Principles of the United Nations." The purposes and principles of the United Nations

Charter, as delineated in the Charter itself,[3] include not only the maintenance of international peace and security, but also "respect for the principle of equal rights and self-determination of peoples,"[4] and "promoting and encouraging respect for human rights and for fundamental freedoms for all."[5] The Charter does contain a strong affirmation of the concepts of territorial integrity and non-interference with sovereign states. However, the Charter also notes that these principles "shall not prejudice the application of enforcement measures under Chapter VII."[6] Moreover, a strong argument can be made that statehood is predicated upon respect for basic human rights. According to this line of thought, UN-sanctioned actions designed to address grave abuses and restore respect for human rights *advance* statehood and *restore* sovereignty.

In its early years and throughout the Cold War, the Council could have interpreted its authority to embrace human rights concerns, but it did not have the political will to do so. Rather, it read the phrase "threats to the peace" narrowly and gave priority to the principle of non-interference in sovereign states over the principle of promotion of international human rights.[7] Since the 1990s, however, the Council has been increasingly concerned with the promotion of internal standards within states, including the advancement of human rights norms. At the same time, it has been increasingly willing to identify human rights violations as threats to international peace and security and to use its enforcement authority to respond to these situations, especially in extremely grave circumstances.[8]

The orientation of the UN toward human rights throughout this period has been greatly influenced by the respective roles played by individual Secretaries-General of the United Nations. The emergence of human rights on the Security Council agenda in the 1990s began with Secretary-General Pérez de Cuéllar's historic report to the General Assembly in 1991. He accused the member states of being "callous" and having an "overly bureaucratic attitude" and warned that "[t]he encouragement of respect for human rights becomes a vacuous claim if human wrongs committed on a major scale are met with lack of timely and commensurate action by the United Nations."[9]

He went on to add:

> I believe that the protection of human rights has now become one of the keystones in the arch of peace. I am also convinced that it now involves a more concerted exertion of international influence and pressure, through timely appeal, admonition, remonstration, condemnation and, in the last resort, a United Nations presence, than what was regarded as permissible under traditional international law.[10]

He cautioned against the selective application of the principle of protection of human rights and warned against unilateral actions and actions undertaken without UN authorization. Secretary-General Perez de Cuéllar challenged the UN to find ways to stop states from using the shield of state sovereignty "as a protective barrier behind which human rights could be massively or systematically violated with impunity."[11]

This challenge was taken up by the UN under the leadership of Secretary-General Boutros Boutros-Ghali. Almost immediately upon assuming the office in early 1992, Boutros-Ghali proved himself a well-reasoned advocate of a stronger UN role in conflict resolution and post-conflict peace-building. His seminal *An Agenda for Peace*, published in mid-1992, called for cooperation amongst states in the post-Cold War era, along with a commitment to human rights.[12] Boutros-Ghali identified the following as the most important goals for the United Nations:

- To seek to identify at the earliest possible stage situations that could produce conflict, and to try through diplomacy to remove the sources of danger before violence results;
- Where conflict erupts, to engage in peacemaking aimed at resolving the issues that have led to conflict;
- Through peace-keeping, to work to preserve peace, however fragile, where fighting has been halted and to assist in implementing agreements achieved by the peacemakers;
- To stand ready to assist in peace-building in its differing contexts: rebuilding the institutions and infrastructures of nations torn by civil war and strife; and building bonds of peaceful mutual benefit among nations formerly at war;
- And in the largest sense, to address the deepest causes of conflict: economic despair, social injustice and political oppression. It is possible to discern an increasingly common moral perception that spans the world's nations and peoples, and which is finding expression in international laws, many owing their genesis to the work of this Organization.[13]

Despite his strong stance on peace-building and his attention to human rights, the legacy of Boutros Boutros-Ghali was damaged by the widely reported failures of the UN in the former Yugoslavia, Rwanda, and Somalia. These supported popular opinion that the UN would only dither while warring factions unleashed genocidal campaigns against their enemies and that, in the rare cases the UN did intervene, it would not result in any great benefit to civilians. The United States clashed with Boutros Boutros-Ghali on several issues and ultimately vetoed his re-election in 1996. Despite the importance of the Secretary-General's role in upholding human rights, this veto provided another reminder that state influence still plays a weighty role in terms of the UN's human rights activities.

The next UN Secretary-General, Kofi Annan, advocated for the expansion of the UN's commitment to conflict resolution and peace-building. From the beginning, Annan was particularly forceful in linking human rights with security issues and repeatedly emphasized the imperative to address human rights issues when addressing conflict situations. In 1999, the Secretary-General electrified and angered much of the UN General Assembly by highlighting the inconsistencies in the international response to humanitarian emergencies and articulating a powerful moral imperative to "do something." In what has come to be known as the "Annan Doctrine," he repeatedly stated that state sovereignty must not shield states in the face of crimes against humanity.[14] In April 2000, Annan issued a Millennium Report entitled *"We the Peoples": The Role of the United Nations in the 21st Century,*

Table 5.1 Security Council responses to human rights

Peace-keeping	Peace enforcement	Peace operations
Chapter VI, UN Charter	Chapter VII, UN Charter	Chapter V and VII
"Pacific Settlement of Disputes"	"Action with Respect to Threats to the Peace, Breaches of the Peace, and Acts of Aggression"	"Chapter VI"
"The use of international military personnel, either in units or as individual observers, as part of an agreed peace settlement or truce, generally to verify and monitor cease-fire lines"[a]	"The coercive use of military power to impose a solution to a dispute to punish aggression, or to reverse its consequences"	Blend of peacemaking, peace-keeping and peace enforcement
Consent of parties; impartiality of peacekeepers; non-use of force	Consent doctrine weakening; force used more commonly	
Original 13 peace operations	Vast expansion of activities	

Note:
a Denis McLean, "Peace Operations and Common Sense," in Chester A. Crocker and Fen Osler Hampson, eds., *Managing Global Chaos* (Washington, D.C.: US Institute of Peace, 1996).

calling on member states to commit themselves to an action plan for ending poverty and inequality, improving education, reducing HIV/AIDS, safeguarding the environment, and protecting people from deadly conflict and violence.[15] In 2001, Annan was awarded the Millennial Nobel Peace Prize and was re-elected as Secretary-General without opposition.

The attention paid to human rights by the Secretary-General and, in turn, the Security Council has inspired not only an increased number of UN resolutions condemning rights violations and addressing certain thematic issues of great interest to human rights advocates, such as the UN resolution calling for greater inclusion of women in peacemaking (Resolution 1325).[16] Attention to human rights has also inspired the development and operation of peace-keeping missions, peacemaking (as with the Gulf War), and other peace-building initiatives, such as truth commissions and war crimes tribunals. The various ways in which the Security Council has responded to human rights concerns are discussed in Table 5.1.

Measures to promote human rights

Non-coercive measures

The Security Council may react to gross human rights abuses through a number of non-coercive measures. First, it may issue non-binding resolutions under Chapter VI of the Charter expressing its opinion on the abuses and their resolution. Although technically non-binding, resolutions made under the Council's Chapter VI powers have a certain value through setting precedents as multilateral statements on human rights.[17] As one commentator has noted, "because non-binding resolutions need not involve the invasions of state sovereignty required by Chapter VII actions, the precedential value of non-binding resolutions for destabilization of the non-interference principle is less threatening." States have a great incentive to take these resolutions seriously because of their potential influence on customary norms. Customary law develops from the consistent practice of states, coupled with the states' feeling of legal obligation to so act.[18] A pattern of state obedience to non-binding resolutions may provide such evidence of both consistent practice and an emerging feeling of obligation.

The second main category of non-coercive measures concerns Security Council-authorized peace-keeping operations. While many forms of peace-keeping today involve military force, traditional Chapter VI peace-keeping is not coercive in the sense that the Council predicates these actions based on the consent of the state subject to the operation.[19] The first classic UN military-observer group was the United Nations Truce Supervision Organization (UNTSO), established in 1948 in Palestine, and the first classic UN peace-keeping operation was the United Nations Emergency Force (UNEF), which ran from 1956 to 1967, first to supervise withdrawal of forces following the Suez Crisis, then to act as a buffer between Egyptian and Israeli forces.

Until 1987, the United Nations had carried out 13 peace-keeping operations. The traditional tasks of these operations included monitoring and enforcing ceasefires; observing frontier lines; and keeping conflicting parties separate. The operations were guided by three key principles: the consent of the parties involved, the impartiality of the peace-keepers, and the non-use of force in most circumstances.[20] While the operations during this time suffered from several weaknesses, including a lack of significant power and authority, they were also successful in many respects, freezing certain conflicts and reducing the risk of expansion of others.

Since 1988, the number of United Nations peace-keeping operations has expanded quickly and drastically. By 2004, the UN was either engaged in or had completed over 55 peace operations. The reason behind this is largely political—with the end of the Cold War, the major powers in the Security Council were less likely to use their veto powers to stop peace-keeping operations for politically motivated reasons. As the number of peace-keeping operations expanded, so too did the mandates of the operations. Peace operations were involved in such activities as monitoring and running elections in countries; protecting inhabitants of a region from the use of force, including protecting citizens from their own governments; protecting designated "safe havens"; assuring the delivery of humanitarian aid and other supplies; assisting in the reconstruction of governmental or police functions; and reporting violations of international humanitarian law.

Numerous successes have come with the expansion of peace-keeping operations. However, there have been numerous problems confronted as well. First, peace-keepers have often found it difficult to maintain impartiality. Second, the troops involved in peace-keeping operations have little experience with the intelligence-gathering and organizational skills needed to establish and enforce safe zones. Third, and most importantly, the expanded use of peace-keeping troops has led to a heated debate regarding the use of force. As soldiers are put into vulnerable situations, or find themselves in a position to protect civilians, questions regarding the degree of force appropriate for UN troops are continually surfacing. Solutions have been applied on a case-by-case basis, but currently there is no specific mandate outlining the degree of force which UN peace-keepers are authorized to use.[21]

The Security Council also engages in numerous consultative and fact-finding missions, often utilizing the Secretary-General's office or its own independent observers. Although not exclusively focused on human rights, these missions often do involve investigation into human rights concerns and contact with both local and international human rights advocates. Other activities of the Council that may be considered non-coercive while being intrusive in state affairs include the establishment of truth commissions and tribunals. These tribunals can be considered a radical innovation in international criminal law. The ad hoc International Criminal Tribunal for the former Yugoslavia was established by a Security Council resolution in 1993, the International Criminal Tribunal for Rwanda in 1994, and the Special Court for Sierra Leone in 2000.[22] The three courts were established in order to bring to justice those responsible for war crimes, crimes against humanity, and genocide in each country. These courts aim not only to bring past perpetrators of human rights abuses to justice; also, their presence conveys a broader message that trials in an international arena will help prevent future abuses from occurring.

Coercive measures

The coercive measures available to the Security Council for enforcement of human rights are governed by Chapter VII of the UN Charter.[23] Article 41 authorizes the Security Council to order economic sanctions against states, while Article 42 permits it to order military action including "demonstrations, blockades, and other operations by air, sea, or land forces of Members of the United Nations." Under Article 48 (1) of Chapter VII, the Security Council may determine whether the action required to carry out its decisions is to be taken by all or only some of the UN member states. Article 53 of the UN Charter specifically allows for "regional arrangements or agencies" to take enforcement action, including military action, with the authorization of the Security Council. In practice, states and collective regional security arrangements (i.e. NATO) have sought Security Council approval for their use of force on human rights and humanitarian grounds.[24]

The UN's ability to take enforcement action under Chapter VII is limited by design. Member states are not required to assist the Security Council in taking action, unless an agreement negotiated between the Security Council and the member so specifies. Additionally, the threshold for abuses triggering enforcement action has been set quite high. In order for the UN to take forceful measures, the situation must constitute a "threat to the peace, breach of the peace, or act of aggression," and the Security Council must determine that the relevant parties cannot peacefully resolve the situation. Although the threshold is couched in terms of "the peace" rather than "international peace," it is generally understood that international rather than domestic peace must be threatened or breached in order to spark forceful action by the UN.[25]

Moreover, the willingness and ability of the Security Council to exercise its Chapter VII powers against states that have engaged in gross and persistent violations of their citizens' human rights have been tempered by the ability of the Council's five permanent members to veto any such measures.[26] There have been some exceptions, however. The first case in which the Security Council found a state's violations of human rights to constitute a threat to the peace warranting economic sanctions occurred in 1966, when the Council imposed mandatory economic sanctions against Southern Rhodesia.[27] Intense international outrage against human rights abuses under South African apartheid also led the Council to invoke the "threat to the peace" rationale in order to impose a mandatory arms embargo against South Africa.[28] Yet these cases did not start a trend, and the Security Council remained silent as long as human rights violations took place primarily or exclusively within state borders.

The turning point did not come until the end of the Cold War. After Iraq invaded and occupied Kuwait, in 1990 the Council sanctioned an enforcement action by member states. Security Council resolution 678 reaffirmed that Iraq had committed a breach of the peace and authorized member states "to use all necessary means to uphold and implement [the Council's resolutions concerning the invasion] and to restore international peace and security in the area."[29]

The key words here were "all necessary means"—United Nations language for permitting the use of force. This resolution was followed by Resolution 688 (1991), which sanctioned the creation of "safe havens" in Iraq at the conclusion of the "first Gulf War." This measure was announced as a method of protecting Kurds from further repression by Saddam Hussein.[30] Recognizing the connection between humanitarian crises and violent conflict, Resolution 688 expressed concern that Iraq's actions had "led to a massive flow of refugees towards and across international frontiers and to cross-border incursions, which threaten international peace and security in the region." In agreeing to this resolution, the allies in the first Gulf War committed themselves to protecting the Kurds, both through the provision of humanitarian assistance and, if necessary, military might. The willingness of the Council to issue such a resolution represented a substantial change of course in articulating the relationship between human rights violations occurring within a sovereign state and international security.[31] While in the past, state consent was required for the delivery of humanitarian assistance across state borders, there could be occasions where consent was not possible but intervention was nonetheless necessary on humanitarian grounds. Based upon Resolution 688 and subsequent practices, a strong argument can be made that the Council has "legal authority to authorize armed action, or lesser coercive measures, to correct human rights violations materially within a territorial state."[32]

Another fundamental landmark validating UN humanitarian intervention for human rights purposes came in December 1992, when through Resolution 794, the Security Council authorized the use of force "to restore peace, stability and law and order" to Somalia.[33] In that case, the Council found that "the magnitude of the human rights tragedy caused by the conflict in Somalia, further exacerbated by the obstacles being created to the distribution of humanitarian assistance, constitute[d] a threat to international peace and security," and resolved "to restore peace, stability and law and order with a view to facilitating the process of a political settlement under the auspices of the United Nations." To achieve these objectives, the Council, this time specifically invoking Chapter VII of the UN Charter, authorized both the Secretary-General and cooperating member states "to use all necessary means to establish as soon as possible a secure environment for humanitarian relief operations in Somalia." Significantly, Resolution 794 focused solely on the human rights and humanitarian crisis within Somalia and made no mention of the potential effects of the crisis on neighboring states. The Somalia intervention was widely considered legal, signaling support for the argument that grave human rights abuses may alone trigger a response by the Security Council.[34]

The deaths of American soldiers and rapid pullout of peace-keeping troops in Somalia, however, ensured that the episode stood more prominently for another principle: that peace-keepers sent to violent intrastate conflicts be armed sufficiently so that they may defend themselves. Soon after Somalia, the failures of the international community to protect civilians in Bosnia[35] and Rwanda[36] led to another new concept: that peace-keepers must be empowered to defend themselves, and civilian victims of war are entitled to legitimate self-defense. As David Malone observes, "Slowly but painfully, the UN system has learnt that impartial peace-keeping cannot be equated with moral equivalence among the parties to a conflict, in extreme circumstances, nor with unwillingness to intervene to prevent atrocities."[37]

Humanitarian intervention and the responsibility to protect

In 1999, Secretary-General Kofi Annan came out firmly on the side of humanitarian intervention.[38] In his annual report on the work of the United Nations, he issued a challenge to skeptics:

> If humanitarian intervention is, indeed, an unacceptable assault on sovereignty, how should we respond to a Rwanda, to a Srebrenica—to gross and systematic violations of human rights that offend every precept of our common humanity?[39]

Following up on his challenge, in March 2000, the Secretary-General asked a panel of international experts led by long-time adviser Lakhdar Brahimi to evaluate UN peace operations. The resulting *Report of the Panel on UN Peace Operations*—known as the Brahimi Report—offered clear advice about minimum requirements for a successful UN peace-keeping mission. These included a clear and specific mandate, consent to the operation by the parties in conflict, and adequate resources. The Brahimi Report was a watershed in that it strongly argued for the abandonment of any idea that UN peace operations should be "impartial" and "neutral."[40]

The next landmark report on UN peace operations was soon issued by the International Commission on Intervention and State Sovereignty (ICISS), a group of eminent scholars and practitioners which, although funded by the Canadian government, remained independent in its study of the issue. Just as Francis Deng et al. had urged that state sovereignty be conceptualized as state responsibility,[41] the ICISS sought to re-conceptualize the intervention debate as a "responsibility to protect." In so doing, they shifted the focus from the security of states to the security of individuals.[42] In the words of the ICISS report:

> State sovereignty implies responsibility, and the primary responsibility for the protection of its people lies with the state itself. Where a population is suffering serious harm, as a result of internal war, insurgency, repression or state failure, and the state in question is unwilling or unable to halt or avert it, the principle of non-intervention yields to the international responsibility to protect.[43]

According to this view, states do not have an unqualified right to non-intervention by other states, but rather the right is conditioned on the state meeting its own responsibility to protect its citizenry. Failure to

Table 5.2 Summary of opinions on humanitarian intervention/responsibility to protect

Opinion type	Opponents	Agnostics and skeptics	Optimists
Principle of opinion	Unequivocally condemn the idea of humanitarian intervention/ responsibility to protect.	Pay little attention to the issue/ believe it to be of little importance.	Support the idea of humanitarian intervention and/or the responsibility to protect.
Lines of argumentation	Doctrine is an excuse for American hegemony;	Attention now turned to terrorism issue;	ICISS report captures workable consensus;
	Implementation is always too selective;		
	Inherent potential to divide world into the "civilized" and "uncivilized";	Dismissal of responsibility to protect as a mere clever twist of vocabulary;	Incremental measures must be taken in line with ICISS report;
	Unworkable—states will not cooperate;	Just war theory never works; and/or	No excuses are left for state failure to abide by responsibilities to world community; and/or
	Responsibility to protect is subject to political manipulation; and/or	Political will cannot be generated.	Humanitarian intervention is needed based on pragmatism— sometimes it is the "lesser evil."[a]
	The use of force is always a poor way of promoting long-lasting peace and justice.		

Source: Adapted from S. Neil Macfarlane, Caroline J. Thielking, and Thomas G. Weiss, "The Responsibility to Protect: Is Anyone Interested in Humanitarian Intervention?" *Third World Quarterly* 25, no. 5 (2004): 977–92.

Note:
a Michael Ignatieff, *The Lesser Evil: Political Ethics in an Age of Terror* (Princeton, N.J.: Princeton University Press, 2004).

accept responsibility to protect the safety and lives of citizens opens states to the possibility of intervention.

In its list of "Principles for Military Intervention," the ICISS report employed a just war framework. According to this interpretation of the typical just war criteria, the criterion of "right intention" may only be fulfilled if the primary motive of such a military action is to halt or avert human suffering. The criterion of "right authority" is fulfilled upon Security Council approval or, if the Council fails to act, upon authorization of either the General Assembly or regional organizations under Chapter VIII of the UN Charter. Other criteria require that military force be a "last resort," that it have "reasonable prospects" of succeeding, and that the scale, duration and intensity of an intervention be proportionate to the humanitarian objective ("proportional means").

While the existence and nature of a right to intervene on humanitarian grounds under the auspices of the UN continue to be debated,[44] the practice continues. UN peace-keeping operations have since occurred in such diverse places as Afghanistan, East Timor, the former Yugoslavia, Liberia, Rwanda and Somalia. Although the motives and articulated justifications for these interventions vary, the human rights dimensions of the cases were important in all of them. Human rights advocates have increasingly targeted the Security Council in their advocacy, arguing that there is if not a legal, at least a moral duty to intervene in cases of gross violations of human rights. The human rights community, however, remains divided on the legality and morality of using military force to address human rights abuses in any circumstances; see Table 5.2.

Box 5.1 Examples of UN peace operations

While the failures of some UN peace-keeping operations have been well publicized, the success stories have not attracted similar attention. Absence of conflict does not often get the big headlines. Some recent examples of successful peace-keeping are:

Bosnia and Herzegovina

When the United Nations Mission in Bosnia and Herzegovina (UNMIBH) ended operations in December 2002, the most extensive police reform and restructuring project ever undertaken by the

Box continued on next page.

UN had been completed. UNMIBH had trained and accredited a 17,000-strong national police force. In addition to maintaining internal security, this force has made progress in curbing smuggling, the narcotics trade and human trafficking.

Timor-Leste

The UN was called in to East Timor (now Timor-Leste) in late 1999 to guide the Timorese toward statehood in the wake of violence and devastation that followed a UN-led consultation on integration with Indonesia. The United Nations Transitional Administration in East Timor (UNTAET) operated under a multidimensional mandate to provide security and maintain law and order while working with the Timorese to lay the foundations of democratic governance. The UN established an effective administration, enabled refugees to return, helped to develop civil and social services, ensured humanitarian assistance, supported capacity-building for self-governance and helped to establish conditions for sustainable development.

Sierra Leone

The efforts of the international community to end an 11-year civil war and move the country toward peace have enabled Sierra Leone to enter a period of democratic transition and better governance with the assistance of the United Nations Mission in Sierra Leone (UNAMSIL). Since the May 2002 elections, Sierra Leone has enjoyed a much improved security environment and continues to work toward consolidating the peace. Key milestones include completion of the disarmament and demobilization of some 75,000 combatants, including almost 7,000 children, and destruction of their weapons. UNAMSIL peace-keepers have reconstructed roads; renovated and built schools, houses of worship and clinics; and initiated agricultural projects and welfare programs. UNAMSIL is expected to withdraw by the end of 2004, pending careful assessments of regional and internal security.

Democratic Republic of the Congo

Progress has also been achieved by the United Nations Organization Mission in the Democratic Republic of the Congo (MONUC). From a small observer mission in 2000, MONUC evolved to become,

Box continued on next page.

first, a disengagement and monitoring mission; then an assistance and verification mission for disarmament, demobilization, repatriation, reintegration and resettlement programs; and now a complex mission tasked with facilitating the transitional process through national elections in 2005. By remaining in contact with all parties of the transitional government, MONUC has helped create an enabling environment for the adoption of key legislation related to the reform of the army and police and competencies of the various ministries and transitional institutions.

A large portion of the country is now at peace, and steps have been taken toward re-unification: the new national flag flies in territories formerly controlled by belligerents; the Congo River has reopened to traffic; commercial airlines fly between Kinshasa and cities once under rebel control; postal and cellular phone networks have expanded. This has allowed MONUC, which has an authorized strength of 10,800 troops, to deploy contingents to the northeastern district of Ituri, where unrest continued in early 2009.

Liberia

In Liberia, the UN peace-keeping mission, UNMIL, was dispatched in record time to assist in the implementation of a comprehensive peace agreement. Even before UNMIL's full authorized strength of 15,000 uniformed personnel was reached, the security situation in the country improved dramatically. Violence and ceasefire violations decreased, and UN peace-keepers paved the way for the provision of humanitarian assistance and for the demobilization, disarmament and reintegration of ex-combatants. The ongoing deployment of troops, civilian police and civil affairs personnel during 2009 will continue to facilitate the restoration of civil administration.

Source: Adapted from Department of Peacekeeping Operations (DPKO), Questions and Answers, www.un.org/Depts/dpko/dpko/faq/q15.htm (2 September 2008).

Holding the UN accountable

Another dimension of human rights advocacy on security issues concerns the monitoring of the foreign troops tasked with humanitarian missions. Whenever military troops or civilian monitors or other staff are deployed under a UN banner, there is a possibility that they may commit human rights violations. Considerable obstacles exist, however, to holding the UN collectively responsible for human rights violations. The UN is not a party to any of the human rights instruments and indeed, some treaties specify in these provisions that only states may be parties to the instrument, thereby foreclosing participation in these regimes by collectives like the UN. Furthermore, the ability to hold the UN accountable to international standards is complicated by the practice of the UN granting privileges and immunities to actors within UN organizations.[45] In Article 105, the UN Charter recognizes that the organization "shall enjoy in the territory of each of its Members such privileges and immunities as are necessary for the fulfillment of its purposes." The exact nature of the privileges is set through separately negotiated, state-specific agreements.[46]

Nonetheless, several grounds have emerged to support holding the UN accountable to human rights standards.[47] First, the UN is said to be bound by international human rights norms when it is acting as a state. The reasoning here is that "states should not be allowed to escape their human rights obligations by forming an international organization to do their dirty work."[48] The UN enjoys many of the benefits given to states. As already noted, the UN is granted privileges and immunities akin to a state. As the International Court of Justice noted in the seminal *Reparations Case*, the UN has legal personality based on the notion of functional necessity, that is the UN is "exercising and enjoying functions and rights which can only be explained on the basis of the possession of a large measure of international personality and the capacity to operate upon an international plane."[49] The "legal personality" of the UN permits it, like states, to conclude treaties, to make claims on behalf of its agents, and to engage in activities for the fulfillment of its purposes.[50] This approach dilutes the distinction between states and international organizations and emphasizes the role and capacity exercised by an organization, rather than its official status.

A second argument for holding the UN accountable under international human rights standards draws from this notion of "functional necessity." This line of reasoning acknowledges that because an international organization is "obliged to pursue and try to realize its own purpose,"[51] it may exercise the powers implied in its purposes.[52] Article 1 of the UN Charter makes clear that one of the aims of the UN is to achieve international cooperation by "promoting and encouraging respect for human rights and for fundamental freedoms for all without distinction as to race, sex, language or religion." Article 55 identifies three purposes which the states of the United Nations pledge to promote: "(i) higher standards of living, full employment, and conditions of economic and social progress and development; (ii) solutions of international economic, social, health, and related problems; and international cultural and educational cooperation; and (iii) universal respect for, and observance of, human rights and fundamental freedoms for all without distinction as to race, sex, language, or religion." By agreeing to the Charter, Article 56 of the Charter elaborates, "[a]ll Members pledge themselves to take joint and separate action in cooperation with the Organization for the achievement of the [three] purposes set forth in Article 55." The commitment of the UN to promotion of human rights, which is affirmed again and again in the UN Charter, has been explicitly recognized by Secretary-General Kofi Annan to be central to UN peace-building work.[53] The United Nations is bound by the international human rights standards that are part of its constitutive document, and thus it has the power and responsibility to hold itself—and all actors under its authority[54]—accountable under these standards.

Furthermore, the leading international human rights documents—the Universal Declaration of Human Rights (UDHR) and the International Covenant on Civil and Political Rights (ICCPR)—both recognize that obligations may be attached to non-state entities, thus supporting the application of human rights law to the UN. Article 30 of the UDHR and Article 5 of the ICCPR recognize that "any State, group or person" may not derogate from the rights and freedoms enumerated in each instrument. This allows leeway for holding a collective like the UN accountable. At a minimum, the argument can be made that because the UN is bound by customary international law, it must follow those international human rights standards that have reached customary international law status.[55]

In the case of a UN administration of a territory, where the UN is the source of the law, the argument is even stronger that the UN must enforce adherence to international human rights standards and provide a means of remedy for violations. If not the UN, who can apply the law? In the case of Kosovo, for example, attempts to rely somehow on existing domestic mechanisms have proven to be tremendously inadequate. Presently, there is great confusion in Kosovo as to even what law should be applied. As Elizabeth Abraham has pointed out, "[s]ince the Federal Republic of Yugoslavia ('FRY') had only acceded to the conventions to which Yugoslavia had signed, which did not include the ECHR [European Convention on Human Rights], the UN's adoption of the ECHR made applicable conventions that were not binding to FRY as a whole."[56] The application of customary norms of international human rights law, in the very least, provides a base minimum standard.

All of these arguments—the UN acting as the functional equivalent of a state, the human rights mandate of the UN, the application of customary international law—may support the argument that United Nations forces conducting operations under UN command and control must operate in accordance with international humanitarian law.[57]

Reform efforts

Transparency, expansion, and voting

As with other parts of the UN system, Security Council reform has been discussed and debated for many years. The three major reform issues surrounding the Security Council, namely transparency, expansion, and voting, all have great importance for human rights advocates as they would enhance openness to human rights concerns. On all three questions, the five permanent members of the Security Council have a record of acting to block change that could benefit human rights advocates.

In 1965, Council membership expanded from 11 to 15 members, but few find the body representative or accountable. The first time the issue of expansion formally came before the General Assembly was in 1979, when the "Question of Equitable Representation on and an Increase in the Membership of the Security Council" was placed on the agenda of the 34th session of the General Assembly. However, discussion was put off for many years, and it was not until 1993 that the General Assembly asked states for comments on Security Council expansion. A year later, a working group was formed to consider the issue, but no conclusions were drawn that year or the next. Questions have been raised regarding the number of members, consecutive terms, categories of membership, etc.[58] While numerous proposals have now been put forward by the working group and by concerned countries, no action has been taken by the General Assembly and a great many concerns regarding the lack of representation in the Security Council remain.

A focus on membership reform would address the problems inherent in the current voting process where the P-5 of the Security Council (China, France, Russia, the United Kingdom, and the United States) enjoy the privilege of veto power. This power has been intensely controversial since the drafting of the UN Charter in 1945. The United States and Russia would likely not have accepted the creation of the United Nations without the veto privilege. Fifty years later, the debate on the existence and use of the veto continues, reinvigorated by many cases of veto threat as well as actual veto use. A strong argument can be made that an expanded Council with strict guidelines as to operations will provide a stronger backbone for human rights promotion at the United Nations. However, a dramatic change in the composition of the Security Council is not expected in the near future. Since the P-5 have veto power over Charter amendments, they can trump any efforts to weaken formally their veto power.

Reform on the issue of transparency focuses on the openness and accountability of Security Council members for their actions.[59] The issue of Security Council secrecy has only recently been raised as a concern. As David Malone explains:

> Council members, and the P-5 in particular, had always needed to consult privately among themselves. However, with active cooperation among the permanent members increasingly the norm by 1990, the P-5 saw little value in continuing to conduct much of the Council's business in open, public meetings. "Informal consultations" or "informals," closed to all non-Security Council members and most secretariat staff and leaving no formal record, became the norm. Nonmembers were in the dark on the agenda of upcoming informals and had to scramble for information, feeding off scraps provided in the antechamber by those emerging from the consultations, a humiliating experience for the supplicants.[60]

Leading non-Security Council Troop-Contributing Nations (TCNs) such as Canada, the Netherlands, Malaysia, India, Argentina, Pakistan, and some Scandinavian countries used their leverage to push for consultations and other face-saving measures. The Council began to post its agenda on a daily basis,[61] and to provide states that are not currently represented on the Council with better access to information.[62] The main reform related to transparency, however, is the creation of consultations and other informal channels of direct contact with the Security Council. This matter is discussed in the "Arria Formula" section below.

Opening the Council, the Arria Formula, and beyond

The Arria Formula, so named for its inventor, Venezuelan Ambassador Diego Arria, is an informal arrangement that allows the Council greater flexibility in receiving briefings about international peace and security issues.[63] In 1992, during the crisis in the former Yugoslavia, a Bosnian priest came to New York and asked to meet with various Council members individually. Only Ambassador Arria agreed to meet him. Ambassador Arria was so impressed with the priest's story that he felt all Council members should hear it too. When the Council would not agree to hear this testimony in its official sessions, Arria invited Council members to hear the story while gathering over coffee in the delegates' lounge. Many attended, the meeting was a great success, and the Arria Formula was born.

Prior to the Arria Formula, under the UN Charter, only delegations, high government officials (of Council members) and United Nations officials could speak at regular Council meetings and consultations. The Arria Formula enables a member of the Council to invite other Council members to an informal meeting, held outside of the Council chambers, and chaired by the inviting member. The meeting is called for the purpose of a briefing given by one or more persons, considered as expert in a matter of concern to the Council.

Today, Arria Formula briefings allow the Council to open itself in a very limited way to the outside world. Attendance is typically at a very high level, with participation from the permanent representatives or deputies. Only rarely do individual members fail to attend. The meetings are announced by the Council president at the beginning of each month or whenever organized, as part of the regular Council schedule. The meetings are also provided with complete language interpretation by the Secretariat. No Council meetings or consultations are ever scheduled at a time when the Arria Formula meetings take place.

In addition to informal meetings with experts under the Arria Formula, other changes in the operations of the Security Council which demonstrate increased openness include the following:

- The Council has participated in a number of retreats, away from headquarters, with the Secretary-General, other UN officials, and sometimes leading independent experts.
- The Council members have undertaken a number of missions to visit areas where developments are of particular interest or concern to the Council. This has allowed much more extensive contact with government officials, non-governmental groups, and UN personnel on the ground in regions of crisis.
- The Council has met a number of times over the past decade at either the foreign minister or summit level.
- To assist transparency and accountability, it has become common practice for the president of the Council to brief non-members, and often the press, on the results of informal (private) consultations.
- Tentative forecasts and the provisional agendas for the Council's upcoming work are now provided regularly to non-members, as are provisional draft resolutions.
- Consultations among Security Council members and troop contributors, along with key Secretariat officials, are now held on a more regular basis.[64]

While heralding these developments, the 10 non-permanent members of the Security Council urge that they do not go far enough. They call for the institutionalization of the steps that have already been taken, for taking several of them further, and for more public meetings and fewer informal consultations.[65]

Advocacy by non-governmental organizations

The role and interaction of non-governmental organizations with respect to the Security Council both grew significantly and evolved in nature during the 1990s.[66] NGOs have been accorded consultative status with ECOSOC, and have contributed to a broad range of UN activities. Yet for years, NGOs were deemed to be largely irrelevant to the concerns of the Security Council. This thinking changed in the 1990s when NGOs became more operational in conflict areas, working alongside and in partnership with United Nations humanitarian operations. In partnership in the field, NGOs and the United Nations organizations were providing assistance, offering protection, documenting abuses and assisting with civil society-building and other conflict-prevention and peace-building projects. At this stage, a number of governments (including those of Portugal, the Netherlands, Germany, and Canada) believed that it made sense for NGOs to have greater access to the Security Council.[67]

One reason for NGO success in this area is the ability to organize for a common purpose across a diversity of NGOs. In early 1995, a group of NGOs came together in New York to organize the NGO Working Group on the Security Council. At first the Working Group was aimed at influencing Council reform and it sought to gather a large number of NGOs under its banner. Soon it became clear that a smaller, higher-profile group could be more effective and that direct dialogue with state delegates was needed. Thus, the Working Group evolved into a closed membership organization of 30 of the most influential NGOs—largely Western-based and Western in orientation— with emphasis on direct dialogue with delegates.

Today, the NGO Working Group includes representatives from such groups as Oxfam, Médecins sans Frontières, Amnesty International, CARE, and the World Federalist Movement. The group now organizes off-the-record briefings almost every week with one of the ambassadors on the Security Council. The Working Group also organizes informal contacts between NGOs, delegates, experts, and others. It holds an annual holiday reception with delegates in December, and occasionally organizes small private meetings or lunches. Furthermore, it helps to circulate documentation and information about the Council to the NGO community and the wider public. Though it is completely informal and enjoys no official status, the Working Group wields considerable influence over Security Council deliberations, particularly on human rights and humanitarian matters.

One area in which NGOs have had tremendous impact on the Security Council is with regard to child soldiers. Restrictions on child soldiers first found their way into treaty law in 1977 with the Additional Protocols to the four Geneva Conventions of 1949 and, later in 1989, with the Convention on the Rights of the Child ("the Children's Convention"). Yet much to the disappointment of child rights advocates, these agreements set the minimum age at 15 for recruitment and participation in hostilities. For many years, advocates campaigned to increase the minimum age to 18. Instead of creating a separate international treaty to that effect, advocates sought to draft an Optional Protocol to the Children's Convention, focusing specifically on the involvement of children in armed conflict. This tactic made a great deal of sense, given strong international support for the Convention.

Under pressure from child rights NGOs, in 1994 the United Nations Commission on Human Rights formed a working group to draft the text of an "Optional Protocol on the Involvement of Children in Armed Conflict." The drafting process was open to the input of country representatives, non-governmental organizations, United Nations agencies, and independent experts. It was also influenced by the landmark study *The Impact of Armed Conflict on Children*, authored by Graca Machel, an independent expert who had been appointed by the Secretary-General to study the problem. Released in 1996, the report caused a storm at the UN as it pointed to the cynical exploitation of children by militaries in many countries and the willingness of other countries to turn a blind eye to the misuse of children as soldiers.

Two further developments helped create momentum for the Optional Protocol. In 1998, the United Nations Secretary-General appointed a Special Representative for Children and Armed Conflict, a post akin to a public advocate for children affected by war. Immediately, the Special Representative undertook activities to build greater awareness of the problem and to protect children in specific conflicts. The same year, the United Nations Secretary-General also established a new policy that would require that civilian police and military observers in United Nations peace-keeping operations be at least 25 years old.

There is little doubt that the Secretary-General's interest in the issue of child soldiers and the unrelenting NGO lobbying had an impact on both the General Assembly and Security Council deliberations. In May 2000, the United Nations General Assembly formally adopted the Optional Protocol on the Involvement of Children in Armed Conflict; it became legally binding on 12 February 2002. On almost a parallel track, beginning in 1999, the Security Council started adopting a series of resolutions on children in armed conflict. Five of these are summarized in Box 5.2. The impact of children's rights NGOs on Security Council deliberations in the case of their advocacy on the issue of child soldiers is part of a trend in human rights practice wherein the Security Council is increasingly viewed as a site for human rights advocacy.

Box 5.2   UN Security Council and children and armed conflict

Provisions and developments relating to child soldiers

August 1999: Resolution 1261 (first ever)

- strongly condemns recruitment and use of child soldiers;
- calls on UN and governments to intensify efforts to end the recruitment and use of child soldiers, and to facilitate disarmament, demobilization, and rehabilitation (DDR).

August 2000: Resolution 1314

- condemns deliberate targeting of children in situations of armed conflict;
- calls on parties to respect international law, including the Optional Protocol;
- calls on parties to armed conflict to demobilize and reintegrate child soldiers.

November 2001: Resolution 1379

- calls on parties to respect international law, including the Optional Protocol;
- urges governments to ratify the Optional Protocol;

Box continued on next page.

- urges governments to consider "legal, political, diplomatic, financial and material measures" to ensure that parties to armed conflict respect international norms protecting children;
- calls on parties to armed conflict to demobilize and reintegrate child soldiers;
- urges the UN to work to reduce child recruitment in the context of development assistance programs, and to devote particular attention to rehabilitation of children affected by conflict;
- encourages international financial institutions to support DDR of child soldiers;
- urges regional organizations to address cross-border recruitment and abduction of children and expand regional initiatives to prevent the use of child soldiers;
- requests the Secretary-General (SG) to submit a report, attaching a list of parties to armed conflict that recruit or use children in violation of international obligations in situations that are on the Security Council's agenda, or that may threaten international peace and security.

November 2002

SG's report lists 23 parties in 5 countries (Afghanistan, Burundi, Democratic Republic of the Congo (DRC), Liberia, Somalia) for recruiting and using child soldiers. The body of the report also identifies governments and/or groups in Burma, Colombia, Nepal, the Philippines, Sudan, Uganda, and Sri Lanka.

January 2003: Resolution 1460

- calls on parties to armed conflict that recruit or use child soldiers to immediately halt such practices;
- commits to enter into dialogue (or support dialogue by the SG) with parties recruiting or using child soldiers in order to develop clear and time-bound action plans to end this practice;
- calls on parties that were listed in SG's report to provide information on steps they have taken to end the recruitment and use of child soldiers;
- expresses its intention to consider appropriate steps to further address this issue after receiving the next report from the SG, in cases with insufficient progress;

Box continued on next page.

- calls on member states and international organizations to ensure children are included in DDR processes;
- requests the SG to include in his next report progress made by the parties listed in the annex of his previous report, "taking into account" the other parties mentioned in the report;
- requests the SG to include in his report "best practices" on DDR.

November 2003

SG's report includes two annexes of parties recruiting or using child soldiers. The first (situations on the Security Council's agenda) lists 32 parties in 6 situations (Afghanistan, Burundi, Côte d'Ivoire, DRC, Liberia, Somalia). The second lists 22 parties in 9 situations (Burma, Chechnya, Colombia, Nepal, Northern Ireland, the Philippines, Sri Lanka, Sudan, Uganda).

April 2004: Resolution 1539

- strongly condemns the recruitment and use of child soldiers;
- requests the SG to devise within three months an action plan for systematic and comprehensive monitoring and reporting, in order to provide timely, objective, accurate, and reliable information on the recruitment and use of children and other violations against children;
- calls on parties in Annex I (those on the Security Council's agenda—Afghanistan, Burundi, Côte d'Ivoire, DRC, Liberia, Somalia) to prepare within three months concrete, time-bound action plans to halt recruitment and use of child soldiers, in close collaboration with the UN;
- requests the SG to appoint a focal point in each country to engage parties in dialogue leading to time-bound action plans, and to report back to the SG by 31 July 2004;
- expresses its intention to impose targeted and graduated measures, such as a ban on the export or supply of small arms, military equipment and military assistance, against parties that refuse to enter into dialogue, fail to develop an action plan, or fail to meet the commitments in their action plan;
- calls on other parties mentioned in SG's report to immediately halt recruitment and use, and expresses its intention to

Box continued on next page.

consider additional steps to address this issue, based on information received from relevant stakeholders;

• requests a report from the SG by 31 October 2004, including information on compliance and progress made by parties mentioned in his last report in ending recruitment and use of child soldiers, "bearing in mind" all other violations and abuses committed against children affected by armed conflict.

Concluding thoughts

Today, human rights concerns are so integral to the United Nations Security Council that any book on the UN human rights system would be incomplete without a separate chapter on its involvement in these matters. Although the UN Charter's original mandate for the Security Council has not changed, the Council's interpretation of its mandate has decidedly embraced human rights. Informal networks such as the recently strengthened campaign for children caught in armed conflict are highly indicative of this trend. The Council now routinely issues declarations on human rights, and the protection, promotion, and monitoring of human rights form an important part of the mandates of several UN peace-keeping operations.

The Security Council has become much more open to the input of non-governmental organizations, giving particular attention to those advocating for human rights. In addition to advocates for the rights of children, the Security Council responded favorably to the efforts of advocates for women's rights. Most significantly, in October 2000, the Security Council acknowledged that women have a key role in promoting international stability by passing Resolution 1325 on Women, Peace, and Security. It called on all parties to ensure women's participation in peace processes, from the prevention of conflict to negotiations and post-war reconstruction to efforts to address the issue of women, peace, and security broadly, and also to focus on disarmament in particular.[68] This resolution portends the future. As the Security Council continues to be involved in peace-keeping and peace-building efforts around the globe, its involvement in human rights concerns is likely to continue to develop.

6   The International Labour
        Organization[1] and the UN
        Global Compact

The International Labour Organization (ILO) was founded in 1919 under the Treaty of Versailles and became the first specialized agency of the UN in 1946. Today, there are 19 specialized agencies in the UN system. Many of these agencies make substantial and important contributions to the UN human rights system. While not all of these agencies are mentioned in this volume, several reasons exist for according the ILO a more extended treatment. The ILO is not only one of the oldest continuously existing international organizations, but since its founding it has operated according to a rights-based approach. Even though the ILO only explicitly conceptualized its work as human rights promotion in 1998, the ILO has set detailed, widely accepted standards on workers' rights and created an unusual highly participatory system of enforcement since its inception. The standard-setting work of the ILO has long been related to the UN human rights system. Many of the rights enshrined in the early ILO conventions provided language for the ICESCR and ICCPR, and the later conventions have likewise been elaborated upon through recent ILO conventions.

Growing concern over the impact of globalization and debates on trade and labor have drawn greater attention to the ILO in recent years. Protests over the launching of a Millennium round of trade talks of the World Trade Organization in 1999 drew significant media attention to a debate that had been brewing for over a century, but which had become especially heated throughout the previous decade. The debate concerned whether or not to more closely regulate the social dimensions of the exponential growth in trade, that is whether to link labor standards to trade. By the end of the decade, the task of harmonizing labor standards was placed squarely in the hands of the ILO. To this end, the ILO has established universal minimum labor standards and created elaborate enforcement mechanisms to protect the human rights of workers. Nonetheless, compliance has largely been left to private voluntary standard-setting by corporations themselves and monitoring by international non-governmental organizations (NGOs). This has prompted many to call for still greater institutional enforcement mechanisms. Although the ILO remains a relevant and appropriate institution for that task, its compliance mechanisms are significantly underutilized. Highlighting the human rights mechanisms of the ILO encourages their use and, in the very least, invites continued study as to why their potential remains untapped. This chapter's consideration of human rights in the ILO system begins with a general introduction to the ILO and moves on to an illustration of that role through the campaign for the elimination of child labor. The second part of this chapter examines what may be considered one of the contemporary challengers or supporters of the ILO framework for labor standards—the Global Compact, a voluntary measure for urging business compliance with international human rights standards. The Global Compact has quickly become the main regulatory response by the UN to the problem of transnational corporations on human rights.

ILO organizational structure and operations

The unique tripartite structure of the ILO establishes a highly participatory approach to rights enforcement that addresses the rights and interests of governments, employers, and workers. Membership reached 177 countries in 2004.[2] Although the ILO is an intergovernmental organization, workers and employers participate directly in formulating ILO policy and in decision-making through the General Conference and Governing Body, with support from the International Labour Office.

The *International Labour Conference*, the membership body of the ILO, is composed of two representatives of member states, and one representative each of employers and employees of those member states. Each of these representatives votes separately at the annual International Labour Conference held in June in Geneva. This annual meeting provides a world forum for discussions of social and labor problems. Between conferences, the work of the ILO is guided by the Governing Body.

The Governing Body, the executive council of the ILO, determines ILO policy, including the program and budget. Its decisions are then forwarded to the General Conference for adoption. Additionally, the Governing Body elects the Director-General. Composed of 56 titular members and 66 deputy members, the Governing Body retains the tripartite structure of the ILO. Ten permanent members of the body come from states of "chief industrial importance."[3] The other half of the titular members is constituted equally of workers and employers' representatives. Other governmental representatives are elected every three years at the conference with consideration of geographical representation. Committees representing certain industries assist the Governing Body, which also occasionally hosts regional meetings to discuss specific matters (see Figure 6.1).

The *International Labour Office* functions as the secretariat of the ILO. Headed by a director-general, who is elected to five-year renewable terms, the secretariat undertakes the research and technical cooperation of the ILO. Administration and management of the ILO are decentralized throughout offices in 40 countries.[4]

NGOs also play an important role in the work of the ILO. The Constitution of the ILO explicitly provides for consultative relations with "recognized non-governmental international organizations, including international organizations of employers, workers, agriculturists and cooperatives." This constitutional provision has been put into effect with the establishment of three different categories of international non-governmental organizations. First, international NGOs with an important interest in a wide range of the ILO's activities may be granted either general or regional consultative status (at present a total of 8 and 16 organizations, respectively) and be permitted to participate in all

The ILO has three main bodies, each of which works on the basis of a tripartite structure (government, employers and workers). While government delegates outnumber employer and worker delegates, each constituency has the same number of votes in the governing bodies, and each constituency can speak and vote independently of the others.

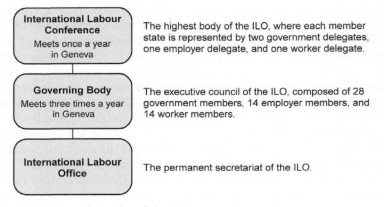

Figure 6.1 The main bodies of the ILO.
Source: Adapted from Canada's Voice in Global Governance at www.foecanada.org/intl/handbook.htm

ILO meetings. A second category, the Special List of Non-Governmental International Organizations, includes international NGOs other than employers' and workers' organizations that demonstrate an interest in the ILO's program of meetings and activities. There are currently more than 150 NGOs on the Special List. In a third category, the ILO Governing Body extends invitations to international NGOs that meet certain established criteria to attend different ILO meetings in which they have demonstrated a particular interest. During the 2004 Conference, the majority of NGO participants represented workers' unions of certain regions or occupations, but a few major human rights groups, such as Amnesty International, were present. The criteria for NGO participation are explained in Box 6.1.

Box 6.1   Criteria for NGO participation

To be represented at a session of the International Labour Conference and other ILO meetings, non-governmental international organizations require an invitation, and they must satisfy the criteria and adhere to the procedure set out below.

The NGO requesting an invitation should:

- demonstrate the international nature of its composition and activities, and in this connection it should be represented or have affiliates in a considerable number of countries;
- have aims and objectives in harmony with the spirit, aims, and principles of the ILO's Constitution and the Declaration of Philadelphia;
- have formally expressed an interest—clearly defined and supported by its statutes and by explicit reference to its own activities—in at least one of the items on the agenda of the conference session to which it requests to be invited, and these details should be supplied with the request for an invitation; and
- have made its request in accordance with the procedure set out in the Standing Orders of the Conference.

Requests by NGOs for invitations to ILO meetings other than the International Labour Conference are considered in light of the

Box continued on next page.

relevant rules and Standing Orders governing those meetings. Requests must be approved by the ILO's Governing Body. NGOs wishing to be observers at ILO meetings should, therefore, submit their requests to the Director-General no later than one month before the session of the Governing Body preceding the meeting for which a request is being made.

Source: International Labour Organization, Information Note: Representation of Non-governmental International Organizations at the International Labour Conference and Other ILO Meetings, www.ilo.org/public/english/comp/civil/ngo/ ilcnote.htm (8 September 2008).

ILO headquarters are in Geneva and regional offices are in Africa, Latin America and the Caribbean, Asia and the Pacific, Europe, and the Arab states. Also, liaison and field offices and multidisciplinary advisory teams work in more than 40 countries. The ILO employs approximately 1,900 officials from over 110 different countries at its Geneva headquarters and in its offices worldwide. Additionally, more than 600 experts undertake missions around the world as part of the technical cooperation program.

The participation of all members is crucial for passing resolutions or new conventions within the Conference, which is also referred to as the International Parliament of Labour. The process for establishing a convention provides a good illustration of this cooperation. First, worker or employer representatives submit a topic for placement on the meeting agenda. The International Labour Office—the secretariat of the organization—then circulates the proposed "law and practice report" among government representatives. Government representatives respond to a questionnaire attached to the report. The officials are mandated (and in the case of States Party to Convention no. 144, legally obliged) to consult with workers and employers' representatives before replying. However, employers and workers may also submit comments regarding the reports directly to the Office. Finally, two-thirds of the Conference must vote to adopt a resolution before it passes, therefore requiring broad consensus among all actors. Nevertheless, it is important to recognize that if governments and employers establish consensus, their 75 percent membership suffices to override any unified workers' opposition. Therefore, although the organization was established with the intent of organizing workers, their goals remain subject to the veto of governments and employer organizations.

The failure to establish stricter core labor standards as trade increased exponentially between developed and developing countries after the Cold War illustrates precisely this point. The International Confederation of Free Trade Unions adopted a unanimous resolution in 1996 calling for a floor of labor rights standards and a joint World Trade Organization/International Labour Organization Advisory Body to oversee a social clause.[5] Nevertheless, the debate about whether or not to link trade and labor standards divided government and employer representatives in the ILO, and as the World Trade Organization consistently tabled the issue, the oversight proposal for the joint advisory board remained unresolved.

Linking trade and labor

Moral obligation and economic incentives to link trade and labor have fueled international debate for over a century, and galvanized the establishment of the ILO.[6] The Organisation for Economic Co-operation and Development "catalogued sixty-six instances of linkage or attempted linkage on trade and labour standards" between 1919 and 1991.[7] Institutional attempts to govern free trade began with the establishment of the International Trade Organization (ITO) by the Havana Agreement after the Second World War. The ITO was to have formal relations with the ILO, but the former organization failed to take shape. Since then, states have repeatedly illustrated a willingness to comply with minimum standards in global trade and social conferences, but attempts to set stricter standards within the ILO in the early 1990s failed. A lack of consensus among industrialized countries and debates as to the economic effects of such standards led to weaker ILO provisions.

In part due to the lack of institutional linkages between trade and labor, the debate continued. In the 1973–79 round of the General Agreement on Tariffs and Trade (GATT), parties considered labor standards but tabled the discussion for the actual establishment of the trade organization. Final negotiations for the birth of the World Trade Organization (WTO) ran concurrent with final negotiations for regional free trade zones in the largest trading zones in the world—the European Union (EU) and North America. In those regional agreements, the link between trade and labor was clearly understood and regulated. After much debate as to whether or not to include labor and environmental rights in the main North American Free Trade Agreement (NAFTA) accord, the USA, Mexico and Canada signed a side accord. Similarly, a social chapter formed part of the EU regional trade agreement, and human rights were incorporated into the EU's Lomé agreement with Caribbean, African, and Pacific countries. Nonetheless, as the Uruguay round of GATT neared completion to establish the WTO, countries debated whether or not to include a social clause. The social clause would have allowed for sanctions or other penalties on countries for inadequate labor standards or other social negligence.

The social clause debate

The WTO was created in 1995 to govern trade worldwide. Nations granted Most Favored Nation status by the WTO enjoy privileges for cheaper and therefore presumably increased trade. Many developing countries seeking increased foreign investment sought to preclude social clauses from the WTO agreement, while many developed nations supported it. Economic arguments against the social clause were based on laissez-faire trade principles; claiming a social clause would allow for protectionism. For other opponents of a social clause, cultural relativism was an obstacle to consensus on labor standards. On the other hand, moral arguments bolstered claims that floor standards are necessary to prevent a "race to the bottom" and economic exploitation.[8] The economic arguments against the social clause prevailed; the WTO was established without a social clause and at its first meeting, officially deferred the issue to the ILO.

Although some scholars have lamented this unwillingness to consider the social aspects of trade within the WTO, others contend that the participation of workers in the ILO makes it more suitable for topics concerning their protection.[9] States had already turned to the ILO to address the human impact of globalization. The preamble to the Declaration on Fundamental Principles and Rights at Work states:

> Whereas economic growth is essential but not sufficient to ensure equity, social progress and the eradication of poverty, confirming the need for the ILO to promote strong social policies, justice and democratic institutions.[10]

Nevertheless, governments not only prevented social restrictions on trade, but likewise blunted potential ILO standards. ILO Declaration paragraph 5 reflects this struggle as it declares that the ILO "[s]tresses that labour standards should not be used for protectionist trade purposes, and that nothing in this Declaration and its follow-up shall be invoked or otherwise used for such purposes; in addition, the comparative advantage of any country should in no way be called into question by this Declaration and its follow-up."[11]

After this, the debate shifted from whether or not to include a social clause to one of how to enforce ILO and other existing labor standards.[12] Effectively, that shift pulled social responsibility out of the domain of trade ministers in governments and placed it back in social and labor departments, thereby weakening the link to corporations. The ILO responded soon after to the global demand for more vigilance over globalization.

The ILO's Decent Work Agenda, announced in 1998, provided an apt response to governments' call for core labor standards. The agenda had been debated for over a decade. Whereas industrialized countries had often argued for minimum standards, developing countries had argued that the standards unfairly stripped them of their comparative advantage and improperly privileged industrialized governments. The lack of consensus led to consideration of alternatives. Already in 1994, the ILO formed a Working Party on the Social Dimensions of the Liberalization of Trade, which soon began considering incentives for private sector compliance. The Decent Work Agenda formed in 1998 embraced these rights-based labor standards explicitly; while they were already enshrined in core ILO conventions that the trade ministers had agreed upon at the Singapore round, the 1998 agenda did signify a forward step for the mainstreaming of human rights. The development of standard-setting in the ILO involves all members, as the process described below illustrates.

Standard-setting

The primary way in which the ILO has worked to improve labor conditions and advance human rights in the workplace has been through the setting of international standards, based on the general consensus of its members. These standards are embodied most prominently in ILO conventions, but also standard-setting occurs through the promulgation of ILO declarations and recommendations, as well as through the issuance of voluntary codes of conduct (see Box 6.2).[13]

Rather than focus on universal ratification, as has been the trend in UN human rights mechanisms, the ILO adopted a different approach designed to draw in large numbers of diverse states and workers' associations, and to encourage the diffusion of new labor standards. Most ILO conventions are "optional" in the sense that members can choose to adopt them. However, once adopted, conventions are binding. Moreover, beginning in 1998, eight principles are said to be so fundamental

Box 6.2   ILO standard-setting mechanisms

- Conventions are adopted by the General Conference after a two-year procedure requiring the participation of governments and social partners. They are subject to ratification by member states, and are binding once states ratify them.
- Recommendations are established in the International Labour Conference to provide guidelines for national practice. They are not binding. ILO recommendations are akin to General Comments expressed by Committees of the various UN treaty bodies. Recommendations and conventions together constitute what are known as the "labor standards."
- Resolutions passed in the International Labour Conference guide the policy and future activities of the ILO. They formally express the will or opinion of the conference on a specific subject.

that all members by virtue of membership in the organization are bound to respect and enforce them. This major change, made formal through the 1998 Declaration on Fundamental Principles and Rights at Work ("the 1998 Declaration"), "establish[es] a universal minimum level below which poverty and lack of employment and educational opportunities should not push either workers or enterprises."[14]

Formal agreement over clarifying which ILO conventions provided for human rights standards occurred through discussion at the World Summit on Social Development in Copenhagen in 1995. The World Summit identified six ILO conventions as essential to ensuring human rights in the workplace: numbers 29, 87, 98, 100, 105 and 111. The Governing Body of the ILO subsequently confirmed the addition of the ILO Convention on Minimum Age, no. 138 (1973), in recognition of the rights of children. The United Nations High Commissioner for Human Rights now includes these conventions on the list of "International Human Rights Instruments." Each of the instruments establishes standards for the four main principles of the ILO: freedom of association and the right to collective bargaining; the elimination of forced and compulsory labor; the abolition of child labor; and the elimination of discrimination in the workplace. Taken as a whole, these principles can be summed up as the means to achieve decent work. The eight core ILO conventions are as follows:[15]

1 *Forced Labour Convention, no. 29 (1930).* The oldest of the core conventions, the Forced Labour Convention entered into force before the labor camps of the Second World War began functioning. The convention defines forced or compulsory labor in Article 2 as "all work or service which is exacted from any person under the menace of any penalty and for which the said person has not offered himself voluntarily," and excludes military conscription, civic responsibility, and work required as punishment.

2 *Freedom of Association and Protection of the Right to Organize Convention, no. 87 (1948).* Associational rights are broadly protected under this convention. Specifically, it provides for the right to join an association that is independent of governmental interference and which cannot be dissolved by governmental administration. It also establishes the right to form confederations or federations.

3 *The Right to Organize and Collective Bargaining Convention, no. 98 (1949).* The convention provides for protection from "antiunion" discrimination, specifically regarding hiring and firing practices. It prohibits interference of workers and employers in each other's unions and requires the establishment of national machinery for collective agreements.

4 *Abolition of Forced Labor Convention, no. 105 (1957).* In prohibiting forced labor, the Forced Labor Convention references previous conventions against slavery, the 1949 Convention on the Protection of Wages, and the UDHR in its preamble. The articles of the convention require States Parties to suppress and abolish forced labor within their territory.

5 *Equal Remuneration Convention, no. 100 (1951).* The Equal Remuneration Convention provides for equal wages for men and women. Article 2 suggests remedies for that assurance.

6 *Discrimination (Employment and Occupation) Convention, no. 111 (1958).* The Discrimination Convention defines discrimination in Article 1 as "any distinction, exclusion or preference made on the basis of race, color, sex, religion, political opinion, national extraction or social origin, which has the effect of nullifying or impairing equality of opportunity or treatment in employment or occupation"; it further stipulates inclusion of laws against discrimination in form or effect. The convention requires positive efforts on behalf of the state to ensure and promote equality, and requires that state remedies exist in the event that an individual is targeted for reasons of security of the state.

7 *Minimum Age Convention, no. 138 (1973).* The Minimum Age Convention establishes a general convention that incorporates 10

other conventions specific to certain sectors, some of which are consequently invalidated by the present convention. The convention requires establishment of a national minimum age for work. It grants significant flexibility for underdeveloped countries, offering them a lower set of standards for work in nearly every instance.

8 *Elimination of the Worst Forms of Child Labour, no. 182 (1999)*. The Child Labour Convention defines the worst forms of child labor to include forced labor, such as forced recruitment of child soldiers; prostitution; drug trafficking; and employment hazardous to the development of the child. Enforcement of the convention involves monitoring, prevention, enforcement, and punishment of crimes.

Follow-up

As a follow-up to the 1998 Declaration, the ILO has focused not on obtaining the consent of member states, but rather on furthering the principles established in each of the conventions. The follow-up to the 1998 Declaration thus is based upon technical assistance, a global report, and annual reports of non-ratifying countries to the eight core conventions. The ILO seeks to ensure that all countries comply with the principles of the core conventions, whether they are States Parties or not. This reporting procedure focuses on transparency, which it rewards with technical assistance. Despite these efforts, so far the Declaration has not had the impact on international corporate behavior hoped for by many of those present at its creation.[16]

In addition to focusing on developing the principles established in each of the core conventions, the ILO follow-up to the 1998 Declaration includes an annual focus on one of the four themes of the Declaration: freedom of association, eradication of child labor, eradication of forced labor, and non-discrimination. The annual theme is reflected in a Global Report. The 2004 Global Report was entitled *Organizing for Social Justice*. Secretary-General Somavia introduced the report by expressing freedom of association as crucial to human dignity and emphasizing the respect of other labor rights and civil liberties.[17] Moreover, the report clearly aims to further freedom of association by, inter alia, highlighting studies that show it actually furthers national productivity in a section called "A rights-based approach to dynamic labour markets."[18] Somavia writes, "[Core standards have] a positive effect on economic development by ensuring that the benefits of growth are shared, and promoting productivity, adjustment measures and industrial peace."[19]

The new agenda follows the traditionally preferred modus operandi of the organization[20] by offering technical assistance and relying on moral persuasion to ensure that states comply with standards. The several enforcement mechanisms already available within the ILO have traditionally been underused, but could feasibly be used to establish greater jurisprudence protecting workers.

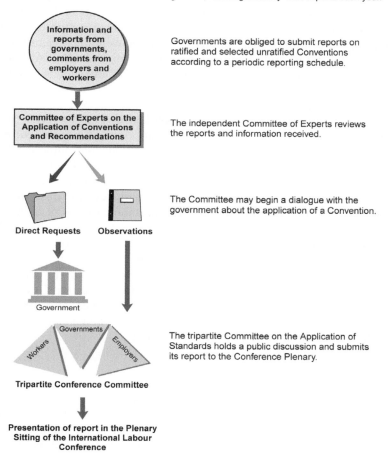

The regular system of supervision is set up to oversee the application of ILO Conventions. Some 6,500 ratifications have been registered, resulting in nearly 1500 reports each year.

Information and reports from governments, comments from employers and workers

Governments are obliged to submit reports on ratified and selected unratified Conventions according to a periodic reporting schedule.

Committee of Experts on the Application of Conventions and Recommendations

The independent Committee of Experts reviews the reports and information received.

Direct Requests   Observations

The Committee may begin a dialogue with the government about the application of a Convention.

Government

Tripartite Conference Committee

The tripartite Committee on the Application of Standards holds a public discussion and submits its report to the Conference Plenary.

Presentation of report in the Plenary Sitting of the International Labour Conference

Figure 6.2 The ILO's regular system of supervision.
Source: Adapted from ILO diagram at www.ilo.org/public/english/standards/norm/enforced/supervis/index.htm

Enforcement mechanisms

ILO implementation of labor standards includes monitoring compliance with conventions through regular state reports and three complaint mechanisms. In addition, technical assistance is used both to reward good behavior and to address problem areas. Each of these will be discussed in turn.

State reports

In a manner similar to the reporting requirement under UN human rights treaties, governments are obligated to prepare reports on the application of ratified conventions, the core conventions (regardless of ratification status) and of action taken on recommendations. Although initially the ILO required annual reports, a 1994 amendment required reporting every second year on the core and priority conventions, and every fifth year on the other conventions.

The Committee of Experts was established in 1926 to review state reports and present an annual report. Comprised of independent jurists, all proceedings of the Committee are confidential, although UN representatives are permitted entry into their process. The Committee writes observations on the application of conventions and recommendations. Unlike the observations of UN Committees, ILO observations are generally used in more serious or long-standing cases of failure to fulfill obligations. Each year, the Committee of Experts on the Application of Conventions and Recommendations examines more than 2,700 reports and makes 1,500 comments, which are then taken up by a standing committee of the conference. The observations are published annually in the report of the Committee of Experts to the Governing Body of the annual International Labour Conference, and form the basis for discussions of individual cases in the Conference Committee on the Application of Standards (see Figure 6.2).

Complaints

Complaints may be brought to the ILO through three mechanisms: complaints, freedom of association special procedures, and representations.

In addition, ad hoc mechanisms are provided at the request of the Governing Body to investigate specific labor concerns, but as of July 2004 they had never been used.

Under the ILO's Article 26 Complaint Procedure, a member state (and, importantly, not an individual) may bring a complaint if it feels another member state has failed to comply with the ILO Constitution. A commission is then formed and, if a violation is found, a report is issued to the offending state recommending that it conform its practices to the ILO Constitution and relevant provisions. Theoretically, when an offending member state refuses to comply, the complaining member state may then refer the matter to the International Court of Justice, although this has never happened. In its 93 years, only six complaints brought under Article 26 have resulted in the commission issuing a report. One of them, a complaint against Burma, is outlined in Box 6.3.

Box 6.3 The Article 26 Procedure in action—the case of Burma

In June 1996, 25 worker delegates to the ILC launched an Article 26 complaint against the government of Myanmar (Burma) alleging that it had failed to observe the Forced Labour Convention of 1930, which it ratified in 1955. The Governing Body set up a three-member Commission of Inquiry to investigate the complaint. The Commission invited submissions from countries, intergovernmental organizations, workers' and employers' organizations, and human rights NGOs, as well as companies that were mentioned in the complaint. In its report the Commission found that the use of forced labor was *systematic, widespread, and increasing*. Far from acting to prevent forced labor, the Burmese government was promoting it, such that "hundreds of thousands of workers ... are subjected to the most extreme forms of exploitation, which all too frequently leads to loss of life."

In response to the Commission's report, the ILC passed two resolutions. The first, in June 1999, deplored Burma's 30-year record of forced labor and suspended the government from receiving any technical assistance from the ILO and from participating in ILO meetings. The second, in June of 2000, did something that the ILO had never done in its 88 year history: it invoked Article 33 of the ILO Constitution, calling upon the constituents of the ILO and other international organizations to "re-examine their relations" with Myanmar to ensure that they did not "contribute directly or indirectly" to the practice of forced labor in that state. In other words, the ILO encouraged economic sanctions.

Box continued on next page.

Armed with the 2000 ILO resolution, civil society and labor groups have campaigned against businesses operating in Burma. Some members of the ILO have imposed new sanctions against Burma—or strengthened existing ones—in response to the ILO resolution: most notably the United States and the EU, with Japan, Australia, the UK, Canada, and Switzerland imposing lesser restrictions on trade and travel. Most countries, however, suspended their sanctions in early 2001 in response to early signs that the Burmese government might cooperate with the ILO, and have since taken a "wait-and-see" approach. Recent debate has centered on whether the ILO should issue a renewed call to its members to "review their relations" with Burma under the 2000 resolution, which remains in force.

Source: www.foecanada.org/intl/handbook.htm (28 September 2008).

The second mechanism for lodging complaints is through the ILO's Fact-Finding and Conciliation Commission on Freedom of Association (FFCC) and Committee on Freedom of Association (CFA). The FFCC operates in a similar manner to the Article 26 provisions, but only receives complaints relating to freedom of association violations which have been referred to it by the ILO's Governing Body or the UN, not by individuals. Complaints based on associational claims may be brought to the CFA regardless of whether the offending member state has ratified the specific convention allegedly violated. If a violation is found, a recommendation is issued to the member state outlining what measures should be taken to conform its practices to the standards promulgated by the ILO. Although the CFA may "follow up" to see if recommendations have been enacted (and this only when the underlying convention has been ratified by the offending member state), the ILO lacks any enforcement mechanism to enforce compliance. In its first 44 years of existence, the CFA reviewed more than 1,800 cases.[21]

The third complaint mechanism is known as "representations." Under this procedure, the ILO Constitution also allows for representations to be filed by an industrial association of employers or workers alleging failure of a state to observe any element of a convention to which they are party. The ILO determines what constitutes an "industrial association," which may not necessarily have a specific affiliation to the state in question.

These complaint mechanisms have great potential to raise labor standards, yet they remain underutilized. In practice, less formal methods of compliance have been developed due largely to pressure and monitoring by advocacy NGOs, especially in the area of trade and labor.

Case study on child labor

According to ILO estimates, over 250 million children between the ages of 5 and 14 work; 120 million of them work full-time.[22] More children work in Southeast Asia than anywhere else, but the rate of child labor is greatest in Africa—at 29 percent.[23] The ILO estimates that over 8.4 million children worldwide suffer "unconditional" forms of labor: forced or bonded labor, sexual exploitation, trafficking, or recruitment as child soldiers.[24] Many of the causes of these egregious abuses of children, including poverty, conflict, and migration, as well as more recent phenomena that facilitate the abuse of children, are linked to such "unconditional" forms of child labor. For example, the internet now facilitates child pornography and commercial sexual exploitation of children such as sexual tourism; cheaper transportation increases availability of human trafficking; and lighter weapons enable child soldiers to perform as exceptional soldiers with their speed, agility, and fearlessness. These are some of the worst forms of child labor. Although the 1973 Minimum Age Convention sought to restrain the use of child labor, a new convention seeks to eliminate those worst forms.

New standards: Convention 182

As the international aspects of child labor have increased alongside globalization, states have increased their cooperation and dangerous forms of child labor have gained increasing prevalence on the agenda of international organizations, with unprecedented speed and intensity. After governments agreed officially to establish the elimination of child labor as a fundamental principle of the ILO in 1995, they established a crime against a child as a universal crime at the Stockholm Conference in 1996.[25] By 1999, they had promulgated a new treaty: Convention 182 on the Worst Forms of Child Labour. Non-governmental organizations can submit information to the ILO on child labor alone, or preferably, through a trade union, when a country has ratified Convention 182 (or the earlier Convention 138).

Convention 182 has enjoyed the most rapid ratification in the history of the ILO and provoked an increase in ratifications of Convention 138; by May 2004, 150 countries had ratified Convention 182 and 134 countries had ratified Convention 138. Yet effective eradication of such prevalent and often covert human rights abuses has proven elusive. The following section reviews one specific ILO project on child labor which was prompted by or otherwise related to Convention 182.

InFocus Programme on the Progressive Elimination of Child Labour

The International Programme on the Elimination of Child Labour (IPEC) was "stepped up" after the elimination of child labor became one of the fundamental principles in 1998 and the new convention was promulgated. It was transformed into the InFocus Programme on the Progressive Elimination of Child Labour, and set children in the worst forms of child labor as the focus. IPEC's mandate is "to work towards the progressive elimination of child labor by strengthening national capacities to address child labor problems, and by creating a worldwide movement to combat it."[26] Established with funding from Germany in 1992, the IPEC program has grown from six countries in 1992 to over 82 beneficiary countries.

IPEC activities to implement its goals have grown from policy assistance and direct services to a broader and more integrated framework. Included among those activities are research, policy analysis, program evaluation and labor monitoring, and direct services. IPEC direct services include prevention of entry into labor, withdrawal from hazardous labor, alternative work provision, and work condition improvements. Children benefiting from IPEC programs are not only removed from hazardous employment, but their futures are supported through programs for school registration and support for their families. Monitoring systems are an example of ILO direct assistance. Throughout the world and in sectors ranging from agriculture to small mines to factories, the ILO has developed partnerships with communities and employers themselves to create child labor monitoring systems. The systems maintain a database, develop necessary legal standards, and coordinate with labor inspectorates to prevent re-entry into hazardous work and to identify children in those conditions.[27]

A review of donor support for IPEC programs suggests that governments are increasingly taking ownership of the projects: whereas during the initial stages of IPEC, NGOs implemented half of the programs, they now provide slightly more than one-quarter. Conversely, governments now implement one-third of programs and fund 37 percent of them.[28] Perhaps research showing a strong negative correlation between child labor laws and labor rates[29] has persuaded governments of the positive economic effects of eliminating child labor.

IPEC reorganized its structure in 2001 to approach more broadly the phenomenon of child labor. It divided its work into four focal areas: vulnerable groups, hazardous work, education, and economic development. The broader focus established through this reorganization is part of an aim to mainstream child labor eradication throughout ILO programs. That explains in part why IPEC is increasingly the venue for ILO technical assistance, having delivered nearly 50 percent of it in 2002. (Another explanation is that funding for IPEC has increased significantly, from the local to the international level.) One IPEC strategy used to implement the mainstreaming of child labor elimination has been promotion of the link between child labor and development. One of several new networks, the Development Policy Network (DPnet) helps establish the link between development and child labor by helping include child labor issues in Poverty Reduction Strategy Papers (PRSPs).[30] Another new strategy provides Child Labour Specialists in Bangkok, New Delhi, Abidjan, and Lima.[31] Time-Bound Programs provide close guidance for governments' fulfillment of these efforts and their obligation established in Convention 182.

Time-Bound Programs illustrate the technical cooperation work of the ILO. In 2001, Tanzania, El Salvador and Nepal became the first three countries to launch a Time-Bound Program (TBP). These programs provide technical assistance for implementation of Convention 182, which calls upon states to "prevent the engagement of children in the worst forms of child labour (WFCL), provide assistance for the withdrawal of children from the WFCL and for their rehabilitation and social integration, and to ensure access to free basic education for all children removed from such activities."[32] Created and led by national governments, TBPs focus on national capacity-building. Additionally, they implement the goal of the DPnet by requiring that child labor be included in national development plans. By the end of 2003, 14 countries had developed programs, 11 of which had secured funding.[33]

The effects of IPEC in India have been enormous. A US$40 million project in India is IPEC's largest—funded equally by the Indian government and the U.S. Department of Labor.[34] Throughout 2002–3, 25 organizations partnered with the government and six country donors to expend US$2.3 million in IPEC projects.[35]

Private compliance efforts

Private initiatives aimed at implementing the ILO's core standards have proliferated along with NGO growth in general. Many criticize the ILO's approach and take it upon themselves to monitor corporations' behavior. Governments' laissez-faire stances throughout the 1990s left corporations independently responsible for regulating their behavior and social responsibility standards. Some have undertaken voluntary codes, often after increased consumer and media attention provoked them to do so. Human rights NGOs exposed such labor rights abuses as child labor, 18-hour work days, and improper safeguarding against chemical hazards. The consequent consumer awareness, especially in industrialized countries, led to stronger calls for greater social consciousness among corporations. Consumer boycotts of products for moral reasons, as was the case with child labor, pushed corporations to at least change their images and attitudes. NGOs remain on the front lines of ensuring that corporate claims of responsibility are realized.

The UN Global Compact

In 1999, Secretary-General Kofi Annan stepped up the UN's complementary commitment to standard-setting by proposing a Global Compact of Corporate Responsibility. The Global Compact is an inter-organizational network designed to facilitate learning and dialogue among social actors and UN organizations on social aspects of globalization: human rights, the environment, anti-corruption, and labor rights. The Compact aims to build a network in which transnational corporations enter into a dialogue to determine best practices in social responsibility. Supporters of the GC argue that it could help to establish standards upon which a compliance mechanism might be based in the future. In his first address outside the UN, in January 2007, Secretary-General Ban Ki-moon underscored the continued centrality of the Global Compact to UN work, calling on businesses to advance universal principles of human rights within their "stream of influence."[36] The two human rights principles to be promoted by the Global Compact are:

- Principle 1: Businesses should support and respect the protection of internationally proclaimed human rights;
- Principle 2: Businesses should make sure that they are not complicit in human rights abuses.[37]

Although, as explained below, the Global Compact will receive and respond to complaints about gross corporate misconduct, it rejects the notion that it is a regulatory instrument—"it does not 'police,' enforce or measure the behavior or actions of companies."[38] Rather, the Global Compact "relies on public accountability, transparency and the enlightened self-interest of companies, labour and civil society to initiate and share substantive action in pursuing the principles upon which the Global Compact is based."[39]

The Global Compact involves a broader set of relevant social actors than does the ILO: governments, who defined the principles on which the initiative is based; "companies, whose actions it seeks to influence; labour, in whose hands the concrete process of global production takes place; civil society organizations, representing the wider community of stakeholders; and the United Nations, the world's only truly global political forum, as an authoritative convener and facilitator."[40] Through dialogue among these diverse actors, the Global Compact seeks to create an understanding within companies that observance of human rights is not only the moral route to take, it is a smart business decision as well. NGO human rights activists are led by Amnesty International and Oxfam;[41] the Corporate Citizenship unit of Warwick University[42] facilitates the dialogue. Relevant intergovernmental organizations, including UNHCR and the ILO, guide the standards that the corporations seek to implement. Finally, the corporations themselves—which included over 3,000 in 2007—agree to three commitments: (1) to post publicly, at least once annually, concrete efforts they have made toward implementing the 10 principles; (2) to publicize the Global Compact and therefore its principles; and (3) to partner with the UN in assisting these efforts elsewhere, especially in developing countries.[43]

The voluntary reports, known as the Communication on Progress Annual Reports (COPs), require all GC participants to describe the ways in which they have implemented the 10 principles and to provide a measurement of outcomes from those actions.[44] After two years of non-communication a company will be declared inactive and removed from the GC website. As of 2008 over 900 companies were delisted.[45]

Structure of Global Compact

In 2005, the governance framework for the Global Compact was reshaped in an effort to be less bureaucratic and to foster greater stakeholder involvement in, and ownership of, the initiative. Governance functions are shared by six entities; the Global Compact Leaders Summit; Local Networks; the Annual Local Networks Forum; the Global Compact Board; the Global Compact Office; and the Inter-Agency Team. Each of these six entities has its own assigned tasks.

The Leaders Summit is held triennially to review the progress of the GC and provide future direction. The Local Networks are comprised of stakeholders at the local level, where they work on projects developing and implementing the principles (over 50 local networks existed as of 2008). The Local Network Forum (hosted by the Barcelona Center for the Support of the Global Compact ("Barcelona Center")) allows members of various local networks around the work to meet and promote learning through sharing experiences. The Global Compact Board is composed of 20 members representing the main constituency groups of the GC; while the Board as a whole holds an annual formal meeting; constituency groups are expected to interact with the Global Compact Office on an ongoing basis. (Members of the Board act in personal, honorary and unpaid capacity.) The Global Compact Office is responsible for the management of the Global Compact logo and implementation of its "integrity measures," including a consideration of specific complaints. The Inter-Agency team is responsible for mainstreaming the GC principles within the UN as a whole. Finally, the Global Compact Foundation is responsible for retaining voluntary contributions from businesses and other sources for non-core related activities. The purpose of each entity is summarized in Box 6.4 below.

Box 6.4   Goals of Global Compact entities

- *Global Compact Leaders Summit*: Provides an opportunity for Global Compact participants to discuss the Global Compact and corporate citizenship at the highest level and to produce strategic recommendations and action imperatives.
- *Local Networks*: Roots Global Compact within different national, cultural and linguistic contexts; facilitates dialogue and action on regional and country-specific basis.
- *Annual Local Networks*: Enables Local Networks from around the world to share experiences, review and compare progress, and identify best practices.
- *Global Compact Board*: Creates an advisory body of four constituency groups—business, civil society, labor, and the United Nations—to provide ongoing strategic and policy advice for the initiative as a whole and make recommendations to the Global Compact Office.
- *Global Compact Office*: Establishes the formal UN offices entrusted with the support and overall management of the Global Compact initiative, including advancing advocacy and

Box continued on next page.

issue leadership initiatives, fostering network development and maintaining the Global Compact communications infrastructure, safeguarding the logo, and implementing "integrity measures."

- *Inter-Agency Team*: Supports the internalization of the principles within the United Nations and among all participants. The six UN agencies represented in the Inter-Agency Team are: the Office of the UN High Commissioner for Human Rights (OHCHR), the International Labour Organization (ILO), the United Nations Environment Programme (UNEP), the United Nations Office on Drugs and Crime (UNODC), the United Nations Development Programme (UNDP) and the United Nations Industrial Development Organization (UNDI).

Awareness raising and practical advice

The Global Compact approach to human rights and business can be characterized as two-fold: it both seeks to raise awareness about the impact businesses can have on human rights and to develop practical ways in which businesses can support human rights within its "sphere of influence." The general understanding of the concept "sphere of influence" includes "the individuals to whom the company has a certain political, contractual, economic or geographic proximity," and also situates the core of the businesses' operation and the center of the sphere.[46] With regards to complicity, the report acknowledges that complicity in human rights abuses "means that a company is participating in or facilitating human rights abuses committed by others, whether it is a state, a rebel group, another company or individual."[47]

The Global Compact has developed practical tools for businesses to integrate human rights into their standard operating procedures. The Global Compact, in partnership with the Business Leaders Initiative on Human Rights, and the Office for the High Commissioner of Human Rights, have developed a practical manual for implementing human rights standards into seven specific management areas. Each year the guidelines draw on the experiences of several large firms who have attempted various methods for integrating human rights into their practices. For example, in 2008, businesses profiled for best practices included: MTV Networks Europe, National Grid, Novartis, Novo Nordisk, Statoil and The Body Shop International. This experience was supplemented with practical examples of human rights implementation from other companies including BP, Carrefour, Cemex, Codelco, Copel, Eskom, Li &

Fung (Trading), MAS Holdings, Shell, Taj Hotels, Tata Enterprises, Telefoncia, and Valeo.[48]

Critics of the Global Compact question the motives of participating corporations, noting the marketing benefits of participation. Human rights advocates participate in the Compact with caution, noting that many of the companies party to it campaigned against the development of the UN norms. One critic stated, "The UN's positive image is vulnerable to being sullied by corporate criminals ... while companies get a chance to 'bluewash' their image by wrapping themselves in the flag of the United Nations."[49] Often, that wrapping may cover otherwise tarnished images.

Complaints for egregious abuses

Complaints against companies that have allegedly engaged in systematic and egregious abuses can be brought to the Global Compact Office, where it will be determined if the complaint is frivolous. If the complaint is not determined to be frivolous then the Office will request that the company respond to the complaints and may include any actions taken to address the complaints. The Global Compact Office then informs the party raising the matter of any actions taken by the Global Compact Office. The Global Compact Office is charged with providing guidance and assistance, as necessary and appropriate, to the participating company concerned, helping them in their efforts to remedy the situation. The Global Compact Office may ask the relevant country/ regional Global Compact network, or other Global Compact participant organization, to assist with the resolution of the matter. The Office may also refer the matter to one or more of the UN entities that are the guardians of the Global Compact Board, drawing in particular on the expertise and recommendations of its business members.

If the participating company concerned refuses to engage in dialogue on the matter within three months of first being contacted by the Global Compact Office, it may be regarded as "non-communicating," and would be identified as such on the Global Compact website until such time as a dialogue commences. If the continued listing of the participating company on the Global Compact website is considered to be detrimental to the reputation and integrity of the Global Compact, the Global Compact Office reserves the right to remove that company from the list of participants and to so indicate on the Global Compact website. Once the participating company concerned takes appropriate action to remedy the situation that is the subject matter of the allegation, the company may seek reinstatement as an "active" participant in the Global Compact and to the list of participants on the Global Compact website.

Concluding thoughts

The future of the Global Compact and the ILO may depend largely on whether they can work to reinforce each other. The four labor principles of the Global Compact are taken from the ILO Declaration on Fundamental Principles and Rights, a declaration adopted in 1998 by the governments, employers and workers in attendance at that year's International Labour Conference. Nonetheless, corporations' design of their own codes of conduct often fails to live up to international standards. In fact, ILO surveys of corporate codes of conduct have found "not infrequently" that the codes are unknown or unavailable in production countries; that only about one-third of such codes surveyed mention international standards; and that often the goals of the codes are self-defined.[50] Moreover, the Global Compact is subject to the main criticism of all voluntary codes: where negative practices are uncovered, voluntary standards fail to provide mechanisms for an adequate remedy.

The inadequacy of the corporate codes of conduct undercuts the legitimacy of the Global Compact. By insisting on the open dissemination of codes of conduct in line with ILO standards, the Global Compact may reclaim its legitimacy and operate more effectively. ILO compliance mechanisms offer a unique yet underutilized forum in which trade union representatives can contribute to the establishment and application of human rights norms that are central to the Global Compact. The ILO's formal incorporation of NGOs through its unique tripartite structure illustrates the effectiveness of participatory rights enforcement.

7 Conclusion
Looking backward, going forward

The architects of the UN human rights system undoubtedly never anticipated the evolution of their project. Their once-negligible cabin at the edge of the woods has grown, albeit in a haphazard and lopsided fashion. Additions small and large have been added, the trees shielding the structure have been cut down, and a maze-like structure has found itself at the city center.

The existence of the human rights system owes itself to a belief that no longer exists. States adopted the Universal Declaration of Human Rights (UDHR) and other early international human rights instruments on the understanding that enforcement would always be a matter of state discretion. Thus, in the early years, spanning roughly from the end of the Second World War to the beginning of the Cold War, states could agree to the establishment of the UN Human Rights Commission and other UN human rights bodies without the sense that they were relinquishing any of their sovereignty. Although many international human rights standards were established by the new human rights bodies during this period, these standards were rarely enforced. No UN body believed itself to be competent to do so. For the first 20 years of its existence, even the UN Human Rights Commission, the central UN human rights body, adopted the position that it had no power to take any action in regard to human rights complaints.

With the influx of new member states to the UN, mainly from Africa and Asia, the composition and focus of the UN human rights organs changed. Greater attention was paid to anti-colonialism and anti-racism. While some developments during this period were positive, such as the adoption of the Convention on the Elimination of All Forms of Race Discrimination, political opportunism cast a pall over this period. Manipulated by the politics of the day, human rights became a central political wedge, first between East and West and then North and South. Many states began demanding more vigorous enforcement of the international human rights standards, though with little effect. Advocates increasingly argued that sovereignty did not shield states from international scrutiny for human rights violations. International outrage over extreme racism in Africa supported the Human Rights Commission's development of a nascent enforcement system, ushering in a new era of international monitoring and reporting on thematic issues and investigation of individual complaints. Yet the UN system of human rights remained troubled. To the extent that human rights advocates were attracted to international organizations as a means of solving international problems, enthusiasm soon waned. As Henry Steiner and Philip Alston observe, "it became clear that [international] institutions could simply incorporate the polarities and conflicts of the 'outside' world, become lethargic administrators through inertia and stale bureaucracy, and experience manipulation and corruption."[1]

The end of the Cold War unleashed a host of communal conflicts and with them, a rash of human rights violations. Technological advancements in communication, enhanced mobility and improved networking and training permitted human rights advocates to draw attention to these abuses with greater skill and impact than before. Human rights advocates not only worked through the UN Human Rights Commission and Sub-Commission, but also found new ways to use the treaty bodies, preparing their own parallel monitoring reports, utilizing individual complaint mechanisms when available, strategizing for their creation when they were not available. The human rights movement was split over the failure of the international community to use non-coercive diplomacy effectively. While some human rights advocates began to abandon their previous absolutist position against the use of force, others continued to decry the morality, legality and/or effectiveness of bombing for human rights. The UN Security Council soon became a target of human rights lobbying, and eventually became so entangled in human rights issues that it could be considered a UN human rights mechanism itself. NGOs successfully lobbied the Security Council to issue resolutions creating international criminal courts to hear cases against alleged war criminals, condemning the use of child soldiers, and promising action in a host of human rights cases.

The 1990s and early 2000s were in many respects an unparalleled era of human rights development. With the exception of the so-called third-generation human rights, the standards had already been set and attention turned to completion of institution-building and improvement of existing enforcement mechanisms. The Office of the High Commissioner for Human Rights, created in 1993, proved to be an effective centerpiece of the UN human rights system. Field and country offices were instrumental in providing technical assistance on human rights and building human rights institutions at a national level. Under the leadership of Mary Robinson, the Human Rights Commissioner grew in stature and influence, changing from an underfunded outpost to a major player. Enhanced attention to the negative impact of globalization also drew renewed attention to one of the earliest actors in the human rights system, the International Labour Organization (ILO). The unique tripartite structure of the ILO, involving employers, trade unions and NGOs, provided under-explored avenues for holding multinational corporations accountable to international workplace standards. Throughout this period, the range of actors active in human rights issues expanded, the field in which they operated broadened, and the issues they addressed diversified.

When the first edition of this book went to press, the UN human rights mechanism was believed to be entering another era, one that was not only post-Cold War, but also post-September 11. The attack on the U.S. Pentagon and World Trade Center in September 2001 and the slaughter of Russian school children on 1 September 2004 created a genuine fear that the world has entered an "age of terror" where human rights must often be set aside in the name of national and even global security. According to this view, the UN human rights system is destined to revert to being a selectively utilized political tool as during the Cold War. Where before anti-communist ideology served to trump human rights concerns, anti-terrorism had become the new trump card. States with a long record of supporting human rights thus had an incentive to tread more gently when monitoring the human rights record of their allies. The temptation was great to overlook the human rights abuses of other states as long as they were actively supporting anti-terrorism efforts.

Those who decry the end of human rights falsely posit human rights and security at odds with one another. Security *is itself* a human right (implicating, among other rights, the right to life and liberty of person). Just as human rights are indivisible, the right to security is linked to and supported by the protection of other human rights. This book has identified the contours of a strong international human rights system which has set international standards and built mechanisms for enforcement. The UN human rights system exists, and NGOs and other agents of civil society are in place to remind states that human rights are part and parcel of any international peace and security agenda. Especially today, when an imbalance of power prevails, strong international human rights institutions are needed. In the absence of competing powers, these institutions hold great promise for imposing limits on state abuse of power and, thus, for promoting peace and justice for all humankind. States are likely to remain the central actors in international relations, but only the states that are disciplined to follow international human rights precepts and that work cooperatively with other states on human rights promotion will have the moral authority to lead.

The drafters of the UN Charter may not have intended to spark all of these responses to human rights, but they did indeed usher in a modern era of human rights institution-building. While the promise of human rights remains as yet unfulfilled, the system itself retains some of the optimism and hope for a better future held by the Charter's founders.

Postscript to the second edition

As the second edition of this book heads to press, the Universal Declaration of Human Rights (UDHR) is marking its sixtieth birthday and, despite continued global threats to world peace, the UN marches on, determined as ever, to advance a transformative global human rights agenda. This occasion leads us to wonder: What can we expect in the next 60 years?

The ability of the UN to promote the principles of the UDHR will be influenced by five factors which place it at the F.R.O.N.T. of UN politics: a complementary balance of *fragmentation and mainstreaming*; a turn toward the *"responsibility to protect"* ("R2P") complementing the traditional human rights framework; the expanded presence of the *Office of the High Commissioner of Human Rights* (OHCHR); the expansion and deepening of *National Human Rights Institutions* (NHRIs); and *treaty development and application* continuing with increased civil society input.

Fragmentation/mainstreaming: The universal nature of human rights is literally written into the title of the Universal Declaration of Human Rights. Its Preamble proclaims the Declaration as a "common standard of achievement for all peoples and all nations." In furtherance of the universal nature of human rights, in 1997, the UN Secretary-General designated human rights as a crosscutting issue in his reform package. The subsequent mainstreaming of human rights has promoted human rights universalism in two ways: first, by integrating human rights within a broad range of UN activities and programs and, second, by decentralization of rights throughout UN bodies and in the day-to-day operations of UN country offices. This twin movement, of mainstreaming and fragmentation, is likely to continue in the future, advancing human rights universalism by providing opportunities for the interpretation and application of human rights norms within different political structures and cultural contexts.

Responsibility to Protect (R2P): According to the R2P model, states are charged with protecting their own population, but if national authorities are unable or unwilling to protect their citizens, then the responsibility shifts to the international community to use diplomatic, humanitarian and other methods to secure protection. When such methods appear insufficient, the Security Council may out of necessity decide to take action under the Charter of the United Nations, including enforcement actions. Widening acceptance of R2P will likely draw the locus of inquiry in human rights and humanitarian scenarios from the victimized and from individual victimizers to the international community. The new trend toward R2P will continue to support the norms embodied in the UDHR as long as it is viewed as a complement and not a replacement to the human rights model.

Office of the High Commissioner for Human Rights (OHCHR): As explained in this text, in recent years, OHCHR has become an important force for advancing the UDHR. In addition to creating numerous country offices, OHCHR has found regional offices to be of great utility for effective human rights monitoring and promotion. Through regional "hubs" OHCHR staff have also developed regional strategies, targeting regional organizations and utilizing, where available, regional systems and mechanisms. Further plans for extended regional work include opening additional offices covering Southwest Asia and North Africa. The degree to which the OHCHR is successful at promoting human rights will continue to be determined both by the qualities of the individual Commissioner and the political willingness of international institutions and individual states to take heed of OHCHR findings and recommendations.

National Human Rights Institutions (NHRIs): The centrality of NHRIs in promoting human rights is now generally recognized and NHRIs are wide spread. In all corners of the globe, NHRIs perform a variety of functions that promote UDHR norms, including: providing advice and assistance to states on human rights compliance; monitoring national institutions such as jails and prisons; investigating specific alleged human rights violations; and promoting human rights education and awareness. Even as UN human rights institutions continue to develop at the international level, the realization of human rights will depend on the establishment of effective institutions at the national level.

Treaty development and application: Although much of the UN work on standard-setting has already been accomplished, human rights advocates still rely heavily on treaties and their implementation processes to raise awareness about a given human rights issue, to build constituencies, and to foster national change through international treaty monitoring advocacy and other local action. The negotiations in recent years over two new treaties—on the human rights of people with disabilities and on forced disappearance—have attracted considerable support throughout the United Nations structure and in many states. The degree to which these and other human rights treaties will succeed in the future depends largely upon the degree to which they are viewed as legitimate and are effectively operationalized at the national level.

Significantly, these five factors move beyond the UN infrastructure that is the subject of this book. Human rights bodies are arguably the most contested and least effective parts of the UN system, and, as described in this book, the new Human Rights Council is no exception. Yet UN human rights bodies exist not just for the achievement of their own predetermined agenda, but also for the parallel universe of NGOs and, more recently, NHRIs. The most important and effective features of human rights bodies are their integrative and participatory processes. States, Observer States, NGOs and NHRIs can work through these bodies to address areas of concern. In engaging in these activities, participants not only advocate for concrete human rights measures but, equally significant, they raise consciousness among all participants and generate impetus for further organizing. For UN human rights bodies to achieve their mandate, however, NGO and NHRI involvement is not enough. The success of UN human rights bodies depends upon states that have been integral to their creation to participate on a consistent, constructive basis. To take one prominent illustration of this maxim, the failure of the United States to engage in the new Human Rights Council according to the same rules that bind all participant states undermines not only that institution, but the UN human rights system more generally.

The UDHR still stands as a signal to the world that human rights are part and parcel of the UN's commitment to furthering world peace and justice, but the promise of human rights remains unfulfilled.

Appendix

Selected directory of UN human rights bodies

Today, virtually every UN body has human rights on its agenda. A brief description and contact information for the central actors are provided below. The entries are divided into two parts: first, United Nations bodies (including treaty bodies, which are listed at the end of the section) and second, selected specialized agencies and bodies affiliated with or otherwise related to the UN.

United Nations bodies

The Secretary-General of the United Nations

The Secretary-General is the "chief administrative officer" of the United Nations. The United Nations Charter (the primary document of the UN) empowers the Secretary-General to "bring to the attention of the Security Council any matter which in his opinion may threaten the maintenance of international peace and security." This includes human rights. The ability of the Secretary-General to use informal diplomatic channels to press states into action is known as the "good offices authority." The Secretary-General can use his "good offices" confidentially to raise human rights concerns with member states, including issues such as the release of prisoners and commutation of death sentences.

United Nations Secretary-General
United Nations Secretariat
New York, NY 10017, USA
Fax: (1) 212 963 7055
E-mail: inquiries@un.org

The Office of the United Nations High Commissioner for Human Rights (OHCHR or "High Commissioner")

Established in 1993, the High Commissioner is the United Nations official with principal responsibility for UN human rights activities. Technically, this office is an extension of the "good offices" of the Secretary-General. The OHCHR serves as the secretariat of the Commission on Human Rights, the treaty bodies and other United Nations human rights organs, and is the focal point for all United Nations human rights activities.

UN High Commissioner for Human Rights, Office of the (OHCHR)
Palais des Nations, 8–14 Avenue de la Paix
1211 Geneva 10, Switzerland
Tel.: (41) 22 917 9000
Fax: (41) 22 917 9016 Urgent-matter fax: (41) 22 917 9022
Website: www.unhchr.ch

The Security Council

The principal UN body in charge of peace and security. In recent years, the Security Council has become more aware of the impact of gross human rights violations on the outbreak and continuation of violent conflict. To some extent, the Security Council has become more open to human rights advocates. For example, the Security Council has been responsive to the issue of child soldiers. Advocates may try to contact individual members of the Security Council.

The General Assembly

The main deliberative body of the United Nations. It may issue its own declarations on human rights or reviews and take action on human rights matters referred to it by its working group concerned with such issues (the "Third Committee") and by the Economic and Social Council (see below).

General Assembly
United Nations Headquarters
New York, NY 10017, USA
Tel.: (1) 212 963 1234
Fax: (1) 212 963 4879
Website: www.un.org/aboutun/mainbodies.htm

The Economic and Social Council (ECOSOC)

ECOSOC is the lynchpin between several other UN bodies considering human rights issues. ECOSOC makes recommendations to the General Assembly on human rights matters, and reviews reports and resolutions of the Commission on Human Rights and transmits them with amendments to the General Assembly. To assist it in its work, the Council established the Commission on Human Rights, the Commission on the Status of Women and the Commission on Crime Prevention and Criminal Justice. Many individuals and NGOs communicate with ECOSOC directly about human rights cases.

Economic and Social Council
c/o ECOSOC Secretariat, United Nations Headquarters
DPCSD Room 2963J
New York, NY 10017, USA
Tel.: (1) 212 963 1234
Fax: (1) 212 963 4879
Website: www.un.org/esa/coordination/ecosoc

The Human Rights Council (formerly the Commission on Human Rights)

In March 2006, the UN General Assembly voted to replace the Commission on Human Rights with a new Human Rights Council. The broad mandate of the Council, which it inherited from its predecessor, is to examine, monitor, advise and publicly report on human rights situations in specific countries or territories, known as country mandates, or on major phenomena of human rights violations worldwide, known as thematic mandates. In addition, various activities can be undertaken by "special procedures," including responding to individual complaints, conducting studies, providing advice on technical cooperation at the country level, and engaging in general promotional activities.

Human Rights Council
Palais des Nations, 8–14 Avenue de la Paix
1211 Geneva 10, Switzerland
Tel.: (41) 22 917 9000
Fax: (41) 22 917 9016
Website: www.unhchr.ch
http://www2.ohchr.org/english/bodies/hrcouncil/

The Sub-Commission on the Promotion and Protection of Human Rights ("the Sub-Commission")

The Sub-Commission was established in 1948 to assist the Commission in its work. Its 26 members are independent experts from all regions of the world who meet each year for four weeks in Geneva. The Sub-Commission has established several working groups and nominated special rapporteurs who focus on contemporary forms of slavery, including forced labor, illegal and pseudo-legal adoptions aiming at the exploitation of children, and sexual slavery during wartime. They also consider human rights issues concerning domestic and migrant workers, and they examine preventive measures for the elimination of violence against women. The Sub-Commission was formerly known as the Sub-Commission on the Prevention of Discrimination and Protection of Human Rights.

Sub-Commission on the Promotion and Protection of Human Rights
c/o Commission on Human Rights
Palais des Nations, 8–14 Avenue de la Paix
1211 Geneva 10, Switzerland
Tel.: (41) 22 917 9000
Fax: (41) 22 917 9016
Website: www.unhchr.ch

The Commission on the Status of Women (CSN)

Prepares recommendations and reports to the Economic and Social Council on the promotion of women's rights in political, economic, social and educational fields. Historically isolated and underfunded, the Commission on the Status of Women may nonetheless be an appropriate target of NGO activity in the field of women's rights.

Commission on the Status of Women
c/o ECOSOC Secretariat, United Nations Headquarters
DPCSD Room 2963J
New York, NY 10017, USA
Tel.: (1) 212 963 1234
Fax: (1) 212 963 4879
Website: www.un.org/womenwatch/daw/csw

The International Court of Justice (ICJ)

The principal judicial organ of the United Nations, functioning according to its statute which is part of the United Nations Charter. Its main purpose is to decide, in accordance with international law, cases which are submitted to it by states. The ICJ gives advisory opinions on legal questions to the General Assembly and to other organs of the United Nations and specialized agencies, when authorized to do so. Members are elected by the General Assembly and Security Council.

International Court of Justice
Peace Palace, Carnegieplein 2
2517KL The Hague, The Netherlands
Tel.: (31) 70 302 2323
Fax: (31) 70 364 9928
Website: www.icj-cij.org

The International Criminal Court (ICC)

The ICC was established by the Rome Statute of the International Criminal Court on 17 July 1998, when 120 states participating in the United Nations Diplomatic Conference of Plenipotentiaries on the Establishment of an International Criminal Court adopted the Statute. This is the first ever permanent, treaty-based, international criminal court established to promote the rule of law and ensure that the gravest international crimes do not go unpunished. The Statute for the ICC entered into force on 1 July 2002.

International Criminal Court
Maanweg, 174
2516 AB The Hague, The Netherlands
Tel.: (31) 70 515 8108/8304
Fax: (31) 70 515 8555
Public Information Office tel.: (31) 70 515 8186
Public Information Office e-mail: pio@icc-cpi.int
Website: www.icc-cpi.int/

Treaty bodies

1 The Human Rights Committee (HRC)

The HRC monitors the implementation of the International Covenant on Civil and Political Rights (ICCPR). In addition to the reporting procedure, Article 41 of the Covenant provides for the Committee to consider interstate complaints, and the First Optional Protocol to the Covenant gives the Committee competence to examine individual complaints.

Web page (as of 8 September 2008): http://www2.ohchr.org/english/bodies/hrc/index.htm

2 The Committee on Economic, Social and Cultural Rights (CESCR)

The CESCR monitors the International Covenant on Economic, Social and Cultural Rights. The Committee cannot consider individual complaints; a draft Optional Protocol to the Covenant is under consideration.

Web page (as of 8 September 2008): http://www2.ohchr.org/english/bodies/cescr/index.htm

3 The Committee on the Elimination of All Forms of Racial Discrimination (CERD)

CERD monitors the implementation of the International Convention on the Elimination of All Forms of Racial Discrimination. In addition to its reporting procedure, CERD performs monitoring functions through an early-warning system and complaint procedures.

Web page (as of 8 September 2008): http://www2.ohchr.org/english/bodies/cerd/index.htm

4 The Committee on the Elimination of Discrimination Against Women (CEDAW)

CEDAW monitors the Convention on the Elimination of All Forms of Discrimination Against Women. In addition to its regular reporting procedure, under the Optional Protocol to the Convention, the Committee is mandated to: (1) receive communications from individuals or groups of individuals submitting claims of violations of rights protected under the Convention to the Committee; and (2) initiate inquiries into situations of grave or systematic violations of women's rights.

Web page (as of 8 September 2008): http://www2.ohchr.org/english/bodies/cedaw/index.htm

5 The Committee Against Torture (CAT)

The CAT monitors the Convention Against Torture and Other Cruel, Inhuman or Degrading Treatment or Punishment. In addition to the reporting procedure, the Convention establishes three other mechanisms through which the Committee performs its monitoring functions: (1) individual complaints or communications from individuals claiming that their rights under the Convention have been violated; (2) "inquiries"; and (3) interstate complaints.

Web page (as of 8 September 2008): http://www2.ohchr.org/english/bodies/cat/index.htm

6 The Committee on the Rights of the Child (CRC)

The Committee on the Rights of the Child (CRC) is the body of independent experts that monitors implementation of the Convention on the Rights of the Child. It also monitors implementation of two optional protocols to the Convention, on involvement of children in armed conflict and on sale of children, child prostitution and child pornography.

Web page (as of 8 September 2008): http://www2.ohchr.org/english/bodies/crc/index.htm

7 The Committee on Migrant Workers (CMW)

The Committee on Migrant Workers monitors the International Convention on the Protection of the Rights of All Migrant Workers and Members of Their Families, which entered into force on 1 July 2003. In addition to its reporting procedure, the Committee will also, under certain circumstance, be able to consider individual complaints once 10 States Parties have accepted this procedure in accordance with Article 77 of the Convention.

Web page (as of 8 September 2008): http://www2.ohchr.org/english/bodies/cmw/index.htm

8 Committee on the Rights of Persons with Disabilities

The Committee on the Rights of Persons with Disabilities (CRPD) is the body of independent experts which monitors implementation of the Convention on the Rights of Persons with Disabilities. The Optional Protocol to the Convention gives the Committee competence to examine individual complaints with regard to alleged violations of the Convention by States Parties to the Protocol.

Web page (as of 8 September 2008): http://www2.ohchr.org/english/bodies/crpd/index.htm

Selected specialized agencies and bodies affiliated with or otherwise related to the United Nations

There are many organizations affiliated with the United Nations. Below is just a sample, with particular attention given to those mentioned in the text of this book. (For further explanations and organizations, see www. unsystem.org, the official website locator for UN system organizations.)

International Labour Organization (ILO)

Founded in 1919, the International Labour Organization is the UN specialized agency which seeks the promotion of social justice and internationally recognized human and labor rights. The unique tripartite structure of the ILO involves workers and employers participating as equal partners with governments in the work of its governing organs. The ILO formulates international labor standards in the form of conventions and recommendations which set minimum standards of basic labor rights.

International Labour Standards Department
4 Route des Morillons
1211 Geneva 22, Switzerland
Tel.: (41) 22 799 7155/799 6111
Fax: (41) 22 799 6771
Website: www.ilo.org

United Nations Development Programme (UNDP)

The UNDP administers and coordinates most of the technical assistance provided through the UN system. Formed by General Assembly resolution, the current Mission Statement declares that its mission "is to help countries in their efforts to achieve sustainable human development by assisting them to build their capacity to design and carry out development programmes in poverty eradication, employment creation and sustainable livelihoods, the empowerment of women and the protection and regeneration of the environment, giving first priority to poverty eradication." Human rights often figure in UNDP programming, often under "good governance" programs, but also in other areas as well.

UNDP
One United Nations Plaza

New York, NY 10017, USA
Tel.: (1) 212 906 5000
Fax: (1) 212 826 2057
Website: www.undp.org

United Nations Educational, Scientific and Cultural Organization (UNESCO)

Founded in 1945, UNESCO includes human rights in its mandate to promote international cooperation in the fields of education, science and culture. Among other matters, UNESCO seeks to forge universal agreements on emerging ethical issues and to serve as a clearing house for the dissemination and sharing of information and knowledge. UNESCO has its own complaints procedure which allows anyone with knowledge of a human rights violation related to education, science or culture to submit a communication to UNESCO.

UNESCO
7 Place de Fontenoy
75700 Paris, France
Tel.: (33) 1 45 68 10 00
Fax: (33) 1 45 67 16 90
Website: www.unesco.org

United Nations High Commissioner for Refugees, Office of the (UNHCR)

The UNHCR addresses human rights concerns as part of its mandate to provide international protection to refugees and others of concern to UNHCR, and to seek durable solutions to their plight. Activities in fulfillment of this mandate include provision of material assistance, legal advice and assistance, and cooperation with other agencies. UNHCR staff work to defend the rights of refugees by providing them with protection and assistance.

UNHCR
94 rue de Montbrillant, Case Postale 2500
1211 Geneva 2, Switzerland
Tel.: (41) 22 739 8111
Fax: (41) 22 731 9546
Website: www.unhcr.ch

164   *Appendix*

United Nations Children's Fund (UNICEF)

In 1946, the General Assembly established the UN International Children's Emergency Fund as a temporary body to provide emergency assistance to children in war-ravaged countries. The name was changed in 1953 when the General Assembly voted to make the fund permanent. Today, UNICEF plays a key role in implementing the rights contained in the Convention on the Rights of the Child. UNICEF programs seek to combine strategies for improving access to and quality of basic social services together with legal policy, and public education initiatives that promote and protect children's rights. In so doing, UNICEF seeks to enhance the ability of children to participate in decision-making processes.

UNICEF
Three United Nations Plaza
New York, NY 10017, USA
Tel.: (1) 212 326 7000
Fax: (1) 212 888 7465
Website: www.unicef.org

United Nations Development Fund for Women (UNIFEM)

Created by the General Assembly to serve as a catalyst for the mainstreaming of women in development and promotion of the human rights of women. Works to ensure the participation of women in all levels of development planning and practice. It acts as a catalyst within the UN system, supporting efforts that link the needs and concerns of women to all critical issues on the national, regional, and global agendas.

UNIFEM
304 East 45th Street, 15th Floor
New York, NY 10017, USA
Tel.: (1) 212 906 6400
Fax: (1) 212 906 6705
Website: www.unifem.org

United Nations Office on Drugs and Crime (UNODC)

Established in 1997, the UNODC is the umbrella organization for the United Nations Drug Control Programme (UNDCP) and the Centre for International Crime Prevention (CICP). It also includes the Terrorism

Prevention Branch and the Global Programmes against Money Laundering, Corruption, Organized Crime and Trafficking in Human Beings. All of these organizations address human rights concerns in the course of their work. The UNODC has approximately 500 staff members worldwide. Its headquarters are in Vienna and it has 21 field offices as well as a liaison office in New York.

United Nations Office on Drugs and Crime
Vienna International Centre
PO Box 500
A-1400 Vienna, Austria

United Nations Drug Control Programme (UNDCP)
Tel.: (43) 1 26060 0
Fax: (43) 1 26060 5866

Centre for International Crime Prevention (CICP)
Tel.: (43) 1 26060 4269
Fax: (43) 1 26060 5898
Website: www.unodc.org

World Bank Group

The World Bank Group addresses human rights as part of its mission to fight poverty and improve the living standards of people in the developing world. The World Bank Group includes the International Bank for Reconstruction and Development (IBRD); the International Development Association (IDA); and the International Finance Corporation (IFC).

World Bank Group
1818 H Street NW
Washington, D.C. 20433, USA
Tel.: (1) 202 477 1234
Fax: (1) 202 477 6391
Website: www.worldbank.org

World Health Organization (WHO)

The World Health Organization is the United Nations specialized agency for health. It was established on 7 April 1948. WHO's objective, as set out in its constitution, is the attainment by all peoples of the highest possible level of health. Health is defined in WHO's constitution as a state of complete physical, mental and social well-being and not merely the absence of disease or infirmity. WHO is governed by 192 member states through the World Health Assembly. The Health Assembly is composed of representatives from WHO's member states. The main tasks of the World Health Assembly are to approve the WHO program and the budget for the following biennium and to decide major policy questions.

World Health Organization
20 Avenue Appia
1211 Geneva 27, Switzerland
Tel.: (41) 22 791 2111
Fax: (41) 22 791 0746
Website: www.who.org

Notes

Foreword

1 See Bertrand G. Ramcharan, *Contemporary Human Rights Ideas* (London: Routledge, 2008); Bertrand G. Ramcharan, *Preventive Human Rights Strategies in a World of New Threats and Challenges* (London: Routledge, forthcoming).
2 See, for example, Thomas G. Weiss and David A. Korn, *Internal Displacement: Conceptualization and its Consequences* (London: Routledge, 2006); Gil Loescher, Alexander Betts, and James Milner, *UNHCR: The Politics and Practice of Refugee Protection Into the Twenty First Century* (London: Routledge, 2008); David P. Forsythe and Barbara J. Rieffer-Flanagan, *The International Committee of the Red Cross: A Neutral Humanitarian Actor* (London: Routledge, 2007); and Peter Walker and Daniel Maxwell, *Shaping the Humanitarian World* (London: Routledge, 2009).

1 A guide to the new UN human rights practice

1 Janet E. Lord and Katherine Guernsey, "It Takes a Treaty: Elbowing into the Human Rights Mainstream," paper presented at the Annual Meeting of the International Studies Association, Montreal, Canada, March 2004, 24.
2 Craig G. Mokhiber, "Toward a Measure of Dignity: Indicators for Rights-Based Development," in *Perspectives on Health and Human Rights,* ed. Sofia Gruskin, Michael A. Grodin, George J. Annas, and Stephen P. Marks (New York: Routledge, 2005).
3 See International Council on Human Rights Policy, *Local Perspectives: Foreign Aid to the Justice Sector* (Geneva, Switzerland: ICHRP, 2000), at Annex III.
4 UN General Assembly resolution 217A (III), UN document A/810 at 71 (1948).
5 General Assembly, GAOR 1966, 2200A (XXI), supplement no. 16, at 52, UN document A/6316.
6 General Assembly, GAOR 1966, 2200A (XXI), supplement no. 16, at 49, UN document A/6316.
7 Scott Long, *Making the Mountain Move: An Activist's Guide to How International Human Rights Mechanisms Can Work for You,* www.hrea.org/erc/Library/display_doc.php?url=http%3A%2F%2Fwww.hrea.org%2Ferc%2FLibrary%2Fmonitoring%2Funguide.html&external=N (1 September 2008).

8 See International Council on Human Rights Policy, *Performance and Legitimacy: National Human Rights Institutions* (Geneva, Switzerland: ICHRP, 2000). Available online at www.ichrp.org/files/reports/17/102-National_Human _Rights_Institutions-2004-Main_Report.pdf (2 September 2008).

9 *Strengthening human rights-related United Nations action at country level: Plan of Action*, www.un.org/events/action2/action2plan.pdf (17 March 2009).

10 Kenneth Roth, the executive director of Human Rights Watch, has emphasized these three factors as critical to traditional human rights fact-finding work. See Kenneth Roth, "Defending Economic, Social and Cultural Rights: Practical Issues Faced by an International Human Rights Organization," *Human Rights Quarterly* 26, no. 1 (2004): 63.

11 Ellen Dorsey and Paul Nelson, "New Rights Advocacy: Origins and Significance of a Partial Human Rights-Development Convergence," paper presented at the Annual Meeting of the International Studies Association, Montreal, Canada, March 2004.

12 U. Baxi, "Voices of the Suffering, Fragmented Universality and the Future of Human Rights," in *The Future of International Human Rights*, ed. B. H. Weston and S. P. Marks (Ardsley, N.Y.: Transnational Publishers, 1999), 101–56, 102.

2 The Office of the High Commissioner for Human Rights

1 Felice D. Gaer, "The United Nations High Commissioner for Human Rights: The Challenges of International Protection" (book review), *American Journal of International Law* 98, no. 2 (April 2004): 391–97.

2 Ibid.

3 Kofi Annan, *Strengthening of the United Nations: An Agenda for Further Change* (GA document A/57/387), 9 September 2002.

4 International Council on Human Rights Policy, *Local Perspectives: Foreign Aid to the Justice Sector* (Geneva, Switzerland: ICHRP, 2000). See www.ichrp.org (2 September 2008).

5 Janet E. Lord, "The United Nations High Commissioner for Human Rights: Challenges and Opportunities," *Loyola of Los Angeles International and Comparative Law Journal* 17 (February 1995): 329. For a detailed history of the early discussions of this issue, see Roger Stenson Clarke, *A United Nations High Commissioner for Human Rights* (The Hague: Nijhoff, 1972).

6 Summary of Information Regarding Consideration by United Nations Organs of the Question of the Establishment of a Post of United Nations High Commissioner for Human Rights, Note by the Secretary-General (E/CN.4/Sub.2/1982/26), 30 July 1982.

7 Andrew Clapham, "Creating the High Commissioner for Human Rights: The Outside Story," *European Journal for International Law* 5, no. 4 (1998): 556–68. Available online at www.ejil.org/article.php?article=1267&issue=63 (2 September 2008).

8 United Nations Economic and Social Council, Commission on Human Rights, 58th session, Working Group on Enforced or Involuntary Disappearances, *Civil and Political Rights, Including Questions of: Disappearances and Summary Executions* (report by Mr. Manfred Nowak) (E/CN.4/2002/71), 10.

9 United Nations Peacekeeping, www.un.org/Depts/dpko/dpko/index.asp (2 September 2008). The website has full information regarding past and present peacekeeping efforts.

10 Gaer, "The United Nations High Commissioner for Human Rights."
11 Clapham, "Creating the High Commissioner for Human Rights."
12 Ibid.
13 *NGO-Forum Final Report to the Conference* (A/CONF.157/7), at 4.
14 Office of the High Commissioner for Human Rights, *The Role of the High Commissioner*, www.unhchr.ch/about/hcrole.htm (5 September 2008).
15 www.ohchr.org/EN/AboutUs/Pages/MissionStatement.aspx (5 September 2008).
16 GA resolution 48/141, UN GAOR, 48th session, supplement no. 49, at 261, UN document A/48/141 (1993).
17 Stephen Marks, "The Human Right to Development: Between Rhetoric and Reality," *Harvard Human Rights Journal* 17 (Spring 2004): 135.
18 Declaration on the Right to Development, GA resolution 41/128, UN GAOR, 41st session, supplement no. 53, at 186, UN document A/41/128 (1986) ("All human beings have a responsibility for development, individually and collectively, taking into account the need for full respect for their human rights and fundamental freedoms as well as their duties to the community").
19 Vienna Declaration and Programme of Action, World Conference on Human Rights, Part I, para. 10, UN document A/CONF.157/23 (1993).
20 GA resolution 50/214, UN GAOR, 50th session, supplement no. 49, at 296, UN document A/50/214 (1995).
21 www.ohcr.org/EN/AboutUs/Pages/WhoWeAre.aspx (5 September 2008).
22 High Commissionner's Strategic Management Plan 2008–9 (Geneva, Switzerland: Office of the High Commissioner for Human Rights, 2003). Available at: www.ohchr.org/Documents/Press/SMP2008–9.pdf (14 September 2008).
23 www.unhchr.ch/html/menu2/techcoop.htm (5 September 2008).
24 See generally *Report of the Secretary-General on National Institutions for the Promotion and Protection of Human Rights*, UN Commission on Human Rights, 53rd session, Agenda Item 9, at 2 (UN document E/CN.4/1197/41), 1997 (explaining the importance of national institutions in the promotion and protection of human rights).
25 International Council on Human Rights Policy, *Local Perspectives: Foreign Aid to the Justice Sector*, June 2000. Geneva, Switzerland. www.ichrp.org/files/reports/9/104-Human_Rights_Assistance-Main_Report.pdf (2 September 2008).
26 OHCHR, "Fact sheet No. 3 (Revd), Advisory Services and Technical Cooperation in the Field of Human Rights," Commission on Human Rights resolution 1996/55, www.ohchr.org/Documents/Publications/FactSheet3Rev.1en.pdf (14 September 2008).
27 www.ohchr.org/EN/Countries/Pages/CountryOfficesIndex.aspx (14 September 2008).
28 Ibid.
29 www.ohchr.org/EN/Countries/Pages/PeaceMissionsIndex.aspx (14 September 2008).
30 Statement of UNHCHR, cited in Margaret Satterthwaite, "Human Rights Monitoring, Elections Monitoring, and Electoral Assistance as Preventive Measures," *New York University Journal of International Law and Politics* 30, no. 2 (1998): 709–68, at 735, n. 1.

31 The Future Directions of Human Rights Field Presences, Address by Bertrand Ramcharan, Acting High Commissioner, at the Opening of the Annual Meeting of OHCHR Field Presences, 17 November 2003, www.unhchr.ch/huricane/huricane.nsf/(Symbol)/HR.48.2003.En?OpenDocument (14 September 2008).

32 High Commissioner's Strategic Management Plan 2008–9 (Geneva, Switzerland: Office of the High Commissioner for Human Rights, 2003), 102. Available at: www.ohchr.org/Documents/Press/SMP2008–9.pdf (14 September 2008).

33 OHCHR, "Special Rapporteur on the former Yugoslavia," www.unhchr.ch/html/menu2/7/a/myug.htm (8 October 2008).

34 United Nations, "United Nations Mission in Bosnia and Herzegovina," www.un.org/Depts/dpko/missions/unmibh/background.html (8 October 2008). On 21 November 1995, in Dayton, the General Framework Agreement for Peace in Bosnia and Herzegovina was initialed along with 11 associated annexes (together, the "Peace Agreement"). On 14 December 1995, the Peace Agreement was signed in Paris by Bosnia-Herzegovina, Croatia, and FR Yugoslavia, as well as other parties thereto. On 20 December 1995, IFOR took over from UNPROFOR. On 21 December 1995, the Security Council decided to establish the United Nations International Police Task Force (IPTF) and a United Nations civilian office, brought together as the United Nations Mission in Bosnia and Herzegovina (UNMIBH).

35 OHCHR, *OHCHR in Bosnia and Herzegovina,* www.ohchr.org/EN/Countries/ENACARegion/Pages/BASummary.aspx (8 October 2008).

36 United Nations, "United Nations Mission in Bosnia and Herzegovina,"www.un.org/Depts/dpko/missions/unmibh/background.html (8 October 2008).

37 The information in this section is gathered from an interview with Madeleine Rees, June 2004, as well as Cees Flinterman and Marcel Zwamborn, *From Development of Human Rights to Managing Human Rights Development: Global Review of the OHCHR Technical Cooperation Programme, Synthesis Report* (Netherlands Institute of Human Rights (SIM), September 2003), www.ohchr.org/Documents/Countries/global-reviewsynthesis.pdf (2 September 2008).

38 OHCHR, *Human Rights Field Presence in Bosnia and Herzegovina,* www.unhchr.ch/html/menu2/5/bosnia.htm (5 September 2008).

39 Craig G. Mokhiber, "Toward a Measure of Dignity: Indicators for Rights-Based Development," in *Perspectives on Health and Human Rights,* ed. Sofia Gruskin, Michael A. Grodin, George J. Annas, and Stephen P. Marks (New York: Routledge, 2005).

40 Author's interview with Madeleine Rees, June 2004.

41 "Europe and Sexual Abuse," *Le Monde Diplomatique* 9 (November 2001): 20–21.

42 Flinterman and Zwamborn, *From Development of Human Rights to Managing Human Rights Development.*

43 Linda C. Reif, "Building Democratic Institutions: The Role of National Human Rights Institutions in Good Governance and Human Rights Protection," *Harvard Human Rights Journal* 13, no. 1 (2000): 1, 2 (stating that, as of the year 2000, most human rights institutions were created in the past two or three decades).

44 Annan, *Strengthening of the United Nations.*
45 *Report of the Second International Workshop on National Institutions for the Promotion and Protection of Human Rights*, (E/CN.4/1994/45), 23 December 1993, www.demotemp360.nic.in/pdf/HRCinternationalworkshopII-E-CN.4-1994-45.pdf (2 September 2008).
46 www.demotemp360.nic.in/old/default.asp (26 September 2008).
47 These categories are drawn from Reif, "Building Democratic Institutions."
48 Office of the High Commissioner for Human Rights, Fact Sheet no. 19, *National Institutions for the Promotion and Protection of Human Rights* [hereafter "Fact Sheet"] (indicating the need to create national institutions for promoting human rights to assist the United Nations in effectively implementing its goals in this area). Available online at www.unhchr.ch/html/menu6/2/fs19.htm (5 September 2008).
49 C. Raj Kumar, "National Human Rights Institutions: Good Governance Perspectives on Institutionalization of Human Rights," *American University International Law Review* 19, no. 2 (2003): 259–90.
50 Commonwealth Secretariat, *National Human Rights Institutions: Best Practice* (London, 2001) (on file with author).
51 International Council on Human Rights Policy, *Performance and Legitimacy: National Human Rights Institutions* (Geneva, Switzerland: ICHRP, 2000). Available online at www.ichrp.org/en/projects/123 (2 September 2008).
52 Asia Pacific Forum, About, www.asiapacificforum.net/about (2 September 2008).
53 Brian Burdekin, "Human Rights Commissions," in *Human Rights Commissions and Ombudsman Offices: National Experiences Throughout the World,* ed. Kamal Hossain, Leonard F. M. Besselink, Haile Selassie Gebre Selassie, and Edmond Volker (The Hague, The Netherlands: Kluwer, 2000), 801, 807–8 (listing advantages of developing national institutions based on human rights instruments).
54 Sonia Cardenas, "Emerging Global Actors: The United Nations and National Human Rights Institutions," *Global Governance* 9, no. 1 (2003): 28.
55 OHCHR, "Fact Sheet."
56 Mary Ellen Tsekos, "Human Rights Institutions in Africa," *Human Rights Brief* 9, no. 2 (Winter 2002): 21.
57 I develop this analysis further in: Julie A. Mertus, *Human Rights Matters: Local Politics and National Human Rights Institutions* (Stanford, Calif.: Stanford University Press).
58 Interview with author, July 2004.
59 International Council on Human Rights Policy, *Performance and Legitimacy: National Human Rights Mechanisms* (Versoix, Switerland, 2000).
60 OHCHR, "Fact Sheet."
61 UNAMIR, "Rwanda Background," www.un.org/Depts/dpko/dpko/co_mission/unamirFT.htm (11 October 2008).
62 See Helena Cook, "The Role of the High Commissioner for Human Rights: One Step Forward and Two Steps Back?" *American Society of International Law Proceedings* 89 (1995): 235.
63 *Opening Statement to the Stockholm Congress*, José Ayala-Lasso, High Commissioner for Human Rights, 27 August 1996, www.csecworldcongress.org/en/stockholm/Reports/Keynote_speeches.htm (2 September 2008).

64 For the North–South divide at the UN at this time, see Michael J. Dennis, "The Fifty-Third Session of the Commission on Human Rights," *The American Journal of International Law* 92, no. 1 (January 1998): 112–24.

65 BBC News, "Mary Robinson: A Career in Quotes," 28 November 2001, http://news.bbc.co.uk/2/hi/europe/1681129.stm

66 "Talking Point," BBC News, 21 November 2002, http://news.bbc.co.uk/1/hi/talking_point/forum/1673034.stm (2 September 2008).

67 Ibid.

68 *Statement by Mary Robinson*, Symposium on HR in the Asia-Pacific Region, UNU, Tokyo, 27 January 1998, www.unu.edu/unupress/Mrobinson.html (14 September 2008).

69 *Statement by Mary Robinson*, UN High Commissioner for Human Rights at the Opening of the 58th Session of the Commission on Human Rights, Geneva, 18 March 2002; Remarks of Mary Robinson at the closing of the 56th session of the Commission on Human Rights, Geneva, 28 April 2000, http://www2.reliefweb.int/rw/rwb.nsf/db900sid/ACOS-64CNTA?OpenDocument (11 October 2008).

70 According to the *Management Review of the Office of the United Nations High Commissioner for Human Rights* (UNGA document A/57/488), 21 October 2002:

> During the last six years, the regular budget appropriations for human rights decreased by 19 per cent – from $48 million in 1996–97 to $39 million in 2000–2001 – and the share of OHCHR in the United Nations regular budget went down from 1.84 to 1.54 per cent. During the same time, its extrabudgetary resources more than doubled – from $36 million to $79 million – and their share in the overall OHCHR budget rose from 43 to 67 percent.

71 "Talking Point," BBC News. See also Salon, "Interview with Mary Robinson," 26 July 2002, http://dir.saloon.com/story/people/interview/2002/07/26/mary_robinson/index1.html (11 October 2008).

72 "Talking Point," BBC News (2). "UN High Commissioner for Human Rights," 6 December 2008, http://news.bbc.co.uk/2/hi/talking_point/forum/2523983.stm (11 October 2008).

73 See "Statement by Sergio de Mello Special Representative of the Secretary General and Transitional Administrator" (not dated), http://web.worldbank.org/WBSITE/EXTERNAL/COUNTRIES/EASTASIAPACIFICEXT/TIMORLESTEEXTN/0,contentMDK:20199996~isCURL:Y~menuPK:294042~pagePK:64027988~piPK:64027986~theSitePK:294022,00.html (11 October 2008).

74 UN News Centre, "Top UN Envoy Sergio Vieira de Mello Killed in Terrorist Blast in Baghdad," 9 August 2003, www.un.org/apps/news/story.asp?NewsID=8023&Cr=iraq&Cr1 (11 October 2008).

75 UN News Centre, "Fight Against Terrorism Must Not Exclude Respect for Rights, UN Official Says," 13 July 2004, www.un.org/apps/news/story.asp?NewsID=11326&Cr=rights&Cr1=committee

76 Louise Arbour, Introductory press briefing, 22 July 2004, www.iris.sgdg.org/actions/smsi/hr-wsis/list/2004/msg00520.html (11 October 2008).

77 Ibid.

78 Ibid.

79 Lorrayne Anthony, "Arbour Stepping Down as UN Rights Chief to Be With Family: Official," *The Canadian Press*, 7 March 2008, http://cknw.com/News/World/article.aspx?id=4565 (8 October 2008).
80 Ibid.
81 Human Rights Watch, "UN: Human Rights Commissioner Should Take Bold Steps to Confront Abusers, Senior Post Needed in New York to Support New High Commissioner," 18 July 2008, http://hrw.org/english/docs/2008/07/18/global19399.htm (14 September 2008).
82 "UN Human Rights Chief Spotlights Plight of Millions of Detainees Worldwide," News Post India, 3 October 2008, www.newspostindia.com/report-61047.

3 UN Charter-based bodies (and other non-treaty bodies)

1 www.unhchr.ch/html/menu2/2/ga.htm (5 September 2008).
2 Philip Alston and Henry J. Steiner, *International Human Rights in Context: Law, Politics, Morals: Text and Materials* (Oxford: Oxford University Press, 2nd edn., 2000), 121.
3 www.un.org/WCAR/e-kit/backgrounder1.htm (8 September 2008).
4 http://www2.ohchr.org/english/issues/racism/DurbanReview/index.htm (8 September 2008).
5 Louis Henkin, "International Law: Politics, Values and Functions," *Collected Courses of the Hague Academy of International Law* 13, no. 4 (1989): 251.
6 United Nations General Assembly, "General Assembly Establishes New Human Rights Council by Vote of 170 in Favor to 4 Against, with 3 Abstentions," Department of Public Information, General Assembly Document GA/10449, 15 March 2006, at www.un.org/News/Press/docs/2006/ga10449.doc.htm (1 May 2008).
7 UN Watch, "Dawn of a New Era? Assessment of the United Nations Human Rights Council and Its Year of Reform," 7 May 2007, at www.unwatch.org/atf/cf/%7b6deb65da-be5b-4cae-8056-8bf0bedf4d17%7d/dawnofanewerahrc%20reportfinal.pdf (24 May 2007).
8 UN General Assembly, Department of Public Information, "General Assembly Establishes New Human Rights Council by Vote of 170 in Favour to 4 Against, with 3 Abstentions," GA/10449, 15 March 2006, at www.un.org/News/Press/docs/2006ga10449.doc.htm (24 May 2007).
9 Peggy Hicks, "Don't Write It Off Yet," *International Herald Tribune*, 21 June 2007, http://hrw.org/english/docs/2007/06/21/global16228.htm.
10 Office of the United Nations Secretary-General, "Secretary-General's Address to the Commission on Human Rights," 7 April 2005, at www.un.org/apps/sg/sgstats.asp?nid=1388 (15 September 2008).
11 "Annan Calls for New Rights Body", *New York Times*, 8 April 2005, A8.
12 The resolution called for one-third of the Council to be elected annually. The 47 members elected in 2006 were randomly assigned terms of one, two, or three years to set the stage for this process. Each member elected in 2007 was to hold its term for the full three years. For a list of members and their terms, see UN Human Rights Council, "Membership of the Human Rights Council" at www.ohchr.org/english/bodies/hrcouncil/membership.htm (24 May 2007).
13 See Anne Bayefsky, "The Oppressors' Club," *National Review*, 18 May 2007, at http://article.nationalreview.com/?q=NDM2NTQ2ODZmNDU3MTA2ZTBiNDFiNGExZWRjMWM2YjQ (24 May 2007).

14 See, e.g., Office of the UN Commissioner for Human Rights, "Working Group on Situations," at www.ohchr.org/english/issues/situations/index.htm (1 May 2008). Also see United Nations Office at Geneva, "Human Rights Council Concludes Fourth Session," 30 March 2007, at www.unog.ch/80256EDD00 6B9C2E/(httpNewsByYear_en)/4587061E2ABAE3F7C1257243005AE242? OpenDocument (21 September 2008).
15 Brett D. Schaefer, "The U.S. Is Right to Shun the U.N. Human Rights Council," 2 May 2008, www.heritage.org/research/internationalorganizations/ wm1910.cfm (21 September 2008).
16 Ibid.
17 "UN: Rights Council Ends First Year with Much to Do," *Human Rights Watch,* 19 June 2007, www.hrw.org/english/docs/2007/06/18/global16208.htm (8 October 2008).
18 For more information, see Brett D. Schaefer, "The United Nations Human Rights Council: A Disastrous First Year and Discouraging Signs for Reform," Heritage Foundation Lecture no. 1042, 5 September 2007, at www.heritage. org/Research/InternationalOrganizations/hl1042.cfm; and Sean McCormack, "Conclusion of the U.N. Human Rights Council's Fifth Session and First Year," 19 June 2007, at www.state.gov/r/pa/prs/ps/2007/jun/86802.htm (1 May 2008).
19 Brett D. Schaefer, "The U.S. Is Right to Shun the U.N. Human Rights Council," 2 May 2008, www.heritage.org/research/internationalorganizations/ wm1910.cfm (21 September 2008).
20 Ibid.
21 Ibid.
22 www.hrw.org/english/docs/2007/06/21/global16228.htm (8 October 2008).
23 UN General Assembly, "Report of the Human Rights Council on Its Second Special Session," 17 April 2006, at www.ohchr.org/english/bodies/ hrcouncil/docs/specialsession/A.HRC.S-2.2_en.pdf (1 May 2008).
24 United Nations General Assembly, "Election: Human Rights Council," at www.un.org/ga/62/elections/hrcelections.shtml#candidates (1 May 2008)
25 Ibid.
26 http://hrw.org/english/docs/2008/06/06/usint19048.htm (21 September 2008).
27 www.unhchr.ch/html/menu2/2/ecosoc.htm (5 September 2008).
28 Additional ECOSOC bodies addressing human rights concerns include the Commission for Social Development, the Commission on Crime Prevention and Criminal Justice and the UN Permanent Forum on Indigenous Issues.
29 Commission on the Status of Women, www.un.org/womenwatch/daw/csw (2 September 2008).
30 Division for the Advancement of Women, www.un.org/womenwatch/daw/daw/ index.html (2 September 2008).
31 The International Criminal Court (ICC), a court created by treaty and through the UN Charter, is also relevant for human rights advocates. The Court, which entered into force in 2002, holds jurisdiction over crimes against humanity, genocide, and war crimes. In the future, it may also have jurisdiction over crimes of aggression. See Mahnoush H. Arsanjani, "The Rome Statute of the International Criminal Court," *American Journal of International Law* 93, no. 1 (1999): 22–43; David J. Scheffer, "The United States and the International Criminal Court," *American Journal of International Law* 93, no. 1 (1999): 12–22.

32 International Court of Justice, "Advisory Opinion on the Continued Presence of South Africa in Namibia (South West Africa)," 1971 I.C.J. 16, 76.
33 For more information, see www.unicef.org (2 September 2008).
34 *Twenty-second Annual Report of the Human Rights Committee,* UN GAOR, 55th session, supplement no. 40, UN document A/55/40 (2000), at para. 24.
35 OHCHR, *Rights-based Approaches: What are Rights in Development?,* www.unhchr.ch/development/approaches.html (5 September 2008).
36 Twenty-second Annual Report of the Human Rights Committee.
37 See Tom J. Farer, "The United Nations and Human Rights: More Than a Whimper, Less Than a Roar," in *Human Rights in the World Community: Issues and Action,* ed. Richard Pierre Claude and Burns H. Weston (Philadelphia, Pa.: University of Pennsylvania Press, 2nd edn., 1992), 227–28.
38 Micheline R. Ishay, *The History of Human Rights: From Ancient Times to the Globalization Era* (Berkeley: University of California Press, 2004), 17.
39 GA resolution 217B, UN document A/810, at 77 (1948), and GA resolution 217E, UN document A/810, at 79 (1948).
40 Commission on Human Rights, www.unhchr.ch/html/menu2/2/chrintro.htm (5 September 2008).
41 Thomas Buergenthal, Dinah Shelton, and David Stewart, *International Human Rights in a Nutshell* (St. Paul, MN: West Group, 2002), 111.
42 Ibid., 111.
43 Elsa Stamatopoulou, "The Development of United Nations Mechanisms for the Protection and Promotion of Human Rights," *Washington and Lee Law Review* 55 (Summer 1998): 687.
44 ECOSOC resolution 1235 states that the Commission may "examine information relevant to gross violations of human rights and fundamental freedoms." Attempts to limit application of ECOSOC resolution 1235 to apartheid failed. The working groups established in contemporary times by the CHR draw their authority from ECOSOC resolution 1235.
45 Nigel S. Rodley, "United Nations Non-Treaty Procedures for Dealing with Human Rights Violations," in *Guide to International Human Rights Practice,* ed. Hurst Hannum (Ardsley, N.Y.: Transnational Publishers, 3rd edn., 1999), 61–84, 65.
46 Ibid., 65.
47 Another remedy to hold states accountable was granted in ECOSOC resolution 1235 of 1967: it permits the CHR to openly discuss and debate country-specific "gross and reliably attested violations of human rights." *United Nations Landmarks in Human Rights: A Brief Chronology,* www.un.org/rights/HRToday/chrono.htm (2 September 2008).
48 www.unhchr.ch/html/menu2/8/1503.htm (6 September 2008).
49 www.unhchr.ch/html/menu2/8/jurispr.htm (6 September 2008).
50 Patrick James Flood, *The Effectiveness of UN Human Rights Institutions* (Westport, Conn.: Praeger, 1998).
51 Thompson and Giffard, *Reporting Killings as Human Rights Violations Handbook.*
52 http://www2.ohchr.org/english/issues/trafficking/index.htm (8 September 2008).
53 http://www2.ohchr.org/english/issues/indigenous/rapporteur/ (8 September 2008); and http://www2.ohchr.org/english/issues/indigenous/groups/groups-01.htm (8 September 2008).

54 http://www2.ohchr.org/english/issues/poverty/expert/index.htm (8 September 2008).
55 http://www2.ohchr.org/english/issues/minorities/expert/index.htm (8 September 2008).
56 "Consultative Relationship Between the United Nations and Non-Governmental Organizations," ECOSOC resolution 1996/31, 25 July 1996.
57 See *NGOs in Consultative Status with ECOSOC*, 31 August 2006, www.un.org/esa/coordination/ngo/pdf/INF_List.pdf (2 September 2008).
58 All quotes in this section are from interviews with author, June and July 2004.
59 Gay J. McDougall, "Decade of NGO Struggle," *Human Rights Brief* 11, no. 3 (Spring 2004): 13.

4 UN treaty bodies

1 See National Council on Disability, *A White Paper: Understanding the Role of an International Convention on the Human Rights of People with Disabilities* (Washington, D.C., 2002), 41–43, 58. Available online at www.ncd.gov/news room/publications/2002/unwhitepaper_05-23-02.htm (2 September 2008).
2 See, for example, Articles in the Convention on the Rights of the Child.
3 http://www2.ohchr.org/english/issues/disappear/index.htm (8 September 2008).
4 See Guidelines of International Human Rights Law Group for Preparing a Shadow Report for CERD (undated, on file with author).
5 Markus Schmidt, "Follow-Up Mechanisms Before the UN Treaty Bodies and the UN Mechanisms," in *The UN Human Rights Treaty System in the 21st Century*, ed. Anne Bayefsky (The Hague, The Netherlands/Boston, Mass.: Kluwer Law International, 2000), 233.
6 Anne F. Bayefsky, *The UN Human Rights Treaty System: Universality at the Crossroads*, April 2001, www.bayefsky.com/report/finalreport.pdf (2 September 2008).
7 Kirsten Young provided this excellent example.
8 Gerison Lansdown, *What Works? Promoting the Rights of Disabled Children: Guidelines for Action*, www.daa.org.uk/RDC%20WHAT%20WORKS.htm (14 September 2008).
9 Ibid.
10 http://www2.ohchr.org/english/bodies/hrc/index.htm (8 September 2008).
11 For a statistical breakdown of individual complaints to the Human Rights Committee, see *Statistical Survey of Individual Complaints Dealt With by the Human Rights Committee under the Optional Protocol to the International Covenant on Civil and Political Rights*, 3 May 2004, www.unhchr.ch/html/menu2/8/stat2.htm (5 September 2008).
12 Kirsten Young makes this point in her book *The Law and Process of the Human Rights Committee* (Ardsley, N.Y.: Transnational Publishers, 2002).
13 See *Workshop on the Justiciability of Economic, Social and Cultural Rights, with Particular Reference to an Optional Protocol to the Covenant on Economic, Social and Cultural Rights* (Palais Wilson, 5–6 February 2001), www.unhchr.ch/html/menu2/escrwkshop.htm (14 September 2008).
14 Article 2(1) of the ICESCR provides:

> Each State Party to the present Covenant undertakes to take steps, individually and through international assistance and co-operation,

especially economic and technical, to the maximum of its available resources, with a view to achieving progressively the full realization of the rights recognized in the present Covenant by all appropriate means, including particularly the adoption of legislative measures.

15 *Report of the Open-Ended Working Group to Consider Options Regarding the Elaboration of an Optional Protocol to the International Covenant on Economic, Social and Cultural Rights*, UN document E/CN.4/2004/44.
16 http://www2.ohchr.org/english/bodies/cerd/early-warning.htm (8 September 2008).
17 The total number of member states that have ratified the Children's Convention has surpassed that of all other conventions. As of August 2004, only two member states had not ratified it: Somalia and the United States. *Status of Ratification of the Convention on the Rights of the Child*, www.unhchr.ch/html/menu2/6/crc/treaties/status-crc.htm (5 September 2008).
18 http://www2.ohchr.org/english/bodies/crc/index.htm (8 September 2008).
19 http://www2.ohchr.org/english/bodies/crc/discussion.htm (8 September 2008).
20 http://www2.ohchr.org/english/bodies/cmw/index.htm (7 October 2008).
21 http://www2.ohchr.org/english/issues/disability/docs/Q&Acommittee.doc (8 September 2008).
22 *Declaration on the Protection of all Persons from Enforced Disappearance*, General Assembly resolution 47/133 of 18 December 1992, www.unhchr.ch/huridocda/huridoca.nsf/(Symbol)/A.RES.47.133.En?OpenDocument (8 September 2008).
23 www.icc-cpi.int/library/about/officialjournal/Rome_Statute_120704-EN.pdf (8 September 2008).
24 Anne F. Bayefsky, *International Law Association Report on the Treaty System*, www.bayefsky.com/report/finalreport.pdf (14 September 2008).
25 Ibid.
26 See, for example, *Report of the Sixteenth Meeting of Chairpersons of the Human Rights Treaty Bodies* (advance unedited version; Geneva), 23–25 June 2004.
27 *Strengthening of the United Nations: An Agenda for Further Change* (A/57/387), and GA resolution 57/300.
28 OHCHR, "Enhancing the Human Rights Treaty Body System," http://www2.ohchr.org/english/bodies/treaty/CCD.htm (8 October 2008).
29 Henry Steiner, "Individual Claims in a World of Massive Violations: What Role for the Human Rights Commission?" in *The Future of UN Human Rights Treaty Monitoring*, ed. Philip Austin and James Crawford (Cambridge: Cambridge University Press, 2000), 15.
30 See Kirsten Young, *The Law and Process of the Human Rights Committee*, xxii.
31 See, for example, Andrew Byrnes, "An Effective Human Rights System in the Context of International Human Rights Law," in Bayefsky, ed., *The UN Human Rights Treaty System in the 21st Century*, 139.

5 The Security Council

1 See David M. Malone, *The UN Security Council: From the Cold War to the 21st Century* (Boulder, Colo.: Lynne Rienner, 2004).
2 UN Charter, Article 1 (10).

3 UN Charter, Article 1 (2).
4 Ibid.
5 UN Charter, Article 1 (3).
6 UN Charter, Article 2 (7).
7 See Sydney D. Bailey, *The UN Security Council and Human Rights* (New York: St. Martin's Press, 1994), 123.
8 David Bills, "International Human Rights and Humanitarian Intervention: The Ramifications of Reform on the United Nations' Security Council," *Texas International Law Journal* 31, no. 1 (1996): 107–35.
9 *Report of the Secretary-General, UN GAOR*, 46th session, supplement no. 1, at 4–5, UN document A/46/1 (1991).
10 Ibid.
11 Ibid.
12 *An Agenda for Peace*, (UN document A/47/277), 17 June 1992. See also *Supplement to An Agenda for Peace: Position Paper of the Secretary-General on the Occasion of the Fiftieth Anniversary of the United Nations* (UN document A/50/60–S/1995/1), 3 January 1995.
13 Secretary-General Boutros Boutros-Ghali, *Report of the Secretary-General: An Agenda for Peace: Preventive Diplomacy, Peacemaking and Peace-Keeping* (A/47/277–S/24111), 31 January 1992.
14 For statements delivered by the Secretary-General of the United Nations Kofi Annan, June 1998 and October 1999, on the subject of intervention, see Kofi Annan, *The Question of Intervention: Statements by the Secretary-General of the United Nations Kofi Annan* (New York: United Nations Department of Public Information, 2000).
15 *"We the Peoples": The Role of the United Nations in the 21st Century* (UN document A/54/2000), 30 March 2000.
16 Security Council resolution 1325, UNSCOR, 55th Session, 4213th meeting, UN Document S/RES/1325 (2000). See also Hilary Charlesworth and Mary Wood, "Mainstreaming Gender in International Peace and Security," *Yale Journal of International Law* 26 (Summer 2001): 313–318.
17 Ibrahim J. Gassama, "World Order in the Post-Cold War Era: The Relevance and Role of the United Nations After Fifty Years," *Brooklyn Journal of International Law* 20 (1994): 255, 266.
18 "Customary international law results from a general and consistent practice of states followed by them from a sense of legal obligation." Restatement (Third), Foreign Relations Law of the United States, section 102.2 (1986). If a state wishes not to be bound by customary law, it must persistently object to the emerging international norm.
19 Sean D. Murphy, "The Security Council, Legitimacy, and the Concept of Collective Security After the Cold War," *Columbia Journal of Transnational Law* 32, no. 2 (1994): 201, 220.
20 Adam Roberts, "The Crisis in UN Peacekeeping," in *Managing Global Chaos,* ed. Chester A. Crocker and Fen Osler Hampson (Washington, D.C.: U.S. Institute of Peace, 1996), 297–320, 298.
21 Ibid.
22 See the Project on International Courts and Tribunals, www.pict-pcti.org/index.html (2 September 2008).
23 States may also use force under extremely limited circumstances. Article 51 of the UN Charter preserves the "inherent right of individual or collective

self-defense" if an armed attack occurs against a member of the UN, until the Security Council has taken measures necessary to maintain "international peace and security." However, the right to self-defense may be claimed by states threatened by other states, not by individuals or groups facing human rights abuses within states.

24 See Thomas M. Franck, *Recourse to Force: State Action Against Threats and Armed Attacks* (Cambridge: Cambridge University Press, 2002), 135.

25 Tania Voon, "Closing the Gap Between Legitimacy and Legality of Humanitarian Intervention: Lessons from East Timor and Kosovo," *UCLA Journal of International Law and Foreign Affairs* 7 (Spring/Summer 2002): 31–91.

26 Richard B. Lillich, "The Role of the UN Security Council in Protecting Human Rights in Crisis Situations: UN Humanitarian Intervention in the Post-Cold War World," *Tulane Journal of International and Comparative Law* 3 (Spring 1995): 1–19.

27 Security Council resolution 232, UN SCOR, 23rd session, 1428th meeting, at 5, UN document S/Res/253 (1968).

28 Security Council resolution 418, UN SCOR, 32nd session, 2046th meeting, at 2, UN document S/Res/418 (1977).

29 Security Council resolution 678, UN SCOR, 45th session, 2963rd meeting, at 1, UN document S/Res/678 (1990).

30 Security Council resolution 688, UN SCOR, 46th session, 2982nd meeting, at 1, UN document S/Res/688 (1991).

31 Kelly K. Pease and David P. Forsythe, "Human Rights, Humanitarian Intervention, and World Politics," *Human Rights Quarterly* 15, no. 2 (1993): 290, 303.

32 Ibid., 304.

33 Security Council resolution 794, UN SCOR, 47th session, 3145th meeting, at 2, UN document S/Res/794 (1992).

34 Susan M. Crawford, "U.N. Humanitarian Intervention in Somalia," *Transnational Law and Contemporary Problems* 3, (1993): 273, 291.

35 *Report on the Fall of Srebrenica* (UN document A/54/549), 15 November 1999.

36 *Report of the Independent Inquiry into the Actions of the United Nations During the 1994 Genocide in Rwanda* (UN document S/1999/1257), 15 December 1999.

37 David Malone, "Ralph Bunche and Peacekeeping," paper presented at the Annual Meeting of the International Studies Association, Montreal, 17 March 2004.

38 Kofi A. Annan, "Two Concepts of Sovereignty," *The Economist*, 18 September 1999.

39 *Report of the Secretary-General on the Work of the Organisation* (UN document A/54/1), 4 October 1999, 48.

40 *Report of the Panel on UN Peace Operations* (UN document A/55/305–S/2000/809), 21 August 2000.

41 Francis M. Deng, Sadikiel Kimaro, Terrence Lyons, Donald Rothchild, and I. William Zartman, *Sovereignty as Responsibility: Conflict Management in Africa* (Washington, D.C.: Brookings Institution Press, 1996).

42 ICISS, *Intervention and State Sovereignty: The Responsibility to Protect* (Ottawa: International Development Research Center, 2001), xi.

43 Ibid.

180   *Notes*

44 See, for example, Thomas G. Weiss, "The Sunset of Humanitarian Intervention? The Responsibility to Protect in a Unipolar Era," *Security Dialogue* 35, no. 2 (June 2004): 135–53.
45 See Convention on the Privileges and Immunities of the United Nations, Article 3, section 9, 13 February 1946, § 2, 21 U.S.T. 1418, 1422, 1 U.N.T.S. 15, 20; UN Charter, Article 105(1) (requiring member states to recognize UN privileges and immunities).
46 "On the Status, Privileges and Immunities of KFOR and UNMIK and their Personnel in Kosovo," UNMIK regulation 2000/47, 18 August 2000, www.unmikonline.org/regulations/2000/reg47-00.htm (2 September 2008).
47 Frederic Megret and Florian Hoffman, "The UN as a Human Rights Violator? Some Reflections on the United Nations Changing Human Rights Responsibilities," *Human Rights Quarterly* 25, no. 2 (2002): 314–42, 315.
48 August Reinsch, "Securing the Accountability of International Organizations," *Global Governance* 7 (2001): 137–38.
49 Reparation for Injuries Suffered in the Service of the United Nations, 1949 I.C.J. 174, 179 (11 April).
50 Ibid.
51 Zenon Stavrinides, "Human Rights Obligations Under the UN Charter," *International Journal of Human Rights* 3, no. 2 (1999): 40.
52 Manuel Rama-Montaldo, "International Legal Personality and Implied Powers of International Organizations," *British Yearbook of International Law* 44 (1970): 111, 147–49.
53 Kofi A. Annan, "Strengthening United Nations Action in the Field of Human Rights: Prospects and Priorities," *Harvard Human Rights Journal* 10 (1997): 1–9, 6.
54 This argument could be applied to hold civilian military subcontractors accountable.
55 Megret and Hoffman, "The UN as a Human Rights Violator?" 317.
56 See Elizabeth Abraham, "The Sins of the Savior: Holding the United Nations Accountable to International Human Rights Standards for Executive Order Detentions in its Mission in Kosovo," *American University Law Review* 52 (October 2003): 1291–1338, 1320.
57 See *Bulletin on the Observance by United Nations Forces of International Humanitarian Law* (UN document ST/SGB/1999/13), 1999, reprinted in 38 ILM 1656 (1999).
58 Carolyn L. Willson, "Changing the Charter: The United Nations Prepares for the 21st Century," *American Journal of International Law* 90 (January 1996): 115.
59 W. Michael Reisman, "The Constitutional Crisis in the United Nations," *American Journal of International Law* 87, no. 1 (1993): 83, 85.
60 David Malone, "The Security Council in the Post-Cold War Era: A Study in the Creative Interpretation of the U.N. Charter," *New York University Journal of International Law and Politics* 35 (Winter 2003): 487–508, 503. See also Edward C. Luck, *Reforming the United Nations: Lessons from a History in Progress*, International Relations Studies and the United Nations Occasional Papers 2003 no. 1, www.acuns.wlu.ca/publications/UN_Reform/Luck_UN_Reform.pdf (2 September 2008).
61 "Adapting U.N. Structures to a Rapidly Evolving World," *U.N. Monthly Chronicle*, December 1993, at 43.

62 "Question of Equitable Representation on and Increase in the Membership of the Security Council and Related Matters," UN GAOR, 49th session, 29th meeting, at 19, UN document A/49/PV.29 (1994).
63 James Paul, "The Arria Formula," *Global Policy*, October 2003, www.global policy.org/security/mtgsetc/arria.htm (2 September 2008).
64 Luck, *Reforming the United Nations*, 13–14.
65 Ibid.
66 "NGO Working Group on the Security Council Information Statement," *Global Policy*, November 2004, www.globalpolicy.org/security/ngowkgrp/ statements/current.htm (2 September 2008).
67 Malone, "The Security Council in the Post-Cold War Era," 508.
68 *United Nations Security Council Resolution 1325* (New York: UNSC, 2000).

6 The International Labour Organization and the UN Global Compact

1 Special thanks to Professor Margaret Bedggood for her assistance with this chapter.
2 For an updated list of member countries, see International Labour Organization, *Alphabetical List of ILO Member Countries*, www.ilo.org/public/ english/standards/relm/country.htm (2 September 2008).
3 Brazil, China, France, Germany, India, Italy, Japan, the Russian Federation, the United Kingdom, and the United States.
4 International Labour Organization, www.ilo.org/wcmsp5/groups/public/- dgreports/-dcomm/-webdev/documents/publication/wcms_082361.pdf (8 September 2008).
5 Nigel Haworth and Stephen Hughes, "Trade and International Labour Standards: Issues and Debates Over a Social Clause," *Journal of Industrial Relations* 39, no. 2 (1997): 192.
6 Ibid., 182.
7 Ibid., 184.
8 The "race to the bottom" argument suggests that competition for foreign investment depresses labor and other social standards in an effort to minimize costs of investment.
9 Haworth and Hughes, "Trade and International Labour Standards," 190.
10 International Labour Organization, *ILO Declaration on Fundamental Principles and Rights at Work* (Geneva, June 1998), Preamble, paragraph 2, www.ilo.org/dyn/declaris/DECLARATIONWEB.static_jump?var_language= EN&var_pagename=DECLARATIONTEXT (2 September 2008).
11 Ibid., paragraph 5.
12 Eddy Lee, "Globalisation and Labour Standards: A Review of Issues," *International Labour Review* 136, no. 2 (Summer 1997): 173–89.
13 For more information on ILO declarations and recommendations, see its website at www.ilo.org (2 September 2008).
14 Kari Tapiola, "The ILO Declaration on Fundamental Principles and Rights at Work and its Follow-up," in *Multinational Enterprises and the Social Challenges of the XXIst Century*, ed. R. Blanpain (London: Kluwer Law International, 2000), 11. Considering that only three of those conventions were customary international law at the time of signing, the agreement of members to a full eight treaties significantly advances international labor norms.

15 In addition to the eight core conventions, another four were designated in 1994 as "Priority Conventions": the Employment Policy Convention, no. 122 (1964); the Tripartite Consultation (International Labor Standards) Convention, no. 144 (1976); the Labor Inspection Convention, no. 81 (1947); the Labor Inspection (Agriculture) Convention, no. 129 (1969).

16 Michele Colucci, "Implementation and Monitoring of Codes of Conduct: How to Make Codes of Conduct Effective?" in Blanpain, ed., *Multinational Enterprises and the Social Challenges of the XXIst Century*, 281.

17 *Organizing for Social Justice: Global Report under the Follow-up to the ILO Declaration on Fundamental Principles and Rights at Work*, International Labour Conference 92nd Session (Geneva: International Labour Organization, 2004), 1, www.ilo.org/wcmsp5/groups/public/-dgreports/-dcomm/documents/meetingdocument/kd00102.pdf (8 September 2008).

18 Ibid., 13–15.

19 Ibid., 1.

20 Rorden Wilkinson and Steve Hughes, "Labor Standards and Global Governance: Examining the Dimensions of Institutional Engagement," *Global Governance* 6, no. 2 (2000): 259–77.

21 "Freedom of Association: Digest of Decisions and Principles of the Freedom of Association Committee of the Governing Body of the ILO" (book review), *International Labour Review* 134, no. 6 (1995): 788.

22 *The ILO: What it Is, What it Does* (Geneva: International Labour Organization, 2003), 16, www.ilo.org/global/About_the_ILO/lang-en/docName-WCMS_082364/index.htm (2 September 2008).

23 *IPEC Action Against Child Labour 2006–2007: Progress and Future Priorities* (Geneva: International Labour Organization, 2004), www.ilo.org/ipecinfo/product/download.do?type=document&id=7650).

24 "Facts on Child Labor," Department of Communication Fact Sheet (Geneva: International Labour Organization, June 2004), 1.

25 Ibid., 2.

26 IPEC/ILO, www.ilo.org/childlabour (2 September 2008).

27 *International Programme on Child Labour*, www.ilo.org/ipec/index.htm (8 September 2008).

28 *IPEC Action Against Child Labour 2002–2003*, 93.

29 See D. Rodrik, "Labor Standards in International Trade: Do They Matter and What Do We Do About Them?" in *Emerging Agenda for Global Trade: High Stakes for Developing Countries*, Overseas Development Council Essay no. 20, ed. R. Lawrence, D. Rodrik, and J. Whalley (Washington, D.C.: Overseas Development Council and Johns Hopkins University Press, 1996).

30 IPEC/ILO, *Facts on Mainstreaming Elimination of Child Labour into Development and Poverty Reduction Strategies*, www.ilo.org/public/english/standards/ipec/publ/download/factsheets/fs_mainstreaming_0303.pdf

31 *IPEC Action Against Child Labour 2002–2003*, 48.

32 Ibid., 56.

33 International Labour Organization, *IPEC Action Against Child Labour: Highlights 2004* (Geneva: International Labour Organization, 2004), www.ilo.org/public/english/standards/ipec/publ/implementation/index.htm

34 *IPEC Action Against Child Labour 2002–2003*, 43–45.

35 Ibid., 105.

36 www.unglobalcompact.org/docs/news_events/8.1/GCAnnualReview2007.pdf (27 September 2008).
37 www.unglobalcompact.org/AboutTheGC/TheTenPrinciples/index.html (27 September 2008).
38 Ibid.
39 Ibid.
40 Ibid.
41 "Human Rights Working Group Members" 2008. UN Global Compact, February 1. www.unglobalcompact.org/Issues/human_rights/index.html (27 September 2008).
42 For a profile of the University of Warwick Corporate Citizenship Program, see http://www2.warwick.ac.uk/fac/soc/wbs/research/ccu (9 October 2008).
43 John Gerard Ruggie, "Global_Governance.net: The Global Compact as Learning Network," *Global Governance* 7, no. 4 (2001): 371.
44 "Policy for 'Communication on Progress'" 2008. UN Global Compact, 13 March 2008. www.globalcompact.org/COP/ (27 September 2008).
45 "Update: Over 900 Global Compact Participants Marked 'Inactive' or Delisted" 2008. UN Global Compact: New York, 28 January 2008. www.unglobalcompact.org/NewsAndEvents/news_archives/2008_01_28.html (27 September 2008).
46 "Embedding Human Rights in Business Practice II" 2008. UN Global Compact and the Office of the UN High Commissioner for Human Rights, January. www.unglobalcompact.org/Issues/human_rights/Tools_and_Guidance_Materials.html (27 September 2008).
47 Ibid., 19.
48 *Embedding Human Rights in Business Practice II—A joint publication of the UN Global Compact Office and the Office of the UN High Commissioner for Human Rights,* January 2008, www.unglobalcompact.org/docs/issues_doc/human_rights/Resources/EHRBPII_Final.pdf (27 September 2008).
49 As cited in ibid., 371, n. 1.
50 Janelle M. Diller, "Social Conduct in Transnational Enterprise Operations: The Role of the International Labour Organisation," in Blanpain, ed., *Multinational Enterprises and the Social Challenges of the XXIst Century,* 24–25.

7 Conclusion: looking backward, going forward

1 Henry Steiner and Philip Alston, *International Human Rights in Context: Law, Politics and Morality* (New York: Oxford University Press, 1996), 343.

Selected bibliography

Books

Philip Alston and James Crawford, eds., *The Future of UN Human Rights Treaty Monitoring* (Cambridge: Cambridge University Press, 2000). Provides detailed analyses of the strengths and weaknesses of the UN human rights treaty system, written by leading participants in the work of the treaty bodies.

Philip Alston, Ryan Goodman, and Henry J. Steiner, *International Human Rights in Context: Law, Politics, Morals: Text and Materials* (Oxford: Oxford University Press, 3rd ed., 2007). A leading law school human rights textbook. Contains sharply edited primary materials ranging from intergovernmental or NGO reports to treaties, resolutions, and decisions; and excerpts from secondary readings in law and legal theory, as well as other pertinent fields such as international relations, moral and political theory, and anthropology.

Philip Alston and Frederic Megret, eds., *The United Nations and Human Rights: A Critical Appraisal* (Oxford: Oxford University Press, 2004). The best comprehensive volume on the UN and human rights. Particularly strong analysis on the relationship between the various bodies and the potential for major reforms and restructuring.

Carol Anderson, *Eyes on the Prize: The United Nations and the African American Struggle for Human Rights, 1944–1955* (New York: Cambridge University Press, 2003). A well assembled historical account of the impact of racism on U.S. human rights policy and the development of the UN human rights system.

Ian Brownlie, *Principles of Public International Law* (New York: Oxford University Press, 4th ed., 2003). A classic teaching and research text, written with great clarity.

Thomas Buergenthal, Dinah Shelton, and David Stewart, *International Human Rights in a Nutshell* (St. Paul, Minn.: West Group, 3rd ed., 2002). Don't be put off by the "nutshell" in the title; this is a serious book. It is not only the clearest and best guide for law students on human rights, but also a tremendous resource for practitioners and academics. This small book is amazingly broad in scope, covering not only UN human rights mechanisms but regional mechanisms as well.

Richard Pierre Claude and Burns H. Weston, *Human Rights in the World Community: Issues and Action* (Philadelphia: University of Pennsylvania Press, 3rd ed., 2006). Excellent introduction to the theory and practice of human rights.

Jack Donnelly, *Universal Human Rights in Theory and Practice* (Ithaca, N.Y.: Cornell University Press, 2nd ed., 2002). The leading introduction to the theory and practice of human rights. This book's discussion of challenges to the universality of human rights is widely cited. Specific topics addressed include humanitarian intervention, democracy and human rights, "Asian values," group rights, and discrimination against sexual minorities.

Tim Dunne and Nicholas J. Wheeler, eds., *Human Rights in Global Politics* (Cambridge: Cambridge University Press, 1999). A good complement to Donnelly, the authors in this collection take a more critical approach in evaluating the philosophical basis of human rights, and reflect on the structures that affect the development of a global human rights culture. The contributors ask whether human rights abuses are a result of the failure of governments to live up to a universal human rights standard, or whether the search for moral universals is a fundamentally flawed enterprise.

Tony Evans, ed., *Human Rights Fifty Years On: A Reappraisal* (Manchester, UK: Manchester University Press, 1998). A critical examination of the power of human rights; includes several landmark essays from leading scholars.

Richard A. Falk, *Human Rights Horizons: The Pursuit of Justice in a Globalizing World* (New York: Routledge, 2000). A leading thinker on human rights offers a historical perspective on human rights and offers his views on the future of human rights, given new challenges in the globalization era. Rwanda and Bosnia case studies provide for provocative discussion. The last section of the book deals with human rights horizons such as civil society, the role of morality in security, and redressing past grievances.

David P. Forsythe, ed., *Human Rights and Comparative Foreign Policy* (New York: United Nations University Press, 2000). A fascinating collection which considers the place of human rights in the foreign policies of a wide range of states.

Hurst Hannum, *Guide to International Human Rights Practice* (Ardsley, N.Y.: Transnational Publishers, 4th ed., 2004). A detailed introduction to human rights mechanisms, with particularly good chapters on "non-treaty" mechanisms, the ILO, and UNESCO.

Michael Ignatieff, *Human Rights as Politics and Idolatry*, ed. Amy Gutmann (Princeton, N.J.: Princeton University Press, 2003). A succinct liberal argument for a pragmatic approach to human rights. Ignatieff's essay is followed by short responses from leading contemporary thinkers, making this a good book for facilitating discussion on the meaning of human rights.

Micheline Ishay, *The History of Human Rights: From Ancient Times to the Globalization Era* (Berkeley: University of California Press, 2008). A brilliant account of historical and intellectual development in human rights. For scholars and activists alike.

William Korey, *NGOs and the Universal Declaration of Human Rights: "A Curious Grapevine"* (New York: Palgrave Macmillan, 2001). A comprehensive examination of the contributions of non-governmental organizations to the human rights movement.

Paul Gordon Lauren, *The Evolution of International Human Rights: Visions Seen* (Philadelphia: University of Pennsylvania Press, 2nd ed., 2004). A clear and compelling account of the history of UN human rights practice.

Julie Mertus, *Bait and Switch: Human Rights and U.S. Foreign Policy, Global Horizons* (New York: Routledge, 2004). A detailed account of post-Cold War U.S. foreign policy practice on human rights, approaching the executive, military, and NGO roles through separate analyses. Mertus argues that human rights are not seen as imperative within the USA, and that human rights are often misused and held as a double standard.

——*Human Rights Matters: Local Politics and Natural Human Rights Institutions* (Palo Alto, Calif.: Stanford University Press, 2008). Explores the impact of local context on the development and implementation of national human rights institutions, with case studies of Bosnia, the Czech Republic, Denmark, Germany, and Northern Ireland.

Julie Mertus and Jeffrey Helsing, eds., *Human Rights and Conflict* (Washington, D.C.: United States Institute of Peace, 2005). A comprehensive collection of essays on the intersection of international human rights and conflict. Among the issues discussed are human rights as a cause or consequence of violent conflict; holding militaries and paramilitaries responsible for violations; peace negotiations and human rights advocacy; the truth vs. justice debate in truth commissions and war crimes trials; civil society as a human rights safeguard; human rights implications of the war on terrorism; and the human rights of refugees and displaced people.

Manfred Nowak, *Introduction to the International Human Rights Regime* (Boston, Mass.: Martinus Nijhoff, 2003). A comprehensive multidisciplinary textbook introducing the idea and significance of human rights, its philosophical and theoretical foundations, historical development, the main structures and procedures of international human rights protection by the United Nations and regional organizations, and modern trends, such as preventive mechanisms, international criminal law, human rights as essential elements of peace-keeping and peace-building operations, humanitarian intervention, and the relationship between human rights and terrorism.

Michael O'Flaherty, ed., *The Human Rights Field Operation* (Burlington, Vt.: Ashgate, 2007). A well organized collection of essays on the human rights field operations of the United Nations.

Samantha Power and Graham Allison, eds., *Realizing Human Rights: Moving from Inspiration to Impact* (New York: Palgrave Macmillan, 2000). This book brings together leading activists, policy-makers and critics to reflect upon 50 years of attempts to improve respect for human rights. Authors include former president Jimmy Carter, who helped inject human rights concerns into U.S. policy; Wei Jingsheng, who struggled to do so in China;

Louis Henkin, the modern father of international law; and Richard Gold-stone, the former chief prosecutor for the Yugoslav and Rwandan war crimes tribunals.

Monroe E. Price and Mark Thompson, eds., *Forging Peace: Intervention, Human Rights, and the Management of Media Space* (Bloomington: Indiana University Press, 2002). Interesting case studies on the relationship between human rights and the media in conflict scenarios.

Burns H. Weston and Stephen Marks, eds., *The Future of International Human Rights* (Ardsley, N.Y.: Transnational Publishers, 1999). A strong collection of essays from scholars and practitioners on the future of human rights.

Nigel White and Dirk Klassen, *The UN, Human Rights and Post-Conflict Situations* (Manchester, UK: Manchester University Press, 2005). Comprehensive and clear explanation of the application of the UN human rights system in post-conflict areas.

Kirsten Young, *The Law and Process of the Human Rights Committee* (Ardsley, N.Y.: Transnational Publishers, 2002). An authoritative and comprehensive account of the procedures of the Human Rights Committee. Essential for practitioners and scholars concerned with questions of legitimacy and accountability in human rights practice.

Web resources

Note: Web resources can change quickly. Prior to publication, each Web resource has been checked. The date in parenthesis at the end of the citation is the date on which the resource was last examined.

Essential UN resources on the Web

Office of the High Commissioner for Human Rights, www.unhchr.ch (28 August 2008). The website of the Office of the High Commissioner for Human Rights, based in Geneva, is the most important source of information in this field, including programs, documents, statements, and publications. It also offers related links within the United Nations system.

Human Development Reports, UNDP, hdr.undp.org (28 August 2008). Provides information about and analysis of human development indicators, in publications that include national, regional, and international foci.

UNHCHR, Training and Educational Materials, www.unhchr.ch/html/menu6/2/training.htm (28 August 2008). Contains guides, training materials, and all documents produced under the UN Decade for Human Rights Education (1995–2004), including curricula, training manuals, and histories of human rights activities.

UNHCHR, Treaty Bodies Database, www.unhchr.ch/tbs/doc.nsf (28 August 2008). Search for international human rights treaties information and reports.

UNHCHR, Website Search Facilities, www.unhchr.ch/search.htm (5 September 2008). Search for United Nations human rights documents.

United Nations Info Quest (UN-I-QUE), http://lib-unique.un.org/lib/unique.nsf (5 September 2008). Search for reports by UN human rights bodies, special rapporteurs and countries.

Universal Declaration of Human Rights, www.unhchr.ch/udhr/index.htm (5 September 2008). The UDHR in over 350 different languages.

WomenWatch, www.un.org/womenwatch (5 September 2008). The United Nations gateway for the advancement and empowerment of women is a joint initiative of the Division for the Advancement of Women (DAW), the United Nations Development Fund for Women (UNIFEM) and the United Nations International Research and Training Institute for the Advancement of Women (INSTRAW).

Other important internet references

AU Human Rights Council, www.american.edu/humanrights (11 October 2008). A particularly good resource for human rights internships, timeline on human rights and specific updates to this book. (This Web page is connected to the author of this book.)

Bayefsky.com, www.bayefsky.com (5 September 2008). This website is a Canadian human rights professor's resource on the UN treaties, aiming to enhance the implementation of UN human rights legal standards. It tells one how to complain about human rights treaty violations and discusses reform efforts on the UN human rights treaty system.

Human Rights Internet (HRI), www.hri.ca (5 September 2008). One of the oldest organizations founded with the explicit goal of human rights information-sharing. Launched in 1976 in the United States, HRI now has its headquarters in Ottawa, Canada. The website provides information on a wide range of human rights topics, but it is particularly strong on human rights and development.

Human Rights Network International (HRNi), www.hrni.org/index_flash.html (5 September 2008). The website provides extensive research articles and resources on human rights, particularly individual rights such as the right to life, due process, cultural rights, to development, and minority rights. Specific discussions on regional protection agencies (such as the European Court of Human Rights, African Commission on Human and Peoples' Rights) and special focus cases (civil society, terrorism, and human rights) are provided.

Human Rights Research and Education Centre, www.cdp-hrc.uottawa.ca/eng/index.php (5 September 2008). An extensive collection of human rights resources from the University of Ottawa. Their virtual library, publications and links are very comprehensive.

Human Rights Resource Center, http://hrusa.org/default.htm (5 September 2008). The Human Rights Resource Center is an excellent source of information on human rights education. These resources include more than 50 curricula, guides, videos, documents, and other educational aids. The site, which is run through the University of Minnesota, also provides a well organized set of links to over 200 other human rights sites.

International Centre for Human Rights and Democratic Development, www. ichrdd.ca/splash.html (5 September 2008). A good source for information on democracy and human rights. Created by the Canadian parliament, the Centre is independent and non-partisan.

Max Planck Institute for Comparative Public Law and International Law, www.mpil.de/ww/en/pub/news.cfm (5 September 2008). The website of the Max Planck Institute for Comparative Public Law and International Law. One is able to search articles and journals through their online database. The website also has a lot of resources concerning international law and German courts.

Security Council Report, www.securitycouncilreport.org (6 September 2008). A good source for accurate and objective information and analysis on the activities of the Security Council. Although not focusing exclusively on human rights, this source provides useful forecasts of Security Council activities of great relevance to human rights advocates.

Training Manual on Human Rights Monitoring, www1.umn.edu/humanrts/ monitoring/index.html (5 September 2008). A superb OHCHR project, drafted principally by David Weissbrodt and available on his human rights website. The comprehensive manual will be of great assistance to anyone undertaking field research. It is complemented by a Trainer's Guide, which is intended to assist trainers in preparing officers for addressing human rights issues.

University of Minnesota Bibliography for Research on International Human Rights Law, www1.umn.edu/humanrts/bibliog/BIBLIO.htm (5 September 2008). A bibliography that lists both print and internet sources by categories such as Compilations of Human Rights Instruments, Status of Human Rights Instruments, Legislative History of Human Rights Instruments, Country Situations, Country Reports, etc. The website also has a comprehensive list of UN documents.

Website of the Victoria University of Wellington's Human Rights Research Guide, www.vuw.ac.nz/library/special/un/researchaids/humanrights.shtml (5 September 2008). The website lists useful UN websites where one can obtain UN documents. The second half of the document lists resources available in the VUW library.

Women's Human Rights Resources, www.law-lib.utoronto.ca/Diana (5 September 2008). A project of the Bora Laskin Law Library at the University of Toronto, Faculty of Law, the site provides excellent guidance for research on women's human rights, and includes advocacy guides, fellowship information, a women's human rights database, and special features on topical issues.

Selected list of NGOs committed to human rights work

ACT (Advocating Change Together), www.selfadvocacy.org (8 September 2008). Information on disability rights advocacy, with a focus on developmental disabilities.

Amnesty International, www.amnesty.org (5 September 2008). Amnesty International is a membership-based independent organization working to campaign for internationally recognized human rights. There are more than 1.8 million members worldwide and Amnesty does work in over 150 different countries.

Arab Association for Human Rights, www.arabhra.org/HRA/Pages/Index. aspx?language=2 (5 September 2008). The core programs of the organization are international advocacy, women's rights, and education. The Palestinian issue is of particular pertinence to this organization, which is based in Brussels.

Australian Human Rights Centre, www.austlii.edu.au/au/other/ahric (5 September 2008). The Centre focuses on the Asia-Pacific region and aims to increase awareness about human rights through providing access to documentation and conducting research on human rights topics.

Casa Alianza, www.casa-alianza.org (5 September 2008). Latin America's leading children's rights organization, Casa Alianza advocates for street children and sexually exploited children to their governments and at the Inter-American Commission on Human Rights. It is a sister organization to Covenant House.

Center for Economic and Social Rights, www.cesr.org (5 September 2008). The Center uses economic and social rights as a platform for creating greater social justice, both in the USA (where they are based) and abroad. They have targeted their advocacy in eight different countries and also have advocacy guides on their internet site.

Citizens for Global Solutions, www.globalsolutions.org (5 September 2008). This is a grass-roots membership organization aiming campaigns at the promotion of human rights through advocacy for a stronger International Criminal Court, reform of UN peace operations, and encouraging U.S. foreign policy to emphasize international cooperation and human rights. They were formerly known as the World Federalist Society.

The Danish Institute for Human Rights (DIHR), www.humanrights.dk (5 September 2008). The DIHR is a large national human rights organization which takes a multidisciplinary approach in its research, projects, documentation, and educational activities.

Derechos Human Rights, www.derechos.org (5 September 2008). Derechos is a human rights organization which has an enormous amount of reports and projects, and its news is thorough and timely, as well as accurate. It is a sister organization to Equipo Nizkor.

Disabled Peoples' International, http://v1.dpi.org/lang-en (6 September 2008). Source for information on treaty implementation.

Earthtrends, http://earthtrends.wri.org (5 September 2008). This project of the World Resources Institute is an online resource containing a wide variety of statistics, maps, and short thematic pieces on environmental, social, and economic issues.

Equality Now, www.equalitynow.org (5 September 2008). This organization has been striving for women's rights and equality since 1992 and works with local activists and with national human rights groups. Their Women's Action Network is also a broad-based awareness project about women's issues.

Equipo Nizkor, www.derechos.org/nizkor/eng.html (5 September 2008). Like Derechos Human Rights, Equipo Nizkor have a huge amount of information and human rights news. They focus especially on South and Central American human rights issues.

Forefront, www.forefrontleaders.org (5 September 2008). Forefront aims to protect human rights defenders through providing a network of support for local human rights activists.

Franciscans International, www.franciscansinternational.org (5 September 2008). In addition to being a leading NGO on the right to development, Franciscans International works on women's rights, trafficking, and religious freedom. Franciscans International relies on the grass-roots work of more than 1 million Franciscans worldwide to inform its human rights lobbying at the UN.

Global Rights, www.globalrights.org (5 September 2008). Global Rights aim their human rights advocacy at partnerships with local advocates. With offices around the world, they aim to "challenge injustice and amplify new voices within the global discourse."

Human Rights Education Association, www.hrea.org (5 September 2008). Human rights educators are well served to know about and check this site, which contains a wealth of resources, forums, and courses, tutorials, publication opportunities, and documentation on human rights topics.

Human Rights First, www.humanrightsfirst.org (5 September 2008). The organization has headquarters in New York and seeks to protect and promote human rights through affecting U.S. policy as well as international practice. Its activities range from protecting human rights advocates and refugees to promoting international justice and accountability structures.

Human Rights Net, www.human-rights.net (5 September 2008). The site offers a launching point to connect with a myriad of human rights research centers and NGOs; it is a project of the Human Rights Education Association.

Human Rights Watch (HRW), www.hrw.org (5 September 2008) is an independent human rights organization seeking to defend and protect the human rights of people around the world. They have been established for more than 20 years in the field, and are the largest U.S.-based human rights organization. HRW bases their advocacy largely on the "name, shame, blame" technique.

International Council on Human Rights Policy (ICHRP), www.ichrp.org (5 September 2008). ICHRP is an organization aiming to produce work of practical relevance through approaching human rights in an international, multidisciplinary, and consultative manner. They work particularly on applied policy research on issues relating to other human rights organizations.

International Federation for Human Rights, www.fidh.org/_news.php3 (5 September 2008). A federation of more than 150 organizations in more than 100 countries, this group has a broad mandate for prosecuting human rights violators, preventing human rights abuses and protecting victims.

International Gay and Lesbian Human Rights Commission (IGLHRC), www.iglhrc.org/site/iglhrc (5 September 2008). Technical assistance, coalition-building, advocacy, and documentation are the main ways in which the

IGLHRC is trying to make the world more equal and safe for those currently experiencing discrimination on the basis of gender and sexual identity or preference and HIV/AIDS status.

International Helsinki Federation for Human Rights, www.ihfhr.org/welcome. php (5 September 2008). A self-governing group of human rights organizations primarily concerned with European, Central Asian, and North American rights violations, the group's specific goal is to monitor compliance with the human rights provisions of the Helsinki Final Act and its Follow-up Documents.

Makerere University Human Rights and Peace Centre (HURIPEC), http://huripec. ac.ug (5 September 2008). The first academic human rights institution in the East African region, HURIPEC was established in 1993. It is devoted to teaching, researching, and compilation of local/regional materials relating to human rights. HURIPEC publishes the *East African Journal of Peace and Human Rights*, an interdisciplinary semi-annual scholarly publication.

Netherlands Institute of Human Rights, www.uu.nl/uupublish/homerechtsgeleer/ onderzoek/onderzoekscholen/sim/english/18199main.html (5 September 2008). Research, documentation, publications and a school for human rights can all be found on this site; however, it may be easier to visit it via a search engine than copying down the address given here.

The Nordic Committee for Human Rights, www.nkmr.org/english (5 September 2008). The Committee works on the protection of family rights in Nordic countries, basing its work on the UDHR, the Convention on the Rights of the Child, and the European Convention for the Protection of Human Rights and Fundamental Freedoms.

Norwegian Centre for Human Rights, www.humanrights.uio.no/english (5 September 2008). A national center for human rights work based at the University of Oslo, Norway. They aim to promote research, rights-based development, and to be a nucleus for human rights education.

Peace Brigades International, www.peacebrigades.org (5 September 2008). This organization contributes to a more peaceful world through the non-violent transformation of conflicts and emphasis on basic human rights. They conduct projects in several countries, and have delegations of monitors participating in their projects. Their Emergency Response Network is also an interesting initiative of theirs.

Physicians for Human Rights, www.phrusa.org/index.html (5 September 2008). The Physicians promote public health through human rights. They investigate and expose human rights violations worldwide, and work to stop them.

World Organization Against Torture, www.omct.org (5 September, 2008). Training, advocacy, and fighting against impunity are the core of this organization's work. It is a very large coalition of organizations (more than 300) working on issues of torture, arbitrary detention, extrajudicial killings, disappearances, and other human rights violations.

Index

Note: Page numbers followed by *f* or *t* indicate figures and tables, respectively.

1235 procedure 53–54, 175n44, 175n47
1503 procedure 53, 55–56

Abidjan 141
Abkhazia 21
Abolition of Forced Labor
  Convention 133
Abraham, Elizabeth 114
Addis Ababa regional office 19
Ad Hoc Working Group on South
  Africa 53
Advisory Opinion on the Continued
  Presence of South Africa in
  Namibia (South West Africa) 48–49
Afghanistan 21, 33, 34, 40, 89, 110,
  121, 122
An Agenda for Peace (Boutros-
  Ghali) 101
Albania 28
Algeria 32, 44
Alston, Philip 149
Al-Thani, Ghalia Mohd bin Hamid
  71
Amnesty International 10–12, 118,
  127, 143
Angola 19, 46
Annan, Kofi 4, 8, 41–42, 102–3, 108,
  114, 142
Annan Doctrine 102
apartheid 53, 106
Arbour, Louise 33–34, 41
Argentina 116
Arria, Diego 116

Arria Formula 116–17
Asia Pacific Forum of National
  Institutions 29
Aung San Suu Kyi 35
Australia 28, 89, 138
Austria 28
Ayala-Lasso, José 31–32

Bahrain 44
Bangkok 19, 141
Beirut 19
Beit-Hanoun 22
Belarus 45
Bishkek 19
Blaustein, Jacob 10
Body Shop International 145
Bolivia 19, 46
Bosnia and Herzegovina 22–26, 28,
  107, 110–11
Boutros-Ghali, Boutros 101–2
BP 145
Brahimi, Lakhdar 108
Brahimi Report 108
Burma 122, 137–38. *see also*
  Myanmar
Burundi 21, 121, 122
business. *see* private corporations
Business Leaders Initiative on
  Human Rights 145

Cambodia 11, 19
Canada 28, 79–81, 108, 116, 118,
  129, 138

CARE 118
Carrefour, Cemex 145
Cassin, René 9, 51
Central African Republic 21
Chad 21
Chapter VI powers 99, 103
Chapter VII powers 99, 105–7
Charter-based bodies 37–63; defined
    38–39; Economic and Social
    Council 46–48; General Assembly
    39–41; Human Rights Council
    41–46; NGOs and 62–63;
    operation of 51–63; protection
    activities of 53–56; special
    procedures of 56–61;
    standard-setting activities of
    51–53. *see also* Office of the High
    Commissioner for Human Rights;
    United Nations Security Council
Chechnya 33, 122
child labor 134, 139–42
Children's Convention. *see*
    Convention on the Rights of the
    Child
child soldiers 119–23
China 45, 89, 98, 115
CHR. *see* United Nations
    Commission on Human Rights
Clapham, Andrew 12
Codelco 146
Cold War 10, 100, 149
Colombia 19, 122
Committee Against Torture (CAT)
    24, 87–88
Committee on Economic, Social and
    Cultural Rights 83–84
Committee on Enforced or
    Involuntary Disappearance 93–94
Committee on the Elimination of
    Discrimination Against Women
    (CEDAW) 86–87
Committee on the Elimination of
    Racial Discrimination (CERD)
    84–85
Committee on the Protection of the
    Rights of All Migrant Workers
    and Members of Their Families
    (CRMW) 91–92
Committee on the Rights of Persons
    with Disabilities 92–93

Committee on the Rights of the
    Child (CRC) 71–73, 78–79, 88–91,
    95–96
committees of the whole 40
Communication on Progress Annual
    Reports (COPs) 143
communications, treaty bodies and
    73–77. *see also* individual
    communications
complaints 73–77, 136–39, 146–47
Conference on Freedom of
    Information (1948) 47
Consultative Council of Jewish
    Organizations 9
consultative status 62
Convention Against Torture and
    Other Cruel, Inhuman or
    Degrading Treatment or
    Punishment 87–88
Convention on the Rights of Persons
    with Disabilities (CRPD) 65, 92–93
Convention on the Rights of the
    Child 50, 64, 67–73, 86, 88–91,
    119–20, 177n17; Optional
    Protocol on the Involvement of
    Children in Armed Conflict 91,
    119–20; Optional Protocol on the
    Sale of Children, Child
    Prostitution and Child
    Pornography 91
Convention 182 on the Worst Forms
    of Child Labour 139–40
Copel 146
Corporate Citizenship unit of
    Warwick University 143
corporations. *see* private
    corporations
Costa Rica 10
Côte d'Ivoire 21, 122
country mandates 43
country-specific procedures 56–57
Croatia 28
Cuba 45
customary international law 103,
    178n18
Czech Republic 44

Dakar 19
Days of Discussion on Children with
    Disabilities 78

days of general discussion 78, 89, 92
Dayton General Framework
  Agreement for Peace (1995) 23
Decent Work Agenda 131
Declaration on Fundamental
  Principles and Rights at Work
  130, 132
Declaration on the Protection of All
  Persons from Enforced or
  Involuntary Disappearance 93
Declaration on the Rights of the
  Child 40
Declaration on the Right to
  Development 14
declarations 66
Democratic Republic of the Congo
  21, 32, 111–12, 121, 122
Deng, Francis 108
development: human rights and 2,
  14, 25–26; OHCHR and 13–14
Development Policy Network
  (DPnet) 141
disabilities. *see* Convention on the
  Rights of Persons with Disabilities
Disability Awareness in Action 78
Disabled People's International 78
disappearances 11, 65, 93–94
discrimination, defined 84
Discrimination (Employment and
  Occupation) Convention 133
Dorsey, Ellen 5–6

East Timor. *see* Timor-Leste
ECOSOC. *see* United Nations
  Economic and Social Council
Ecuador 19
Egypt 46, 104
Eliasson, Jan 41
Elimination of the Worst Forms of
  Child Labour 134
El Salvador 11, 141
enforced disappearances. *see*
  disappearances
enforcement 103–12, 148–49, 153
Equal Remuneration Convention 133
Eritrea 21
Eskom 146
Ethiopia 21
European Convention on Human
  Rights 114

European Union 129–30, 138
European Union Police Mission 23
exhaustion requirement 76
experts. *see* independent experts

Fiji 29
force, use of 104–7, 149, 178n23
forced disappearances. *see*
  disappearances
Forced Labour Convention 133
fragmentation of human rights 152
France 98, 115
freedom of association 138
Freedom of Association and
  Protection of the Right to
  Organize Convention 133
FRY Macedonia 19

Gaer, Felice 8
gender 24, 26. *see also* women
General Agreement on Tariffs and
  Trade (GATT) 129–30
general comments 77–78
general consultative status 62
Geneva Conventions 119
genocide 21–22, 35, 39, 45
Georgia 20, 21, 28
Germany 118, 140
Ghana 29
Global Compact of Corporate
  Responsibility 142–47; actors in
  143; awareness-raising function of
  145; complaint process in 146–47;
  criticisms of 146; goals of 144–45;
  and human rights 142; ILO and
  147; nature of 142–43; practical
  role of 145–46; structure of 143–44
globalization 130–31
Guantánamo Bay detention center
  33, 35
Guatemala 11, 19, 29
Guinea-Bissau 21
Guyana 19, 71–73

Haiti 11, 21
Havana Agreement 129
Heritage Foundation 43
High Commissioner for Human
  Rights. *see* United Nations High
  Commissioner for Human Rights

Holocaust 9
humanitarian intervention 108–12
Human Rights Advisers 19
human rights commissions 28
Human Rights Committee 51,
  67–69, 82–83
Human Rights Field Operation in
  Rwanda (HRFOR) 21–22
Human Rights Watch 30, 41, 45
Hungary 28
Hussein, Saddam 106

ICCPR. *see* International Covenant
  on Civil and Political Rights
ICJ. *see* International Court of Justice
ILO. *see* International Labour
  Organization
immunity 113
*The Impact of Armed Conflict on
  Children* (Machel) 119
Inclusion International 78
independent experts 57
India 28, 116, 141
individual communications 73–77,
  82–88, 91–93
Indonesia 19, 29
InFocus Programme on the
  Progressive Elimination of Child
  Labour 140
Internally Displaced Persons 20–21
International Bill of Rights 51–52
International Commission of Jurists
  10
International Commission on
  Intervention and State Sovereignty
  (ICISS) 108, 110
International Confederation of Free
  Trade Unions 129
International Convention on the
  Elimination of All Forms of
  Racial Discrimination 84–85, 148
International Convention on the
  Protection of the Rights of All
  Migrant Workers and Members of
  Their Families 91–92
International Coordinating
  Committee of National
  Institutions 28
International Council on Human
  Rights Policy 18

International Court of Justice (ICJ)
  48–49, 113, 137
International Covenant on Civil and
  Political Rights (ICCPR) 2–3, 9,
  51, 52, 67, 82–83, 114, 124
International Covenant on
  Economic, Social and Cultural
  Rights (ICESCR) 2–3, 52, 83–84,
  124, 176n14
International Criminal Court (ICC)
  174n31
International Criminal Tribunal for
  Rwanda 35, 105
International Criminal Tribunal for
  the former Yugoslavia 105
International Human Rights
  Council 30
International Labour Conference
  125, 128, 147
International Labour Office 126, 128
International Labour Organization
  (ILO) 3, 47, 124–42, 150; and
  child labor 139–42; Committee of
  Experts 136; Committee on
  Freedom of Association 138; and
  complaints 136–39;
  convention-establishing process in
  128; core conventions of 133–34,
  181n14; enforcement mechanisms
  of 136–39; Fact-Finding and
  Conciliation Commission on
  Freedom of Association 138;
  founding of 124; and freedom of
  association 138; and Global
  Compact 147; and human rights
  124–25; and labor standards
  124–25, 129–35; membership of
  125; NGOs and 126–28;
  organizational structure and
  operations of 125–29, 126*f*;
  principles of 132; priority
  conventions of 182n15; private
  compliance with 141–42; and
  representations 138;
  standard-setting mechanisms of
  132; and state reports 136;
  supervisory system of 135*f*; and
  technical assistance 141
international law 39. *see also*
  customary international law

International Law Association 94
International Monetary Fund (IMF) 4
International Parliament of Labour. *see* International Labour Conference
International Police Task Force 26
International Programme on the Elimination of Child Labour (IPEC) 140–41
International Trade Organization (ITO) 129
interstate communications 73
Iraq 21, 33, 34, 106
Israel 45, 104
Italy 28

Japan 69–70, 138
Judgment of the International Military Tribunal at Nuremberg (1945) 39
just war 110

Kalin, Walter 20
Ki-moon, Ban 142
Kleine-Ahlbrandt, Stephenie 30
Kosovo 19, 114
Kurds 106
Kuwait 106
Kyrgyzstan 19

labor standards 124–25, 129–35
Latvia 29
Lebanon 22
legal personality, of UN 113
Li & Fung 146
Liberia 21, 22, 110, 112, 121, 122
Lima 141
Lindqvist, Bengt 78
Lomé agreement 130
Long, Scott 4

Machel, Graca 119
mainstreaming of human rights 152
Malaysia 116
Maldives 19
Malik, Charles 51
Malone, David 107, 116
Marks, Stephen 14
MAS Holdings 146

McDougall, Gay 63
Médecins sans Frontières 118
Mexico 19, 29, 129
Migrant Workers Convention 91–92
Minimum Age Convention 133–34, 139
Mokhiber, Craig 25
Moldova 28, 29
Most Favored Nation status 130
MTV Networks Europe 145
Myanmar 35. *see also* Burma

National Grid 145
National Human Rights Institutions: Best Practice 28–29
national human rights institutions (NHRIs) 27–31; categories of 27–28; characteristics of 27; and Children's Convention 90–91; OHCHR and 28–31; Paris Principles for 28; and UDHR, 153; UN involvement with 27
national plans of action 79–81
Nelson, Paul 5–6
Nepal 19, 122, 141
Netherlands 116, 118
New Delhi 141
new rights advocates 5
New Zealand 28
NGOs. *see* nongovernmental organizations
NGO Working Group on the Security Council 118–19
NHRIs. *see* national human rights institutions (NHRIs)
Non-Aligned Movement (NAM) 14
nongovernmental organizations (NGOs): and Children's Convention 90–91; consultative status of 62; and general comments 77; and human rights 5; and ILO 126–28; lobbying activities of 62–63; and OHCHR 10–12; shadow reports by 68–69; strategies and tactics of 5–6; and UN Security Council 118–23
non-state actors 2–3
North American Free Trade Agreement (NAFTA) 129
Northern Ireland 122

North Korea 45
Novartis 145
Novo Nordisk 145

Office of the High Commissioner for
    Human Rights (OHCHR) 3, 8–36,
    149; in Bosnia and Herzegovina
    22–26; and country/regional offices
    18–19; establishment of 8, 12–13;
    evaluation of High Commissioners
    of 31–35; expectations for 8;
    expenditures of 16; field presence
    of 19, 21–23; and general comments
    77; growth of 14; mandate of 13;
    and NHRIs 27–31; organization
    of 14, 15*f*; origins of 9–12;
    protection activities of 55; Rapid
    Response Units 22; and regional
    human rights organizations 29,
    153; significance of 3; and
    technical assistance 16–18; and
    treaty reporting 69, 96; and
    UDHR, 153; UNDP and 51
ombudsmen 27–28
optional protocols 73
Organisation for Economic
    Co-operation and Development
    129
Oxfam 118, 143

Pakistan 19, 45, 116
Palestinian territories 19, 22, 45, 104
Panama 19
Paris Principles 28
peace enforcement 102*t*
peace-keeping operations 102*t*,
    103–5, 107–8, 110–12
peace operations 102*t*
Pen-Chung Chang 51
Pérez de Cuéllar, Javier 100–101
Permanent Court of Arbitration 48
Permanent Court of International
    Justice 48
Philippines 122
Pillay, Navanethem 35
Poland 28
Portugal 118
poverty 25–26
Poverty Reduction Strategy Papers
    (PRSPs) 141

Pretoria 19
private corporations: and Global
    Compact 142–47; and ILO 141–42
procedures of inquiry 77
protection activities 53–56

Qatar 46
Quebec 28

Race Discrimination Convention
    84–85, 148
race to the bottom 130, 181n8
racial discrimination 84–85
rapporteurs 56–57, 60–61
Rees, Madeleine 24, 25
refugees 49
regional human rights organizations
    29
Reparations Case 113
*Report of the Panel on UN Peace
    Operations* 108
representations 138
reservations 66, 86, 89
Resolution 48/141 (1993) 39
Resolution 49/184 (1994) 39
Resolution 56/115 (2001) 39
Resolution 56/176 (2001) 40
Resolution 688 106–7
Resolution 794 107
Resolution 1261 (1999) 120
Resolution 1314 (2000) 120
Resolution 1325 on Women, Peace,
    and Security 123
Resolution 1379 (2001) 120–21
Resolution 1460 (2003) 121–22
Resolution 1539 122
responsibility to protect 108–12, 153
Rights-based Municipal Assessment
    Programme (RMAP) 25
Rights for Disabled Children 78
Right to Organize and Collective
    Bargaining Convention 133
Robinson, Mary 32–33, 150
Romania 28
Roosevelt, Eleanor 51
Roster status 62
RUDs 66, 97
Russia 19, 20, 28, 33, 45, 98, 115, 150
Rwanda 19, 21–22, 29, 31–32, 101,
    107, 110

safe havens 104, 106
Santiago 19
Saudi Arabia 45
Save the Children Alliance 78
Scandinavia 116
security 150
Security Council. *see* United
　Nations Security Council
September 11, 2001 terrorist attacks
　2, 6, 150
Serbia 19, 26
shadow reports 68–69
Shell 146
Sierra Leone 21, 111
Slovenia 28
social clauses 130–31
Somalia 19, 21, 101, 107, 110, 121,
　122, 177n17
Somavia (ILO Secretary-General) 134
South Africa 28, 29, 48–49, 53, 106
South Caucasus 19
Southern Rhodesia 106
sovereignty 100, 108, 148–49
Soviet Union 37
Special Adviser to the High
　Commissioner for the
　Establishment and Strengthening
　of National Institutions for
　Human Rights 29
special consultative status 62
Special Court for Sierra Leone 105
Special Rapporteurs. *see* rapporteurs
Special Representative for Children
　and Armed Conflict 119
Sri Lanka 19, 28, 29, 122
standard communications 57, 60
standard setting 51–53
state reporting 66–73, 94–96, 136
states: and human rights 4–5, 27–31,
　148–51; responsibility of 108, 110,
　153; sovereignty of 100, 108,
　148–49. *see also* States Parties
States Parties: and children's rights
　88–90; defined 52; and disabilities
　92–93; and migrant worker rights
　91–92; and national plans of
　action 79; procedures of inquiry
　for 77; and racial discrimination
　85; reporting on treaties of 66–69,
　94–96; and torture 87–88

Statoil 145
Steiner, Henry 149
Strengthening of the United Nations
　(UN Secretary-General) 96
Sub-Committee on Prevention of
　Torture and Other Cruel,
　Inhuman or Degrading Treatment
　of Punishment 88
Sudan 21, 45, 122
Suez Crisis 104
Suva 19
Swedish International Development
　Cooperation Agency (SIDA) 78
Switzerland 138

Taj Horels 146
Tajikistan 29
Tanzania 141
Tata Enterprises 146
technical assistance 6, 16, 17*t*, 18,
　50–51, 141
Telefoncia 146
terrorism 150
thematic discussions 78–79
thematic mandates 43
thematic procedures 56–57, 58–59*t*
third-generation human rights 149
Time-Bound Programs 141
Timor-Leste 21, 22, 110, 111
Togo 19
torture, defined 87
Torture Convention 87–88
trade: labor standards and 124,
　129–30; social clauses and 130–31
trafficking in persons 26
treaties: reform of processes for
　94–96; reporting and monitoring
　processes for 64–65; role and
　function of 64; RUDs pertaining
　to 66, 97; and UDHR, 153–54.
　see also treaty bodies
treaty bodies 64–97; Committee
　Against Torture 87–88;
　Committee on Economic, Social
　and Cultural Rights 83–84;
　Committee on Enforced or
　Involuntary Disappearance 93–94;
　Committee on the Elimination of
　Discrimination Against Women
　86–87; Committee on the

Elimination of Racial
Discrimination 84–85; Committee
on the Protection of the Rights of
All Migrant Workers and
Members of Their Families 91–92;
Committee on the Rights of
Persons with Disabilities 92–93;
Committee on the Rights of the
Child 88–91; and communications
73–77; composition of 65;
effectiveness of 97; functions of
97; and general comments 77–78;
Human Rights Committee 82–83;
list of 66*t*; and national plans of
action 79–81; and procedures of
inquiry 77; and reform 94–96; role
of 65; state reporting by 66–73,
94–96; thematic discussions by
78–79
treaty congestion 64
treaty fatigue 64–65
Treaty of Versailles (1919) 124
tribunals 105
Troop-Contributing Nations 116
truth commissions 105
Tunisia 44

UDHR. *see* Universal Declaration
of Human Rights
Uganda 19, 28, 29, 122
understandings 66
UNDP. *see* United Nations
Development Programme
UNHCHR. *see* United Nations
High Commissioner for Human
Rights
UNHCR. *see* United Nations High
Commissioner for Refugees
UNICEF. *see* United Nations
Children's Fund
United Kingdom 28, 44, 98, 115, 138
United Nations: founding of 37;
legal personality of 113
United Nations Assistance Mission
for Rwanda (UNAMIR) 22
United Nations Centre for Human
Rights 11
United Nations Charter 37–38, 38*t*,
99–100, 113–14, 151, 153. *see also*
Charter-based bodies

United Nations Children's Fund
(UNICEF) 24, 49–50, 69, 90
United Nations Commission on
Human Rights (CHR) 10, 28, 41,
47, 51–57, 60, 62–63, 84, 93, 119,
148–49. *see also* United Nations
Human Rights Council
United Nations Commission on the
Status of Women 47–48
United Nations Decade for Human
Rights Education 39
United Nations Department of
Peacekeeping Operations (DPKO)
19
United Nations Department of
Political Affairs (DPA) 19
United Nations Development
Programme (UNDP) 2, 3, 25, 29,
50–51, 69
United Nations Division for the
Advancement of Women 48, 86
United Nations Economic and
Social Council (ECOSOC) 10,
46–48, 52, 53, 55, 62, 83, 118
United Nations Emergency Force
(UNEF) 104
United Nations General Assembly
12–14, 39–41, 52, 115, 120
United Nations Guiding Principles
on Internal Displacement 20
United Nations High Commissioner
for Human Rights (UNHCHR) 3,
31–35, 132, 150. *see also* Office of
the High Commissioner for
Human Rights (OHCHR)
United Nations High Commissioner
for Refugees (UNHCR) 49
United Nations Human Rights
Commission. *see* United Nations
Commission on Human Rights
United Nations Human Rights
Council 40–46, 52, 154, 173n12;
Complaint Procedures 43;
criticism of 43–46; establishment
of 41–43; mandate of 43;
membership of 42; organization of
42; Special Procedures 43–45;
Sub-Commission on the
Promotion and Protection of
Human Rights 46; themes

addressed by 52–53; Working Group on Communications 43; Working Group on Situations 43
United Nations human rights practice: actors in 4–6; broadening mandate of 2–3; context of 3–4; and development 2; effectiveness of, 154; enforcement in 148–49; local context for 4; and non-state actors 2–3; significance of, 154; traditional 1–2; treaty-based 10 (*see also* treaty bodies); UN Charter and 37–38, 38*t*; victims' participation in 6
United Nations Mission in Bosnia and Herzegovina (UNMIBH) 110–11
United Nations Mission in Bosnia (UNMIK) 23
United Nations Mission in Liberia (UNMIL) 112
United Nations Mission in Sierra Leone (UNAMSIL) 111
United Nations Office of the High Commissioner for Human Rights. *see* Office of the High Commissioner for Human Rights
United Nations Organization Mission in the Democratic Republic of the Congo (MONUC) 111–12
United Nations Secretary-General 96, 100–103, 105, 107, 119, 152
United Nations Security Council 3, 98–123, 153; authority of 99–100; Chapter VI powers of 99, 103; Chapter VII powers of 99, 105–7; coercive measures of 105–7; expansion of 115; human rights accountability of 112–15; human rights activities of 102*t*, 103–12; and human rights issues 98–103, 123; informal meetings of 116–17; mandate of 98; membership of 98, 115; NGOs and 118–23; non-coercive measures of 103–5; peace-keeping operations of 103–5, 107–8, 110–12; political will of 100–103; reform of 115–18; Secretaries-General and 100–103, 105, 107; transparency in 116–18; voting process in 115–16

United Nations Technical Cooperation Programme in the Field of Human Rights 16
United Nations Transitional Administration in East Timor (UNTAET) 111
United Nations Truce Supervision Organization (UNTSO) 104
United Nations Working Group on Enforced or Involuntary Disappearances 11
United States: and Boutros-Ghali 101–2; and Burma 138; and child labor 141; and children's rights 177n17; development opposition by 13–14; human rights abuses by 33, 35; and NAFTA 129; and UN Human Rights Council 45–46, 63, 154; and UN Security Council 98, 115
Universal Declaration of Human Rights (UDHR) 2–3, 9, 39, 51–52, 114, 148, 152–54
urgent appeals 57, 60
Uruguay 9, 89
use of force 104–7, 149, 178n23
Uzbekistan 29

Valeo 146
victims, role of 6
Vieira de Mello, Sergio 33
Vienna Declaration 12, 14
violations of human rights: increasing numbers of 11, 149; UN accountability for 112–15

Warwick University 143
Western Sahara 22
"We the Peoples" (Annan) 102
women: discrimination against 86; and international peace and stability 123; OHCHR and 24, 26; UN Commission on the Status of Women 47–48
Women's Convention 86–87
working groups 56–57
Working Party on the Social Dimensions of the Liberalization of Trade 131
World Bank 4, 25

World Blind Union 78
World Conference against Racism,
  Racial Discrimination,
  Xenophobia and Related
  Intolerance (Durban, 2001) 40
World Conference on Human Rights
  (Vienna, 1993) 12
World Federalist Movement 118
World Federation of the Deaf 78
World Summit on Social
  Development (Copenhagen, 1995)
  132

World Trade Organization (WTO)
  124, 129–30
World Veterans Association 10

Yearbook on Human Rights 47
Yugoslavia, former 11, 101, 110,
  114, 116

Zimbabwe 45

An environmentally friendly book printed and bound in England by www.printondemand-worldwide.com

PEFC Certified

This product is
from sustainably
managed forests
and controlled
sources

www.pefc.org

PEFC/16-33-415

This book is made of chain-of-custody materials; FSC materials for the cover and PEFC materials for the text pages.

#0210 - 120516 - C0 - 216/138/12 - PB - 9780415491402